The Kings

Suzy Gershman's
born to shop
hong kong,
shanghai & beijing

The u... ...
for people...

D0696685

5th Edition

Wiley Publishing, Inc.

For Peter & Louisa with double thanks and double happiness

Published by:

WILEY PUBLISHING, INC.

111 River St.
Hoboken, NJ 07030-5774

ISBN 978-0-470-53769-5

Editor: Stephen Bassman
Production Editor: M. Faunette Johnston
Cartographer: Anton Crane
Production by Wiley Indianapolis Composition Services

For information on our other products and services or to obtain technical support, please contact our Customer Care Department within the U.S. at 877/762-2974, outside the U.S. at 317/572-3993 or fax 317/572-4002.

Wiley also publishes its books in a variety of electronic formats. Some content that appears in print may not be available in electronic formats.

Manufactured in the United States of America

5   4   3   2   1

Contents

Map list

About the Authors

Suzy Gershman is a journalist, author, and global-shopping goddess who has worked in the fashion and fiber industries for more than 25 years. Her essays on retailing have been used by the Harvard School of Business; her reportage on travel and retail has appeared in *Travel + Leisure, Travel Holiday, Travel Weekly,* and most of the major women's magazines. Suzy is also the author of *C'est La Vie* (Penguin Paperback), the story of her first year as a widow living in Paris, and *Where to Buy the Best of Everything: The Outspoken Guide for World Travelers & Online Shoppers.* She and her two long-haired dachshunds, Toffee and Junior Mint, divide their time between San Antonio, Texas (Suzy's childhood home); a small house in Provence; and the airport.

Suzy also gives shopping tours. Visit www.suzygershman. com or write to suzygershman@gmail.com for details. Suzy blogs at www.borntoshoplady.blogspot.com.

Sarah Lahey is editorial director of the *Born to Shop* series. Sarah lives with her husband, Tom, and two dogs, Bentley and Beckham, in Tiburon, California, when she isn't traveling to research and rewrite *Born to Shop* editions.

Although every effort has been made to ensure the accuracy of prices appearing in this book, please keep in mind that prices can change. In this edition, prices are quoted in U.S. dollars ($), or Hong Kong dollars (HK$), or Chinese Yuan (¥). Dollar estimates have been made at the exchange rate of $1 = HK$7.7 = ¥6.8.

To Start With

Hong Kong has long been the door to the Orient. It's an important destination for those who will be visiting mainland China as well. Many go on to Bangkok; trendy travelers are keen on Cambodia and Laos. This is the first edition with an entire chapter devoted to Hanoi. I have also expanded the Shenzhen coverage and added lodging information; shopping Shenzhen is a lot more than running across the border for a fake handbag and it's time people realized that the New China is less than an hour from Honkers.

This edition still has a whole lotta Hong Kong. Despite threats from the mainland to outpace it, I find that Honkers is still the brightest star in the sky and the one where the most people speak English.

Hong Kong continues to amaze me with its ingenuity and determination to be recognized and to give visitors the most for their money. Here's hoping you have as much shopping fun as we did, enjoy as many great family travels, and do not pay as many overweight charges. And yes, we have a way around some of that, so read on, read on.

Suzy Gershman
January 2010

Acknowledgements

Although by now I consider myself an old China Hand, I am extremely indebted to the team in Asia that continues to help me, guide me, and translate for me. Carole Klein at Inter-Continental Hotels is my constant source and is the creator of the "*Born to Shop* & Spa Tours" done each year in conjunction with InterConti. Everyone at InterContinental Hong Kong helps me invaluably—I thank you all.

At The Pen, I am also grateful for a full team of support from front desk to behind the stoves/ovens to upstairs with the careful touch of Stella and Sian, as well as the Bonnie girls.

In the twenty-some odd years I have been a regular in town, I have come to depend on the Vessas, the Peter Chans, and a handful of woman friends who keep me up-to-date. I thank all of you from the bottom of my cheongsam and say *Shishi* to one and all.

Chapter 1

The Best of Hong Kong & Beyond

A Chinese Blessing

There is an old Chinese curse that says, "May you live in interesting times." I'd like to amend the ancient curse into a prayer for you and yours:

May you shop in somewhat dirty street markets but contract no disease. May you never pay more than 100 of anything (yuan, Hong Kong dollars, euros—whatever). May you gaze at the new China and understand that you see the future—and it is powerful. May you return often, in joy and safety.

With the 2008 Beijing Olympics considered to be a turning point for the Chinese government, everything has become cleaner and more generic, brighter, and even garish. Hong Kong still shimmers as an oasis, although prices are higher on most items (except designer goods, which cost 20% less than in mainland China). This is the new China, and it has been built by the world's finest architects. You can't help but be impressed. Stay tuned for World Expo 2010, opening in Shanghai as you open these pages.

If you're antsy about the rate of exchange on the dollar against the euro, Asia is your new best friend. The rush is on, so get going now. This chapter will help guide you to the best, the brightest, and the most brilliant according to budget.

1

This is a short chapter with short sentences. If you also like pictures, please see my blog, www.borntoshoplady.blogspot.com, and go to the portions on the various explorations done for research trips. There's little repeat information, so you won't get bored and you can see some snapshots of the merchandise available.

Please remember that coming up with a single best of anything is difficult. "Best" is a subjective thing. Each choice here is based on a combination of location, value, and convenience.

Also note that I find little crossover in merchandise in the cities this book covers; once you have left a destination, you may not have the luxury of another crack at a particular item, often resulting in the "Why didn't I buy more?" syndrome. Remember the Moscow Rule of Shopping and grab it when you see it—after bargaining, of course.

The 10 Best Stores

Along with my alphabetical list below comes the usual disclaimer—these choices are based on my personal visits. China is changing fast. As soon as we go to press, a bigger or better store might pop up.

Ashneil

Far East Mansions, 5–6 Middle Rd., shop 114 (up the stairs), Tsim Sha Tsui, Kowloon, Hong Kong (MTR: TST).

Calling this a store may lead you to believe it is bigger than a postage stamp, which it is not. More than two shoppers make it feel crowded. But that's only because it's piled high and deep with handbags of all sorts. These babies are no fakes either. They're excellent-quality items that look like styles you know and love—but, with no phony parts; they're totally legal. Prices begin at around $250 and go up (sometimes way up), but you often can't tell the difference between these bags and the $2,000 versions. You can have your purchases delivered to

THE 10 BEST STORES

the U.S. (saving on the Customs allowance), order something made in a custom color, or buy small leather goods such as belts and wallets. Credit cards accepted. Yes, Birkin.

Blanc de Chine

Pedder Building, 12 Pedder St., room 201, Central, Hong Kong (MTR: Central).

Armani meets Shanghai Tang (see below). Expect to pay $500 or more for a jacket, but the quality and appearance will melt you. Men's, women's, and home-styles.

City Super

Times Square mall (MTR: Causeway Bay); Ocean Terminal, Harbour City, Kowloon (MTR: TST); IFC2 mall (MTR: Central); all Hong Kong.

As the name implies, this is a supermarket. The branches are not all equal—the one at Times Square is the best—but all are good enough to qualify for this list. You can buy Asian products (which make great gifts) as well as bath and beauty items and housewares.

Hu & Hu Antiques

1685 Wuzhong Lu, Shanghai (no nearby Metro).

If you aren't interested in furniture, then you can skip this establishment. If you love to look at pretty things and adore high style with ultrapanache, this is the most chic furniture store in all of China. The woman who runs it is American-Chinese and speaks English like few others in Shanghai. In addition to two warehouses filled with furniture, you'll also find smaller tabletop and gift items. I bought an ancestor scroll once. Have your taxi wait...even if it's for a few days.

Maylin

Peninsula Hotel Shopping Arcade, Salisbury Rd., Kowloon, Hong Kong (MTR: TST).

The Birkin bags are all gone but the store has expanded and is now heavy into woven leathers that look surprisingly like, hmmmm, what was that Italian brand? Prices hover around $250 for a nice sac. They take credit cards but are not big on charm.

Shanghai Tang
Pedder Building, 12 Pedder St., Central, Hong Kong (MTR: Central).

This is undoubtedly one of the must sees, must dos of Hong Kong, even if you don't buy anything. In fact, there is a good chance you *won't* buy anything. Still, the store is gorgeous to look at and inspirational in its creativity.

Shanghai Tang stocks souvenirs and fashions, Mao mania, and original artwork by contemporary artists—all imported from China. Get a load of the gift wrap! Wander, drool, buy, have a cigar, sit down for tea, or shop 'til you're late for your next appointment.

Note: In Kowloon, Tang has moved out of the Pen and into its own little cutie-pie building (was that a police station?) in the Heritage 1888 complex at Salisbury Road and Canton Road. It's not as glam as the flagship, but worth a look-see.

Shiatzy Chen
7 the Bund, Shanghai.

Religious encounter of the fourth dimension. Okay, so that's a little glib, but I am sincere. The first few times I walked into this store it was truly a religious experience; the earth moved. The Taiwanese designer makes men's and women's clothes as well as accessories; they have stores all over Asia. The look is "Armani meets Blanc de Chine" kicked up many notches into couture. In short, this is gorgeous clothing, usually beginning at $1,000.

Airports & You

Many businesspeople are in such a great hurry getting from meeting to meeting that they wait to shop at the airport duty-free shops as they're leaving town. Depending on your point of departure, this may or may not be such a hot idea.

The **Hong Kong** airport may be a virtual shopping mall, but note that prices are not the same as in town. Even duty-free prices are high. I suggest hitting the gift shop at your hotel in Hong Kong if you're willing to pay top dollar anyway. Gift shops will have slightly more budget-friendly prices and less pressure of the "Oh my, I'd better grab it" variety.

The **Beijing** airport's duty-free shop is excellent for last-minute shopping. I can't tell you that the prices are the lowest in town, but the selection is wide enough for all of you last-minute shoppers to at least accomplish all of your shopping goals.

Shanghai's Pudong airport gift shops are even more sophisticated in the TT (tourist-trap) department. I've stocked up on chocolate-covered litchis and the most extraordinary embroidered satin bedroom slippers. Yes, there is a Shanghai Tang here, so you know this place is with it. Shanghai's Hong Qiao airport is neither new nor spiffy but has some basics for giftables.

Taipei's airport, which you will use if you fly EVA Air, is the biggest surprise—the old-fashioned CSK airport is gone and this new beauty has tons of shopping and eats. Yep, even a Starbucks. Note that this airport may have better shopping than in town and is a far better hub to Asia than Narita (Tokyo), so worship for awhile if you can.

The **Hanoi** airport has some kiosks and stands, but really, folks, forget it in terms of anything other than a way to stretch your legs or avoid boredom before boarding. Bring your Kindle or a paperback.

Space 798

Dashanzi Art District (no nearby Metro).

Yes, I know it's off the beaten path; but this trendsetting reclaimed factory is well worth it, with all sorts of shopper's delights in store for you: photography, art, and a little bit of clothing. Look, touch, and splurge. You can even grab a drink or a light meal to reward yourself for making it out there. (See p. 292 in chapter 10 for tips on how to get there and make the most of your excursion.)

Suzhou Cobbler

3 Fuchow Rd., Shanghai.

Don't sneeze or you will miss this tiny shop that specializes in a sophisticated twist on an old Chinese art: the embroidered slipper. About $50 a pair, but they look like a million.

Urban Tribe

133 Fuxing Rd. W., Shanghai.

This is a lifestyle brand that sells ethnic Chinese, nomadic, north country almost looks Tunisian (I know, I know) fabulous clothes, and home-style. If you can't get to the flagship, pop into the boutique in the Portman Ritz-Carlton.

Great Inexpensive Gifts

- **Hello Kitty!** I do not happen to be a Hello Kitty freak; I don't even like cats very much. That said, I adore pop culture and am impressed by the destination specific Hello Kitty merchandise I found in various Chinese cities. I got Post-it notes with Kitty at the Pearl Tower as well as Hello Kitty Shanghai wallets. My best buy was a group of Hello Kitty Hong Kong spiral-bound mininotebooks, each with a different local scene—I love Kitty with the dim sum.

- **Chinese tea.** From high-end brands and makers (such as Fook Ming Tong, in Hong Kong) to any old brand in a great-looking package sold on the street or at a Chinese department store, tea makes a very traditional gift, and it doesn't break. Prices vary with brand and venue. If tea strikes you as old hat, look for the flower teas that are the size of a Ping-Pong ball and open into a beautiful blossom inside the cup as you make the tea. Excellent party trick. Buy flowering tea (of the jasmine variety, for example) in a gift bag for about $10 to $12.

- **"Jade."** I buy "jade" doughnuts by the dozen at the Jade Market in Hong Kong and then string each one individually as a gift. They cost about $1 each and are not real jade. If you're willing to pay $10 to $15 per gift, you can purchase animal figurines. At $15 to $20 there are calligraphy brushes with jade handles...very chic but heavy in the luggage.

- **Chops.** You can be sure that no one else has one of these. A chop, or Chinese signature stamp, costs about $25 and can usually be carved while you wait.

- **Chopsticks.** Okay, so more people in your social circle are likely to have a few sets of these. But I found some really chic ones—pearl inlay and all that—in Hanoi (not in China, incidentally). They are indeed a bargain at about $2 per pair.

- **Perfume bottles.** Many people like perfume bottles painted on the inside, but I prefer the fake antiques that look like smoked glass from the 1920s for $10 to $20. I have a collection of tiny cinnabar bottles for which I paid about $15 each. They are fake antiques, true, but good-looking nonetheless.

The Best Shopping Experiences

- Trolling for bargains on Fa Yuen Street, Hong Kong
- Having a garment made-to-order in Hong Kong
- Having a garment copied in Hanoi
- Any flea market in China
- Shenzhen and the new China

Best Alternate Retail Concepts

Insider Concierge

InterContinental Hotel, Salisbury Rd., Tsim Sha Tsui, Hong Kong (MTR: TST).

Insider Concierge is an InterContinental trademark for a program in which the chain's superduper concierges locate whatever you need. Actually, any good hotel concierge can provide this service, but InterConti backs this up with a fabulous team and an international marketing plan. The concierge can even arrange for potential purchases to be brought to your hotel room for you to look at, or for fittings to be done in your room.

Xintiandi

Huai Hai Rd. E., Shanghai (Metro: Huang Pi Nan Rd.).

Maybe it's not fair to call this an urban-renewal effort—it's an entire city of stone houses that have been renovated into bars, restaurants, and shops with walkways in between and the most chic customers in all of China. You don't come here so much for the shopping as for the whole package, usually at night, when the stores stay open late and you drink and stroll and then have dinner. The concept proved so exciting that there are now five of these villages dotted around China—the newest is in Foshan, in the Pearl River Delta.

Best Twist on an Old Theme

Jade and antiquey doodads hung from a silken cord is not a new look and can be found in markets and stores in Hong Kong and China. Yet we never found another source besides I Tre, in Hong Kong, that is doing such thick and elaborately knotted cords; they are sold with pendants for about $100. New World Centre, no. L063, Kowloon, Hong Kong. © 852/2722-4617.

Best Postcards

For old-fashioned-style postcards with a fun technology, find the **3-D** postcards of the Great Wall at any of the TTs at Badaling. The one I keep posted on my office wall is from China National Publications Import & Export Corp.

For new graphics and hot Chinese fashionsitas, the postcards from **Shanghai Tang** can't be beat. Sometimes you can get one free with a purchase.

The Best Sources for Antiques

Antiques in China are tricky—you simply don't know what's real and what isn't. Hong Kong's Hollywood Road is an excellent stroll for antiques shopping, getting an overview of what is available, and learning about the prices. Don't buy anything serious from a dealer who is not known in the trade.

Macau is an excellent source for antiques—that is, if they weren't just made right there!

Both Shanghai and Beijing abound with shopping ops for small decorative items and antiques, real and fake. Prices can be half those in Hong Kong. But then, reliability can be, too.

The Best PVC

If you're looking to save bucks on a handbag, you can spend time looking for a leather wannabe made of PVC. Finding a good one is hard. Shenzhen's LoWu Commercial Center is filled with bad ones but there's a tiny store in Hong Kong that carries both leather and PVC bags and will honestly tell you which is which. Stop by **St. Louis Boutique,** New World Centre, no. LO40GF, Kowloon (© **852/2368-2707**). Real leather bags will cost $150 to $300, as elsewhere, but the PVC stuff is around $100 and worthy of your sniff.

Best Markets

Jade Market

Kansu and Battery sts., Yau Ma Tei, Kowloon, Hong Kong (MTR: Jordan Rd.).

Two tents' worth of dealers with beads, jade, more jade, and a few antiques. Do-it-yourselfers will go wild. Check out Jenny Gems. To reach the market from the Metro, walk or take a taxi.

Panjiayuan Antique and Curio Market/Dirt Market

Huaweiqiaxi Nan Dajie, Beijing (no nearby Metro).

If you are a flea-market person, you owe it to yourself to arrange your trip so that you have a few hours here. Also known as the Dirt Market (it once had a dirt yard), the market includes some aisles of dealers under tin rooftops, and masses of real people with their goods laid out on the ground. Beware of fakes. The best time to shop is before 10am, before it gets very crowded. Open Saturday and Sunday only.

Pearl Market (Hong Qiao Market)

Near the Temple of Heaven, Beijing (no nearby Metro).

This indoor mall sounds a lot more romantic than it looks, but if you can adjust your expectations, you'll be on your way to heaven…and the Temple of Heaven is conveniently across the street.

The first floor has watches and small electronics (including Mao lighters), along with leather goods and fakes. Also on this floor is luggage, which comes in handy when you run out of packing space and are desperate for cheap new bags. At the far end of this floor is a series of stalls selling Chinese arts and crafts and souvenir items. Next up is a floor of pearls and pearl wannabes, beads, gemstones, clasps, and more beads. The rear of this floor holds a small mall of antiques shops.

There are two more floors of jewelry stores. *Note:* Another building stands virtually next-door—new and modern and spiffy. I do not include it in my "best of" thoughts.

Most Overrated Market

Go to **Hangzhou** for many things, including the heart-stopping, more-than-magical *Impression Westlake* performance (nights only; www.hzyxxh.com) but do not make the trip for the Night Market.

The Best Tailors

Prices in China for custom-made clothing may be less than in Hong Kong, but don't be tempted. If you want top-of-the-line quality that competes with the best of Savile Row, you want a Hong Kong tailor whose family probably came from Shanghai and who does things the old-fashioned way, by hand.

W. W. Chan & Sons Ltd.
Burlington House, 92–94 Nathan Rd., 2nd floor, Kowloon, Hong Kong (MTR: TST); 129A–2 Mao Ming Rd., Shanghai (Metro: Shi Men Rd.).

Best City for Cheapie Copy Tailors

Hanoi. We tested tailors in Bangkok (not in this book), Shenzhen, and Hanoi, and Hanoi won hands down.

MY BEST FINDS
by Suzy Gershman

- **Shinco DVD Player:** I thought Shinco was a no-name Chinese brand, but the Sony store near me in Paris also sells it. So do Fortress and Broadway, two reliable electronics chains in Hong Kong. My latest score is a portable DVD player the size of a CD player for $135. It's dual voltage (110–220), so I can use it anywhere in the world.
- **Face Cream:** I can't tell you that wrinkle creams and moisturizers really work, but I'm not taking any chances. I like the big-name brands, the ones that cost about $100 a jar (sorry, I can't afford the ones that cost $1,000). I used to buy them at duty-free stores. Now I buy from the stands at the Pearl Market in Beijing.
- **Eyeglasses:** I have bought eyeglasses and had the prescription filled at the Eye Mart in Beijing and been pleased with the adventure and the quality. But my best treat is to go to **New Fei Optical** in Kowloon (Hong Kong), where I can get designer frames plus my prescription for about $100 per pair.
- **Chinese Shirts:** From Kenki, a small chain of arts-and-crafts clothing stores in Hong Kong, I bought reversible velvet-silk Chinese big shirts for $40.
- **Custom-Made Jewelry:** I brought a set of aquamarines that I bought in Brazil to Hong Kong and had a pair of David Yurman–like earrings made in sterling. It took 1 week and cost $250, not counting the price of the stones.
- **Designer Fashion:** Not just any designer mind you, but Taiwanese legend **Shiatzy Chen.** I fell into a sale with prices marked down 20%, and I got a men's tailored black silk Chinese-style jacket that would make the door gods weep (for a total of $455).

MY BEST FINDS
by Sarah Lahey

- **Armani Sweater:** I found a Giorgio Armani Collezione pale sage double-breasted cotton tunic at the **Joyce Warehouse** in Aberdeen, Hong Kong, for $40.
- **Embroidered Silk Tote:** Lots of vendors at the **South Bund Soft Spinning Material Market** sell accessories along with yard goods; here, I bought several stunning tote/carry-on bags for $10 each. Large enough to hold my computer, travel pillow, and other necessities, the bags are made of jewel-toned heavy-duty embroidered silk.
- **Eyeglasses:** I brought my prescription (and my husband Tom's, too) from home and had several pairs of eyeglasses made. The best selection of frames and best prices (under $75/pair) were at **New Fei Supply** in Hong Kong, but I also had a pair ($90) made for my husband Tom at **Ming Jin Yuan,** at the Beijing Eye Mart. Glasses for my daughter Meredith, who has a simple Rx, cost $20 a pair in Shanghai!

MY BEST FINDS
by Aaron James

- **CDs:** In Shanghai you can find cheap and legal CDs in local stores—just weed through racks of Backstreet Boys and eventually you may find something decent.
- **Video Games:** I found Game Boy and other game system cartridges and cassettes in the Shanghai street market. Video-game cassettes are cheap and contain several games in one. Of course, they may not be legal, and they may repeat the same game over and over.
- **Mao Bags:** Street vendors, especially in Shanghai, sell these. An over-the-shoulder Mao bag is a must for any young revolutionary.

- **Custom-Tailored Shirts:** In Shanghai I visited the show-room of W. W. Chan & Sons Ltd. (my father's tailor from Hong Kong) and was fitted for my first custom shirts. The quality of the shirts is unmatched. I work in the music business in L.A., so I like to wear a good shirt, with a simple, almost invisible monogram on the cuff, with a pair of jeans. If I'm really going to dress up, I can throw on a blazer.

MY BEST FINDS
by Jenny McCormick

- **Hair Sticks:** Plastic chopstick-style fashion statements that you poke into your hair—everything from faux tortoise shell to Burberry plaid. Talk 'em down to $1 each. Best selection: ground floor of the Pearl Market, Beijing.
- **Fake Jade "Doughnuts":** The Pearl Market and elsewhere, about $1. These babies are great for stringing individually onto a cord or chain of your choosing to make a striking pendant.
- **Bamboo Handbag:** About $10 at the Dong Tai Market in Shanghai.
- **Mao Watch:** About $2. Available at most street markets but sold by the dozens at Hong Qiao and in the booths along Wangfujing, both in Beijing. Extra points awarded for their excellent kitsch value.

Chapter 2

Orientation

Years of Chinese Magic

Whether it's the year of the Tiger (2010) or of the Rabbit (2011) or of the Dragon (2012), it is always the year for China and its neighbors, from Hong Kong to Macau and beyond. Bring your family. China owns the world, so it's time we caught up on the new China.

Note these updates:

- **Delta** and **Northwest** (now merged) have been awarded new routes from the U.S. to China and Vietnam.
- Low-cost airlines, à la the U.S. brand Southwest Air, have come to Asia. Check out **AirAsia, Shenzhen Air,** and **Shanghai Air.**
- **Dragonair** has been granted more and more routes into the People's Republic of China (PRC)—now there are twice daily flights from Hong Kong International. Airport (HKG) to Guangzhou.
- **Sofitel** decided to open five-star luxury hotels in Beijing. Their hotels all over Asia are fabu.
- The Kowloon-Canton Railway (KCR) train has become part of Hong Kong's Mass Transit Railway (MTR) and now has two border crossings into the PRC. LoWu has been cleaned up and modernized, but the new **Lok Ma**

Chau is gorgeous and so easy to use you will want a visa just to enter China and use this station.

- **Fairmont,** the luxury brand from San Francisco, has taken to China as well and is opening up more deluxe beds.

- Beijing opened Terminal 3 at the **Capital Airport** as the cherry on top of the cake of all the new architecture, innovative buildings, and jaw-dropping changes that have spiffed up the city.

- Not to be outdone by Beijing, Hong Kong is on a building spree that wreaks devastation everywhere. As prime real estate in Kowloon has gone under the bulldozer, new buildings and even new neighborhoods are as populous as dim sum. We're standing in awe, as we wait for the new **Ritz-Carlton** in Kowloon to open—it's right near the Western Tunnel in a whole new part of Kowloon—and directly across from the International Finance Center (IFC) and Star Ferry in Central. **Ritz-Carlton** has also just opened in Shenzhen and Guangzhou (p. 147 and 165).

- **Shanghai Tang** has redone stores all over Asia and opened new ones. See their little redbrick house in Kowloon, their new digs in Pacific Place, and also another airport store in Pudong.

- **Wah Tung,** the maker of Chinese porcelain, has followed the trend to moving into new 'hoods as they shift from their warehouse environment in far-out Aberdeen to a gorgeous showroom in the Western District.

Everything is up-to-date in China and getting hotter, and cooler, every day. Make that wei cool.

The Magic of Hong Kong

Much talk has been made of Shanghai being the new Hong Kong, or that Shenzhen will merge with Hong Kong into a single metropolitan district. The way I see it, despite all that the new China has to offer, Hong Kong has not lost out. Hong Kong is, in fact, going gangbusters with new stuff.

Sure, China's big cities offer plenty of European designer goods, but they cost 20% more than in Hong Kong, and they probably won't fit you. And the linen sheets at the Mandarin Oriental? The bar at the InterConti? The E-Spa system at all Peninsula Hotels and anchored in Hong Kong? The fact that W has arrived and there's soon going to be a diamond as big as the Ritz-Carlton? Oh, my dear.

Hong Kong is still the gateway to China, and the best place to begin and end any trip to the area. It's the center of Asia for transportation, for getting the big picture, and for understanding tourism. There is some very good shopping, but prices keep going up so you will have to shop carefully and follow me to the magic.

The Lure of China

This book covers the most obvious cities a tourist will visit, but I don't want you to think that Shanghai and Beijing are the only chic cities in China. The new China is spreading and growing; money and sophistication are out there where tourists even wander.

To make this clear, I'll list the cities where the Italian brand Max Mara has stores: Beijing, Changchun, Chandu, Chongqing, Dalian, Guangzhou (Canton), Hangzhou, Harbin, Kunming, Qingdao, Shanghai, Shenyang, Shenzhen, Urümqi, Wuhan, and Xi'an.

Welcome to the new China. Get out there and shop. Study a map, learn these cities, and book another ticket to come back. Remember that if price is your bottom line, you may find that Hong Kong is more expensive than other cities.

Welcome to China

I try to put politics aside when I write about China; after all, my mission is to shop. I can't help but note, however, that the Chinese are the most capitalist communists I've ever seen. They grasp the big picture and, my God, it's impressive.

Beijing and Shanghai are masterworks of marketing, in all senses and subtexts of the word. To market, to market, to score some fine buys. To market, to market, to influence the world. Napoleon was right: When China awakes, the world will indeed tremble. China is the future.

GETTING A VISA

U.S. citizens do not need a visa to enter Hong Kong or Taiwan. They do need a visa to enter the People's Republic of China (PRC), even on a day trip from Hong Kong. It is virtually impossible for a U.S. citizen to get a visa to enter China outside of the U.S. except through London, or in Hong Kong after you arrive. *Note:* Visa prices and systems have recently changed.

American and British passport holders living in Hong Kong will pay a dear price for their visas. The most expensive is the 1-year, multiple-entry visa, which a tourist probably will not need. Tourists, however, can now get a single or multiple-entry visa for a flat fee of $130 from a Chinese embassy or consulate. A visa service will charge you more. If you allow yourself 48 hours in Hong Kong, you can possibly get the visa there for a little less.

You can get a visa in a number of ways:

- Apply for a visa through the Chinese consulate in your city; you can pay with cash or credit card.
- If you carry a secondary passport from a country other than the U.S. or U.K., present it at the Chinese Embassy (or consulate) to secure your Chinese visa. It can be much less expensive.

- If you are willing to pay the money or you live in a city that does not have a Chinese consulate, contact a visa service. Download the necessary papers, fill them out, then send off your passport, one passport-size photo, and a big fat check via FedEx or other provider that offers package tracking. I sometimes use **Zierer Visa Service** (© 866/788-1100; www.zvs.com).
- Zierer charges about $100 in service fees (the price of the visa is additional), but you are paying for convenience and will get your passport back, with a hologram visa, in about a week.
- Get your visa in Hong Kong. This can be pricey, especially if you need fast service. Visa services are offered in the airport and throughout town. It's a cinch at the airport and costs about $175, but it takes about 4 hours, which means hanging out at the airport or schlepping back and forth.
- But wait, there are other ways. For me, it was far easier to have my hotel concierge do all the work, though that's more expensive. When the concierge obtains your visa, your total bill is usually divided in two: the cost of the actual visa and the service charge. *Note:* You do not have to add a tip to a service charge. My friend Toby just got a visa in Hong Kong from her hotel concierge for $50. Go figure.

CHINESE ARRIVAL DETAILS

1. The amount of foreign cash you can legally bring into the PRC is unlimited. However, if you have more than US$5,000, you must declare it.
2. No pornographic materials, guns, or bombs. Duh.
3. No live animals for short-term visits. Regulations on pets are being eased, however for longer stays; dogs are quarantined for 30 days upon entry, and must have proof of rabies vaccine and a health certificate issued by the U.S. government. (The new Chinese chic is to walk your dog—but dogs are prohibited from most public spaces.)

China

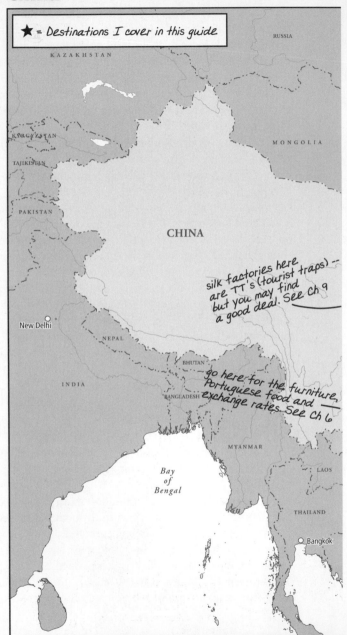

★ = Destinations I cover in this guide

RUSSIA

KAZAKHSTAN

KYRGYZSTAN

TAJIKISTAN

MONGOLIA

PAKISTAN

CHINA

silk factories here
are TT's (tourist traps) --
but you may find
a good deal. See Ch 9

New Delhi

NEPAL

BHUTAN

go here for the furniture,
Portuguese food and
exchange rates. See Ch 6

INDIA

BANGLADESH

MYANMAR

LAOS

Bay
of
Bengal

THAILAND

Bangkok

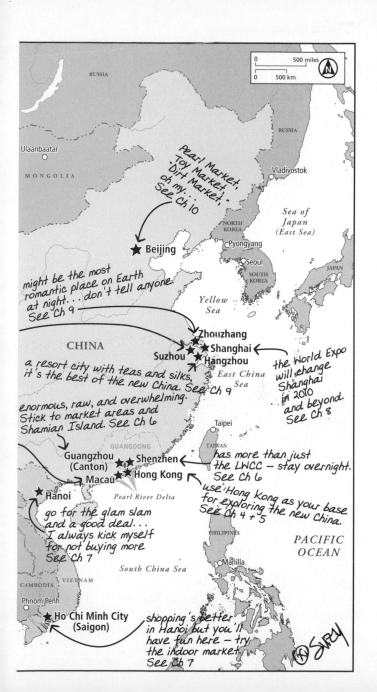

Flying Concepts

With the PRC opening up, demand has created more plane routes into China. More and more airlines are fighting for hubs and for the loyalty of business and leisure travelers. The number of flights into China has doubled in the past few years. The number of airline alliance relationships is also increasing. Code shares are on the takeoff.

The type of craft flying long-haul routes is also changing. In fact, after my most recent trips, I can't tell you how important it is to check the kind of craft making the haul and adjust your plans accordingly. The difference of a 12-hour flight in a new 777 versus an old 747 is enormous. Airlines are working to make the trip more comfortable with the addition of a new class of service: executive economy, extended economy, economy plus—whatever they want to call it.

Note also that technology has now made it possible for a plane to fly for about 18 hours nonstop. (A direct flight from New York to Hong Kong is slightly over 17 hrs.) You may not want to sit that long, but at least it's your choice.

Finally, if you are doing a Pacific Rim or multidestination visit, choose your hub city carefully. Both Hong Kong and Taipei are good choices (even if you don't want to visit Taiwan, the Taipei airport is great and we adore EVA Air), but avoid Narita if you can. Depending on the routing and the carrier, it may pay to fly nonstop to Shanghai or to Ho Chi Minh City (formerly Saigon) and use that as a hub for southern Asia.

The destination chapters that follow include specific tips on carriers, flights, and savings. Below are some concepts that will help you organize your trip.

If you are planning on exploring China or are looking for promotional deals, don't forget to check out the international airports of the Pearl River Delta, which include Baiyun International Airport in Guangzhou. Shenzhen also has a new, modern international airport as does Macau.

Petty Pekin Announcement

For those of you who will book all or part of your trip through Beijing, be aware that most airlines refer to Beijing as Pekin (PEK). When checking flights listed in alphabetical order, look under P for Pekin. I even had trouble getting tickets to Beijing when the agent told me that the carrier served only Shanghai and Pekin in China, and I had to choose one.

TRANSPACIFIC FLYING

Many flights from the major West Coast cities (Los Angeles, San Francisco, Seattle, Vancouver) connect through Narita, Taipei, Seoul, and even Hawaii. Travelers increasingly prefer transpacific nonstops, most with flying times of 13 to 16 hours.

Continental Airlines (www.continental.com) flies nonstop from Newark Liberty International Airport to Hong Kong. Its BusinessFirst service offers a first-class experience at a business-class price.

Cathay Pacific (www.cathaypacific.com) also flies a transpacific route from New York, and they have two flights a day from both Los Angeles and San Francisco.

From the South or Midwest, you may want to travel through the major West Coast gateway cities listed above.

I like **Northwest** (www.nwa.com)—now merged with **Delta** (www.delta.com)—for several reasons, including the possibility of a layover in Minneapolis, not far from the Mall of America. Northwest also uses its Detroit hub for flights to China—it's less crowded than other U.S. international airports, and a secret worth remembering.

Smart shoppers and travelers know about **EVA Air** (www. evaair.com), which flies the Taiwanese flag. EVA offers service from major cities around the world, including several U.S. West Coast cities (even Seattle) and is known for the excellent luxury-coach section of the plane. Trust me on this: Taipei is a great city for making connections, and EVA has the best value in the skies. For my money, if you are not on a nonstop to HKG, Taipei is the best hub city in Asia.

Finally, see specifics of travel to each destination in this book in subsequent chapters.

TRANSATLANTIC ROUTES

You can get to Hong Kong or the PRC from a variety of European hubs that offer ongoing flights to Asia. The transatlantic approach from the U.S. makes sense only if you take the time to layover for at least 1 night; the next 6 hours of jet lag will be a lot easier to handle.

Lufthansa (www.lufthansa.com) operates many flights a week to Asia, so check their options on a transatlantic route. **KLM** (www.klm.com), which code shares with Delta, Continental, Northwest, and Air France, has flights from Amsterdam.

Competition on U.K.-to-China routes is fierce, so deals abound. **Virgin Atlantic** (www.virgin-atlantic.com) flies to Hong Kong, Beijing, and Shanghai, with three classes of service. **British Airways** (www.britishairways.com) and **Cathay Pacific** (www.cathaypacific.com) also fly from London. Each airline will match the others' promotional deals. I've heard of round-trips from London for $400. But note that if you have an economy ticket (poor you) on British Airways, you can only check one valise. **Singapore Air** (www.singaporeair.com) has amazing choices in routes and in comfort levels.

Note: When you are departing China, be sure to show your U.S. through ticket even if you are laying over in a European destination. If you have a ticket to the U.S., the less rigid U.S. luggage allowance will apply.

UNUSUAL CONNECTIONS

* **Hawaii:** Service from Hawaii to Hong Kong is available, as is service to China. This means that those who want to break up the flight and avoid Narita can stop over in Hawaii.

- **Tel Aviv:** This route is unusual, but it works. El Al uses Tel Aviv as its hub city and has ongoing service to Beijing and Hong Kong as well as other major cities in the Far East. It's not as strange as it sounds—the flying time from New York to Tel Aviv is about the same as New York to Tokyo. A layover in Israel goes a long way toward eliminating jet lag once you get to China. Furthermore, El Al has a code share with American Airlines, so you can use frequent-flier miles, book through American, or perhaps connect an around-the-world deal with American, El Al, and Cathay Pacific, also a partner.
- **Detroit:** This U.S. hub is not as well-known as Chicago, so you have a better chance of using frequent-flier miles. Northwest Airlines flies from Detroit to Guangzhou. But, speaking of Chicago, it has nonstops to the mainland.
- **Salt Lake City:** I love this connection because coming home through U.S. Customs and Immigration is so easy— fly nonstop to Narita and then carry on from there.
- **Seattle:** Count on EVA Air to make this connection easy.

FLYING ON MILES

While you may indeed be able to use frequent-flier miles for your ticket to Asia, do check if the routing is worth it. My friend Mary had to fly West Palm Beach to Atlanta, Atlanta to L.A., L.A. to Seoul, and Seoul to Hong Kong. On one of her other trips, she had a 6-hour layover in Tokyo before the 5-hour flight to Hong Kong. In booking the trip, she was able to get only certain legs in business or first-class and had to endure portions of her 30-hour journey in an economy seat.

TICKET DEALS

Because they buy in bulk, wholesalers often get a better price. Enter **Lilian Fong,** Pacific Place, 288 W. Valley Blvd., Ste. 206B, Alhambra, CA 91801 (© **626/943-1212;** pacplace@att. net.com), my personal secret weapon in the U.S.

It was Lilian who first introduced me to EVA Air, by the way. I have, in fact, been using Lilian for over 20 years; during this time a few things have gone wrong, but you might want to talk to her and see what she's got.

Other thoughts:

- Talk to your travel agent about coupons or deals that can upgrade you to first-class. Lilian once offered me first-class upgrade tickets if I paid the full fare for business class; that's a pretty good deal. The deals come and go with the seasons and the world news. Note that travel to Asia is up, so deals are not as easy to come by as they once were.

- Airlines have so many code-share partners these days that you can have seamless ticketing; however, you may want to know which carriers are taking you on which legs.

- Do look for new carriers, new routes, and new connections that might offer promotional deals. EVA Air, a Taiwanese airline, is only a few years old but has gotten a lot of attention for its price, comfort, and snazzy lounges.

- Airlines often wage "mile wars"; I once found a deal offering a coach ticket to Hong Kong for 40,000 miles.

- As the PRC loosens up and technology allows airliners to fly farther, possibilities multiply. Watch for flights like Detroit–Shanghai, Minneapolis–Beijing, Houston–Taipei, and so on.

- Look for flights into unfamiliar Chinese cities, such as Shenzhen or Guangzhou (Canton), both of which are near Hong Kong but in the PRC.

- Hunt down little-known promos. For example, if you hold an American Express platinum card, you qualify for a free ticket to any destination when you buy a full-fare business-class ticket for yourself.

- Online fares may offer deals. Cathay Pacific's newsletter provides e-mail updates about contests, deals, and even auctions. Ask to receive their "dings" (instant updates via a program you can download).

About Your Luggage

More and more airlines are going by weight rather than piece, but several international carriers have recently created new rules that combine the two.

For example, most U.S. flag carriers allow you two pieces of checked luggage, each weighing 50 pounds, no matter what class of service you travel. If you travel business class, first-class, or have premium status, you may get additional perks, weight allowance, or pieces. It goes downhill from there. If you are a shopper, you're going to be sick over this.

As you research airfares, also check out the luggage allowances and charges for additional pieces of luggage.

If you are doing some intra-Asian visiting, especially on local carriers, expect a different luggage weight allowance than the long haul! This can make life tedious and expensive.

When we fly Air Asia, we pay for the highest ticket with luggage, which is a specified category.

- Check if the airline will let you buy a coach seat and a confirmed upgrade at the same time. To get a deal on these, you have to fly on certain days of the week and may not get the upgrade in both directions.
- Use your miles to upgrade, but only if the upgrade can be confirmed.
- Choose your premium status with a single airline carefully. Sarah and I are devoted to United because as Premium members, we get seats in extended economy without paying extra for them. These four seats have 7 extra inches of leg room, which on a long haul, makes a big difference.
- Around-the-world fares may offer you the best price, especially in business and first-class. They are allegedly more forgiving on jet lag because you continue going in the same direction. Fares vary with the airline and the point of departure.

- A multiple-city trip around the Far East can be a great deal. Cathay Pacific's All Asia Pass costs less if you buy it on their website. *Note:* A pass may not earn mileage points.
- If you want to try some of the newer Asian discount airlines, pick a hub city that serves the carriers you want to connect with. We've been booking a lot on AirAsia (www.airasia.com).
- Check out age-related discounts. Cathay Pacific considers you a senior starting at age 55, and you get a $100 discount. Also inquire about price breaks for students and children.

CHINESE CARRIERS

AirChina (www.airchina.com.cn) is the best-known Chinese airline; it has code shares with a variety of well-known airlines and flies some 260 routes within China and over 50 international routes. Other brands to know about—especially for domestic flights in China—include **China Eastern** (www.ce-air.com) and **China Southern** (www.cs-air.com). China Southern also serves international routes.

All About EVA

EVA Air (www.evaair.com) is a Taiwanese carrier that flies to Hong Kong, Taipei, and various Southeast Asian/Australian destinations. I heart EVA. They have a fleet of various planes (the 747s seem a bit tatty these days), including brand-new 777s and airbuses. This airline offers "extended coach"—as good as business class at half the price—plus Taipei as their hub city, a much better choice than Narita (Tokyo). Even if you just change planes here, you will love the Taipei airport. It not only has a Starbucks, and plenty of good shopping, but also a museum store.

Fares are excellent. If you buy a promotional business-class ticket (the best deals are available online), it's less than $4,000 round-trip. Executive coach goes for about $2,000. U.S. cities served include Los Angeles, San Francisco, Seattle, and Newark. EVA also flies from Paris.

Cathay Pacific flies the Hong Kong flag and is part owner of **Dragonair** (www.dragonair.com), the best and most trusted of the short-haul carriers from Hong Kong into China. It is also my main choice for a long haul if I am coming from Paris or San Francisco. Dragonair has recently won rights to fly within China, so count on them as needed.

I also like EVA and fly them often, especially when money is tight (see below).

Sleeping Matters

Each city chapter of this book includes specifics on hotels in the area. As China becomes increasingly accessible, more hotels want part of the action. Where there are openings, there are promotional deals. **W Hotels,** a division of Starwood, has sprouted up across the country, along with W Retail, the store that sells objects modeled in the rooms themselves.

Sofitel has brought French charm to China and Southeast Asia. Peninsula Hotel Group has several new hotels in Asia, including the brand-new Pen in Shanghai. As always, the Pen's hotels offer luxuries, amenities, cooking and crafts lessons, and (usually) one of the best locations in town.

Note also the trend for big hotel chains to open two locations in the same city. When you book any hotel, be sure you know which is where. **InterContinental** has opened two hotels in Beijing, on opposite sides of the city. InterConti's hotel in Shenzhen is totally amazing—it's alongside a theme park and has a theme of its own (Spain) and is really a resort.

Ritz-Carlton has made a dramatic entry into the area. Their Hong Kong hotel, right at the mouth of the Kowloon side of the Western Tunnel, was not open as this book went to press, but we've checked out Shenzhen and Guangzhou and been floored by the luxury, the attention to detail, and the service.

Hilton is expanding like mad, especially in China. **Hyatt** has one of the most dependable businesses in terms of consistent product, achieved elegance, good spas, and solid business amenities. There are assorted different Hyatt brands, Regency, Park, and so forth. Hyatt on the Bund in Shanghai, Park Hyatt in Pudong, Grand Hyatt in Wanchai (Hong Kong), and so on.

If you are interested in discounts, check out **www.asia-hotels.com**. (Hey, you never know.)

Websites for the major hotel chains represented in Hong Kong and the main cities in China are as follows:

- www.accorhotels-asia.com
- www.fourseasons.com
- www.hilton.com
- www.hyatt.com
- www.interconti.com (includes InterContinental and Holiday Inn)
- www.landishotelsresorts.com
- www.mandarinoriental.com
- www.peninsula.com
- www.ritzcarlton.com
- www.starwood.com (includes Sheraton, St. Regis, Westin, and W)

Money Matters

The major currencies in this part of the world are

- Hong Kong dollars, represented by HKD or HK$ preceding the amount.
- Chinese yuan, often represented by a ¥ symbol following the amount. Yuan are also called RMB.
- Dong, official Vietnam currency; U.S. dollars are preferred.
- Patacas, used in Macau and written MP$.

MONEY TIPS

Having watched the fall of the dollar over the past few years, I can't begin to stress how important it is to shop in foreign destinations that are not affected by the rise of the euro. Well, it's important if you care about price.

So just being in Asia and shopping smart is **Tip #1**.

Tip #2: Hong Kong dollars are no longer accepted in eastern China. If you can get someone to take them, they will charge you 6% to 10% more.

Tip #3: If you visit Hong Kong before heading into the PRC, some banks will allow you to withdraw Chinese yuan, which appear on the screen as RMB. That means you won't have a money crisis as soon as you land or cross the border. But there's no need for a money crisis; ATMs are located at most border stations.

Tip #4: The yuan is being artificially suppressed by the Chinese government and may increase. Expect the yuan to go to 6 to the $1; as we go to press it is 6.83.

CURRENCY RATES

As this book goes to print, the **U.S. dollar** is equal to approximately 7.7 Hong Kong dollars (HKD) or about 6.8 Chinese yuan (RMB). The **euro** is at HK$11.52 or about RMB10.15. Note that the exchange rate varies widely depending on where you exchange your money; hotels and currency-exchange offices often have the worst rates.

CHARGE IT, PLEASE

Credit cards are more widely accepted in China than in the past. That doesn't mean you can use your card with wild abandon in the PRC, however. You will actually find it easier to bargain and to pay in cash. ATMs are readily available.

In fact, ATMs are all over China and Hong Kong and they are beginning to get more popular in Vietnam, so you can get cash relatively easily. Be aware, however, that your bank may charge a high fee for international withdrawals. Bank cards usually add a 3% surcharge on international purchases as well. Look into **Capital One** (© 877/812-4600; www.capital one.com) for fewer charges—no international fees, they say.

King of Bargaining Tells All

One of the things that make shopping in China so unbelievably great is the all-out, excessive bargaining. Honestly, you will buy things you didn't even want just because you got caught up in the bargaining process.

I became the King of Bargaining because of my take-no-prisoners attitude. I was cheated on my first shopping adventure in China and was terribly upset because I was dumb. After that, I felt compelled to make up all that I had overpaid.

At the time of my first shopping/bargaining foray, I was convinced that I was making out like a bandit. It wasn't until later that I added up all the prices and realized that I could have bought the same stuff for the same price at Wal-Mart. After that, I honed my skills and managed to buy twice the amount of merchandise for half the price.

I try to be polite. I don't criticize the merchandise, but I like to pay 12% to 25% of the asking price. I tell the vendors I'm poor, I'm a student, I don't have that kind of money, and I know they are offering tourist prices.

The important thing is to not let them know that you are too interested. In fact, it works better if there are two of you to play good cop, bad cop, or, in this case, good shop, bad shop. For instance, you examine the item and get an initial price from the vendor. The bad-cop friend says, "No way, man. You don't really want that, and it's waaaay too expensive."

The vendor jumps in and lowers the price. It's very important at this point that you express genuine interest. Once they know you will buy, all they have to do is close the sale, which is a matter of price.

The biggest problem is that the prices you are quoted at first are good prices compared to those we are used to in America. It's just that these are very high prices for China and for the quality of the merchandise. —Aaron James

ABOUT TIPPING

In mainland China, a communist country, tipping is frowned upon. Yet in Western-style hotels and service businesses, everyone seems to want or expect a tip. Therefore, I have noted specific tips in sections of this book in local currency.

For my part, I think tipping helps to teach capitalism. You can tip in U.S. dollars in any of these countries. If I were you, I'd sit on the euros—they're more expensive for you and less convenient for the recipient.

CHEAT SHEETS

If you are mathematically challenged, go to **www.oanda.com** or **www.xe.com** and make yourself a currency cheat sheet. For me, I just divide by seven and let the difference flap in the breeze. (Except in Vietnam!)

FINAL MONEY NOTE

Prices given in this book are in U.S. dollars unless otherwise specified.

Phoning Home

If you're not connected to Skype, what is wrong with you? Use a Skype handset with your laptop, put $10 in your Skype account, and talk to people all over the world for pennies.

Otherwise, please use a phone card. You have to dial a lot of numbers, but you can talk for an hour at a cost of about $10. You can usually buy a phone card from your hotel concierge or business center, as well as any convenience store (such as 7-Eleven) in Hong Kong or China.

My international travel phone accepts a SIM card, so I buy a new one for most destinations. You will pay about $20 for activation and can then buy blocks of time as needed. In Hong Kong you can buy a single SIM card that will also ring in China with a different number—this is easier than changing cards and handing out multiple numbers.

Buyer beware: On my last trip, someone talked me into getting a single SIM and phone number for use all over Asia. This seemed genius at the time but turned into a disaster. Minutes were sucked away and I was stuck without phone service for days.

You can rent a global mobile phone through Zierer's (the visa folks) but it's actually cheaper to buy an international phone when you arrive and install a SIM card. A simple Nokia phone is less than $50. Also note that in Asia the phone is "unlocked," which means you can exchange the SIM card for one from France or Italy or anywhere else.

Comparison Shopping

People often ask me what city has the best deals or what to buy where in order to save money. Unfortunately, there are no clear answers to those questions. To confuse you more, a chart I found in the *Wall Street Journal Asia* compared prices for a 700-milliliter (1½-pint) bottle of Chivas Regal: It cost $25 in Shanghai and $42 in Hong Kong. Who would have thunk it?

In terms of goods, I find different things in each city, without much crossover.

As a rule of thumb, China is less expensive than Hong Kong on basics and more expensive on designer goods and imports. Prices for Hong Kong designer goods are competitive with prices in Europe; the same goods in the U.S. may be less expensive in the U.S. if you can find a match up—often the colors or the styles are different.

Getting Around

Every hotel I've ever been to in Asia has a "taxi card" that lists destinations in English and in the local language (Chinese, Vietnamese, and so forth).

If you are doing some serious exploring, find the **Taxi Book**—there is one for about a dozen different cities in China as well as for Hong Kong. This is like a binder filled with places, addresses, and instructions in Chinese.

Getting Around, Part 2

You'll find train-specific information in the Beijing and Shanghai chapters of this book, but note that the fast train connecting these two cities is slated to begin service in 2011. It will travel about 124kmph (200 mph); there will be 100 new trains with 16 carriages each. See p. 215.

Reading Around

A trip to the news kiosk is part of the fun of any international airport, hotel, or destination—note that *Travel + Leisure* has it's own Asian edition that puts the focus on, oh yeah, Asia, and a fabulous regional travel magazine is *Destin-Asia* (it's a pun, get it?). Both provide insider tips and information to places not covered that frequently in the U.S.

Chapter 3

A Dictionary of Chinese Arts, Crafts, Styles & Customs

An Alphabetical Guide

ANCESTOR PAINTINGS

Available on paper scroll or canvas scroll, these large paintings, most often family portraits, are called "ancestor paintings" in English and represent a very specific art form. They are widely copied and reproduced, so fakes abound. The best one I ever saw was of female twins. My guide that day translated the inscription—about what venerable old ladies they were in that, their 42nd year on Earth.

Genuine antique paintings on canvas cost $500 to $3,000 each in China, depending on size and condition. I recently bought two beauties; the canvas was original but had been painted over. Although this totally ruins the investment or resale value, it made for two glorious wall hangings.

ANTIQUES

Ha! I've seen antiques being made right in front of my eyes, and if I can't tell the difference, you can't, either. Be an expert, use an expert, or go to a trusted gallery.

The U.S. government defines an antique as any item of art, furniture, or craft work over 100 years old. If you return to the States with a genuine antique, you pay no duty on the piece.

True antiques are a hot commodity, and unscrupulous dealers take advantage of the demand by issuing authenticity papers for goods that are not antiques. To make matters worse, Hong Kong does not require its dealers to put prices on their merchandise. Depending on the dealer's mood or assessment of your pocketbook, he might quote you a price of HK$100 ($13) or HK$1,155 ($150) for the ginger jar you love. He also might tell you it's 10 years old or 10,000. If "1,000 year-old eggs," sold in all markets, still haven't reached their expiration date, imagine how that translates to antiques.

Pick a reputable dealer and ask a lot of questions about the piece and its period. If the dealer doesn't know and doesn't offer to find out, he probably is not a true antiques expert. Get as much in writing as possible. Even if it means nothing, it is proof that you have been defrauded if you find out later that your Ming vase was made in Kowloon around 1995.

Your invoice should state what you are buying, the estimated age of the item (including dynasty and year), where it was made, any flaws, and any repairs made to the piece.

Expect most, or many, of the antiques in markets in Hong Kong, Macau, and mainland China to be fakes.

BLUE-AND-WHITE

Blue-and-white is the common term for Chinese export-style porcelain, which reached its heyday in the late 17th century, when the black ships were running "china" to Europe as if it were gold. After 1750, craftspeople in both England and continental Europe had the secret of bone china and were well on their way to creating their own chinoiserie styles and manufacturing transfer patterns for mass distribution and consumption.

The untrained eye needs to look for the following: pits and holes that indicate firing methods, the nonuniform look of hand drawing versus stencils, the truer shades of blues of the best dyes, and the right shades of weathered gray-white as opposed to the bright white backgrounds of new wares (not to mention new replications of the former color). Marks on the bottom are usually meaningless. Designs may have European inspiration (look for flowers and arabesques), which will help you determine if you are looking at a Chinese or a European good.

BRONZES

Several Hong Kong museums, such as the **Hong Kong Heritage Museum**, 1 Man Lam Rd., Sha Tin (© **852/2180-8188;** www.heritagemuseum.gov.hk; Metro to Sha Tin or Che Kung Temple stations), for one, feature antique Chinese bronzes, making the art form an easy one with which to commence your education in Chinese art. Visit several local museums to sharpen your eye; you'll want to completely understand the difference between what will cost you thousands of dollars and what you can buy for a few hundred. The lesser price indicates a fake. As with all Chinese art, you must be able to recognize subtle changes in style and form that indicate time periods and dynasties in order to properly date your fake.

CARPETS

Carpets come in traditional designs or can be special ordered to your specifications directly from factories. The price depends on knots per square inch, fiber content, complexity of design, the number of colors used, and the city or region of origin. Any of the **Chinese Arts & Crafts** stores is a good place to look at carpets and get familiar with different styles and price ranges.

When considering the material of the rug, think about its intended use. Silk rugs are magnificent but impractical. If you're going to use the carpet in a low-traffic area or as a wall hanging, great. Silk threads are usually woven as the warp (vertical) threads, with either silk or cotton as the weft (horizontal). The pile in either case will be pure silk. Wool rugs are more durable.

CERAMICS & PORCELAIN

Ceramic and porcelain wares available in Hong Kong and China fall into three categories: British imports, new Chinese, and old Chinese. For a short lesson in buying blue-and-white, see above.

New Chinese craft pottery and porcelain is in high demand. Although much of the base material is being imported from Japan and finished in Hong Kong, it is still considered Chinese. In fact, the better wares are coming out of Hong Kong, and the mass-market stuff is more likely coming from China. Most factories will take orders directly. Numerous factories in Hong Kong will allow you to watch porcelain wares being created and to place a personal order.

Porcelain is distinguished from pottery in that it uses china clay to form the paste. Modern designs are less elaborate than those used during the height of porcelain design in the Ming dynasty (a.d. 1368–1644), but the old techniques are slowly being revived. Blue-and-white ware is still the most popular. New wares (made to look old) can be found at various Chinese government stores, including **Chinese Arts & Crafts**... zillions of little shops on and off Hollywood Road in Hong Kong, in Hong Kong's **Stanley Market,** in Macau, and just about everywhere else. Fakes abound, so buy with care. When you order ceramics or ceramic lamps, you may even be asked whether you want "antique finish."

CHEONGSAM

You already know what a cheongsam is, you just don't know the term, so you're temporarily thrown. Close your eyes and picture Suzie Wong. She's wearing a Chinese dress with a Mandarin collar and silk knot buttons that run from the neck across the shoulder and then down the side, right? Possibly in red satin with a dragon print, but that's an extra. The dress is called a cheongsam. Really touristy ones come in those silk or satin looks, but you can buy a chic one or you can have one custom-made. In Shanghai a cheongsam may be called a *quipo*.

CHINESE SCROLLS

Part art and part communication, Chinese scrolls are decorative pieces of parchment paper rolled around pieces of wood at each end. They contain calligraphy and art relating to history, a story, a poem, a lesson, or a message. Some scrolls are mostly art, with little calligraphy; others are just the opposite. It is usually not possible to identify the author or artist, but doing so makes the scroll more valuable. Chinese scrolls make beautiful wall hangings and are popular collector's pieces.

CHINOISERIE

Exports from Asia were so fashionable in Europe in the late 18th century, and again in the Victorian era, that they started their own trend. Western designers and craftspeople began to make items in Asian styles. Much was created from fantasy and whimsy; the influence of Indian and other styles mixed with the purely Chinese. Decorative arts and furniture in Asian style, made in Europe, are considered chinoiserie. Chinoiserie is not actually made in China.

CHOPS

A chop is a form of signature stamp on which the symbol for a person's name is carved. The chop is then dipped in dry dye and placed on paper, much like a rubber stamp. The main difference between rubber stamps and chops is that rubber stamps became trendy only in the 20th century, whereas chops were in vogue about 2,200 years ago. Because chops go so far back, you can choose from an antique or a newly created version.

CLOISONNÉ

The art of cloisonné involves fitting decorative enamel between thin metal strips on a metal surface. The surface is then fired at just the right temperature, and the finish is glazed to a sheen. It sounds simple, but the work involved in laying the metal strips to form a complicated design and then laying in the paint so that it does not run is time-consuming and delicate. It is an art requiring training and patience.

Antique works by the finest artists bring in large sums of money. Most of what you'll see for sale in Hong Kong (outside of the finest galleries) is mass-produced cloisonné that is inexpensive—a small vase sells for about $20; bangle bracelets are $3. You can also find rings, mirrors, and earrings for good prices at most markets. These make good souvenir gifts. Frankly, I prefer the Hermès version.

EMBROIDERY

The art of stitching decorations onto fabric is known as embroidery. Stitches can be combined to make abstract or realistic shapes, sometimes of enormous complexity. Embroidered goods sold in Hong Kong include bed linens, chair cushions, tablecloths, napkins, runners, place mats, coasters, blouses, children's clothing, and robes. All of those items are new. Another market deals in antique embroidered fabrics (and slippers), which, of course, can be very expensive.

Traditionally, embroidery was hand sewn. Today machines do most of the work. Embroidery threads range from the finest silk to the heaviest yarn. Judge the value of a piece by whether it is hand stitched or machine stitched and by the fineness of the thread or yarn.

FAKES

China has seriously cracked down on makers of fake name-brand goods. Officials mostly go after the factories that produce the goods, so vendors still have the items, which they sell when conditions appear to be safe. Often the branded fakes are put away and you must ask to see them.

Buying a fake doesn't make you safe, however—many are confiscated when you leave the area or when you enter the U.S. and E.U. countries.

Buyer Beware

Not all of the fakes for sale are handbags or DVDs. I swear that the Ambien I bought with a legal French prescription from a pharmacy in Kowloon is totally fake—and I paid a lot of money for those little pills.

FURNITURE

Chinese styles in furniture once caused a major sensation in the European market. Teak and ebony were imported from the Far East and highly valued in the West. Yet the major furnishing rage was for lacquered goods, usually in the form of small chests of cabinets. The cabinets sat on top of stands, which were built to measure in Europe.

Antique furniture is a hot collector's item. True Chinese antique furniture is defined by purity of form, with decorative and interpretive patterns carved into the sides or backs. Dealers and collectors alike scour the shops and auction houses. It is better to find an unfinished piece and oversee its restoration than to find one that has already been restored. If it has been restored, find out who did the work and what was done. Some unknowing dealers bleach the fine woods and ruin their value. Others put a polyurethane-like gloss on the pieces and make them unnaturally shiny.

Because Asian furniture is used to the local climate, be certain that your hometown weather will not damage the furniture you buy and that you have the proper humidifiers. Many shoppers say it's better to buy furniture from cities farther south in China and Asia, and not to buy in Beijing.

If you decide to buy, decide beforehand how you will get the piece home. If you are having the shop ship it, verify the quality of the shipper and insurance. If you are shipping it yourself, call a shipper and get details before you begin to negotiate the price of the piece. Ask about duty. I once paid $250 for a small piece and ended up paying an additional $425 to get it to my door—the shipping wasn't very expensive, but the duty was.

HORN

Tortoise shell is illegal to buy and import into the U.S., but most Asian tortoisey-looking items are made out of buffalo horn. Ask.

IVORY

A warning: Articles made from raw ivory will not be allowed into the United States. Only antique pieces made from carved ivory are allowed, and only if the dealer provides the proper paperwork and provenance. It is not smart to try to run raw ivory. It's risky on several levels, so you may want to forget this category of goods.

Another warning: New items that look like ivory are made of other materials, including walrus bone and even nut. Carvers in Hong Kong are currently using dentin from walruses, hippopotamuses, boars, and whales as substitutes for elephant ivory. If you want to make sure you are not buying elephant ivory, look for a network of fine lines that is visible to the naked eye. If the piece you are buying is made of bone, it will not have any visible grain or luster. Bone also weighs less than ivory. Imitation ivory is made of plastic but can be colored to look quite good. It is a softer material and less dense than real ivory.

JADE

The term *jade* is used to signify two different stones: jadeite and nephrite. The written character for jade signifies purity, nobility, and beauty. Some consider it a magical stone, protecting the health of the wearer. The scholar always carried a piece of jade in his pocket for health and wisdom. Jade is also reported to pull impurities out of the body; old, red-brown jade reputedly has absorbed the blood and impurities of its deceased former owner.

Jadeite is chemically different from nephrite and tends to be more translucent. For this reason, jadeite is often considered to be more valuable. Furthermore, really good jade—sometimes called "imperial jade"—is white, not green.

In Chinese, *chen yu* is real jade, and *fu yu* is false jade. Jadeite comes in many colors, including lavender, yellow, black, orange, red, pink, white, and many shades of green. Nephrite comes in varying shades of green only.

The value of both is determined by translucence, quality of carving, and color. Assume that an inexpensive carving is not jade. "Jade" factories work in soapstone or other less valuable stones. Poor-quality white jade can be dyed into valuable-looking shades of green. Let the buyer beware.

Jade should be ice-cold to the touch and so hard it cannot be scratched by steel. Some shoppers make it common practice to quick touch or lick touch a piece. This is not a real test of good jade, although stone will certainly feel different to the tongue than plastic. You may also want to "ring" a piece, because jade, just like fine crystal, has its own tone when struck.

If you are interested in carved jade figures, bring out your own jeweler's loupe and watch the dealer quake. If the carving is smooth and uniform, it was done with modern tools. Gotcha! A fine piece and an old piece are hand cut and should be slightly jagged on the edges.

What are those green circles you see in the market and often in the street? They are nephrite and should cost no more than $1 per circle. These "jade doughnuts" make fabulous gifts when tied to a long silken cord and turned into a necklace.

KITES

On one of my trips to China, I bought two very similar kites: One cost $26 in a hotel gift shop, and one cost $2 in Tiananmen Square. If you are buying the kite for a child who will most likely destroy it, get smart.

It is believed that kites appeared about 2,400 years ago, first made of wood and bamboo and later refined in silk or paper, which had better draft. While kite flying is a hobby and an entertainment, it is also a science based on aeronautical engineering. In fact, early kites were used for military purposes, but around the year 784 and the start of the Tang dynasty, people began to fly kites for entertainment.

Among the most common folk motifs in kites are dragons and bats—bats being a figure for good luck, based on a pun with the Chinese word *fu*, which means "bat" and "blessing."

The value of a kite depends on the construction of the frame, the fabric, and the artistic merit of the designs.

LACQUER

No, I don't mean nail varnish. I'm talking about an ancient art form dating as far back as 85 b.c. Baskets, boxes, cups, bowls, and jars are coated with up to 30 layers of lacquer in order to make them waterproof. Each layer must be dried thoroughly and polished before another layer can be applied. After the lacquer is finished, decoration may be applied. Black (on the outside) and red (on the inside) is the most common color combination.

You may be able to date an item by the colors used; metallics in the decorative painting were used by the Han dynasty. Modern (post-1650) versions of lacquer may be European-inspired chinoiserie: Beware.

LANTERNS

Several styles of lanterns are for sale in Hong Kong and China. Because they have become a fashion statement in home-style lately, reproduction lanterns abound. Antique lanterns are available in some markets in Beijing and Shanghai; they are most often made from wire with red fabric inserts.

Plastic lanterns are popular in Hong Kong during the Mid-Autumn Festival and are sold on the street for the night parades.

MONOCHROMATIC WARES

You may adore blue-and-white porcelain, but remember that it was created for export because locals thought it was ugly.

The good stuff was usually monochromatic. Go to a museum and study the best and brightest before you start shopping, because fakes abound.

Celadon is perhaps the best known of the Chinese porcelain monochromes. It is pale gray-green and gained popularity because of the (false) assumption that poisoned food would cause a piece of celadon pottery to change color. The amount of iron in the glaze determines the amount of green in the piece.

MOONCAKES

Just as Anglo-Saxons associate fruitcake with Christmas, the Chinese give mooncakes for the Mid-Autumn Festival. The mooncake is the food that inspired Americans to invent the fortune cookie. It dates to a successful revolt against Mongol warlords. The Chinese communicated with messages that were baked into the little cakes. Now the cakes are a form of celebration, and the design and packaging play a big part of the shopping process and the price.

More than 30 brands are sold in Hong Kong; one large department store sells 10,000 mooncakes a day. Types include those made with lotus flour, bean paste, and even with a hard-boiled duck egg as the prize in the center.

OPALS

Hong Kong is the opal-cutting capital of Asia. Dealers buy opals, which are mined mainly in Australia, in their rough state and bring them to their factories in Hong Kong. There they are judged for quality and cut either for wholesale export or for use in local jewelry making. Black opals are the rarest and most expensive. White opals are the most available; they are not actually white, but varying shades of sparkling color.

The opal has minuscule spheres of cristobalite layered inside; this causes the light to refract and the gem to look iridescent. The more cristobalite, the more "fire." An opal can contain up to 30% water, which makes it very difficult to cut.

Buyer Beware

Dishonest dealers will sell sliced stones, called doublets or triplets, depending upon the number of slices of stone layered together. If the salesperson will not show you the back of the stone, suspect that it is layered.

PAPER CUTS

An art form still practiced in China, paper cuts are handpainted and hand-cut drawings of butterflies, animals, birds, flowers, and human figures. Often they are mounted on cards; sometimes they are sold in packs of six, delicately wrapped in tissue. I buy them in quantity and use them as decorations on cards and stationery.

PEARLS

The first thing to know about shopping for pearls in Hong Kong is that the best ones come from Japan. If you are looking for a serious set of pearls, find a dealer who will show you the Japanese government inspection certification that accompanies every legally exported pearl. Many pearls cross the border without one, and for a reason.

Pearls are usually sold loosely strung and are weighed by the *momme* (pronounced like "mom"). Each momme is equal to 3.75 grams ($\frac{1}{10}$ oz.). The size of the pearl is measured in millimeters. Size 3s are small, like caviar, and 10s are large, like mothballs. The average buyer is looking for something between 6 and 7 millimeters (about ¼ in.). The price usually doubles every half millimeter after 6. Therefore, if a 6-millimeter pearl is $10, a 6.5-millimeter pearl would be $20, a 7-millimeter pearl $40, and so on. When the pearl gets very large, prices often triple and quadruple with each half millimeter.

Most pearls you will encounter are cultured. The pearl grower introduces a small piece of mussel shell into the oyster and then hopes that Mother Nature will do her stuff. The annoyed oyster coats the "intruder" with nacre, the lustrous substance that creates the pearl. The layers of nacre determine the luster and size. It takes about 5 years for an oyster to create a pearl. The oysters are protected from predators in wire baskets in carefully controlled oyster beds.

There are five basic varieties of pearls: freshwater, South Sea, *akoya*, black, and *mabe* (pronounced *maw*-bay). Freshwater pearls, also known as Biwa pearls, are Rice Krispies shaped and come in shades of pink, lavender, cream, tangerine, blue, and blue-green. Many of the pearls that are larger than 10 millimeters are known as South Sea pearls. They are produced in the South Seas, where the water is warmer and the oysters larger: The silver-lipped oyster produces large, magnificent silver pearls, while the golden-lipped oyster produces large golden-colored pearls.

The pearls you are probably most familiar with are akoya pearls. They range from 2 to 10 millimeters in size. The shapes are more round than not, and the colors range from shades of cream to pink. Some of these pearls have a bluish tone.

The rarest pearl is the black pearl, which is actually a deep blue or blue-green. Black-lipped oysters in the waters surrounding Tahiti and Okinawa produce these gems, which range in size from 8 to 15 millimeters. Putting together a perfectly matched set is difficult and costly.

Pearls are judged by their luster, nacre, color, shape, and surface quality. The more perfect the pearl in all respects, the more valuable. Test pearls by rolling them—cultured pearls are more likely to be perfectly round and will, therefore, roll more smoothly.

> **Shop & Save**
> You needn't be interested in serious pearls, whether natural or fake. In fact, prices being what they are, I'm in favor of fakes. Fake versions of cultured pearls are readily available in Hong Kong.

SILK

Anthropologists will tell you that silk is China's single greatest contribution to world culture. The quality of Chinese silk has always been so superior that no substitute has ever been deemed acceptable. The trade routes that brought silk around the world also brought cultural secrets from ancient worlds into Europe.

The art of weaving silk originated some 4,000 years ago in China and has spread throughout Asia and the world. China, however, remains the largest exporter of silk cloth and garments. Hong Kong receives most of its silk fabric directly from China. Fabric shops in the markets sell rolls of silk for reasonable prices, although silk is not dirt-cheap and may be priced competitively in your home market.

When buying silk, be sure that it is real. Many wonderful copies are on the market. Real silk thread burns like human hair and leaves a fine ash. Synthetic silk curls or melts as it burns. If you are not sure, remove a thread and light a match. If the dealer has a fit, ask him to do it or walk out. Vendors who are proud of their merchandise will often do the test for you. Ask.

SNUFF BOTTLES

A favorite collector's item, snuff bottles come in porcelain, glass, stone, metal, bamboo, bronze, and jade. They also come in old and new old-style versions. They are hard to distinguish from perfume bottles, especially if they have no tops. In short, watch out; because of tourist demand, fakes flood this category.

A top-of-the-line collectible snuff bottle can go for $100,000; if you think you are buying a fine example of the art form for $10, think again. Glass bottles with carved overlays are rare and magnificent, one of the specific schools of design and style in snuff bottles that are especially valuable to collectors.

You can find more ordinary examples in any market. If you just want a few ornaments for the house (or Christmas tree), the markets or shops on Hollywood Road in Hong Kong will have plenty.

SOY SAUCE

Ongoing disputes about soy-sauce manufacturing have become a big brouhaha for grocery shoppers in the U.S., where Japan is demanding specific labels and a possible name change. The real thing must be made from real soy products and fermented for at least 3 months.

SPIRIT MONEY

Colorful fake paper money that is to be burned for the dead, spirit money is sold in old-fashioned paper shops, which are (sadly) fast fading out. You can still find a string of such paper shops lining Shanghai Street in Kowloon, in Causeway Bay near Jardine's Bazaar, and in Macau, in the antiques-stores neighborhood.

TEA

The **Museum of Tea Ware in Flagstaff House,** 10 Cotton Tree Dr., Hong Kong (© **852/2869-0690;** www.lcsd.gov.hk), is a good place to start exploring the mysteries of tea. Tea has been cultivated in China for more than 2,000 years and reflects the climate and soil where it is grown, much as European wines do. Three categories make up the tea market: unfermented, fermented, and semifermented.

It is customary to drink Chinese tea black, with no milk, sugar, or lemon. Cups do not have a handle, but often do have a fitted lid to keep the contents hot and to strain the leaves as you sip. Because Hong Kong was a British colony, many hotel lobbies and restaurants serve English high tea (a great opportunity to rest your feet and gear up for a few more hours of shopping).

Chapter 4

Hong Kong

Welcome to Hong Kong

It's not that times are bad in Hong Kong, or worse than elsewhere, but my heavens, how the stores and showrooms are moving about town, finding new (lower rent) areas and downsizing their floor space. Locals are worried about whether the tourists will come and when they get to Honkers, well, will they shop? Many big brands cater to wealthy mainland Chinese; many nonluxury brands are worried.

Who cares? We didn't come for the big brands or to spend megabucks. And there is still plenty to buy at a reasonable price...often, prices are lower than in the PRC (People's Republic of China). So pack a suitcase, grab that empty duffle bag, and get a move on; Hong Kong is waiting.

Hong Kong is the center of the universe, the diamond in the Asian crown. Auctions at Christie's and Sotheby's Hong Kong branches have set record prices for specialty sales in Asian art. **Ashneil** still has great handbags for relatively low prices ($300–$500). **Honeychurch** is hanging onto that 18th-century, hand-painted amoire and will ship it for you, door-to-door. Hong Kong has come out of all of this as a star...and speaking of stars, the word on the water is that the **Star Ferry** will be relocated back to its original pier. Watch this space.

I Remember Mamasan

Use Hong Kong as your base for exploring the new China. Remember these facts:

- Designer goods are 20% less expensive in Hong Kong than in mainland China.
- Hong Kong has been doing luxury and customer service for so long that they are second nature.
- For 99 years, English was the official language.
- In a recent price comparison of similar merchandise at places such as the Hong Kong Jade Market versus similar markets in the PRC, Hong Kong prices were the same.
- If you are looking for Chinese atmosphere, you may find it more readily in parts of Hong Kong than in China's big cities, where the past is being torn down at an alarming rate. Hong Kong is a lot more than the Star Ferry and the skyline you've seen on billboards—there are scads of nearby islands and destinations that will send you over the mooncake when it comes to charm.

THE LAY OF THE LAND

Hong Kong encompasses Hong Kong Island, the city of Kowloon, the New Territories, and a few hundred islands. Technically speaking, what we commonly refer to as Hong Kong is now part of the People's Republic of China (PRC), but because it has separate but equal status, its address is written as "Separate Administrative Region," or "SAR" (not to be confused with SARS, the disease).

When people discuss addresses in the Hong Kong area, they may cite a particular number on a particular street, but more often than not, you'll hear your fellow travelers simplifying directions by just naming a building and a neighborhood. And they play fast and loose with what constitutes a neighborhood. Some people call all of Victoria Island "Central" and all of the Kowloon Peninsula "Kowloon."

Hong Kong Regional Transportation

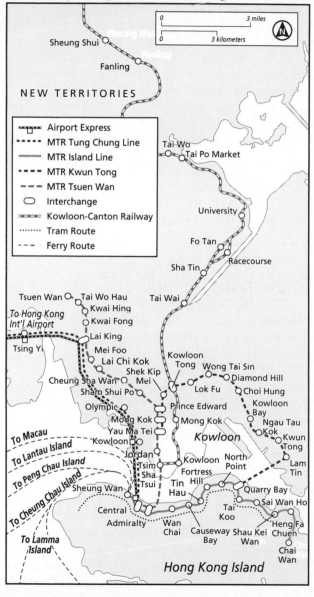

Shopping in Hong Kong concentrates heavily on two areas: Central, the main business "downtown" area on the Hong Kong Island side, and Tsim Sha Tsui in Kowloon. Central is very upscale, civilized, businesslike, and modern. Tsim Sha Tsui (often written TST) is grittier and more frenetic.

As the building and development boom widens, there is new interest in Mong Kok, the area of Kowloon just north of TST, which now has some luxury hotels and a mall. Hotter still is the area around the new Financial Center and the Western Tunnel, which has two luxury hotels (Ritz-Carlton and W), and Elements, a deluxe mall.

See "Shopping Neighborhoods," later in this chapter for a detailed discussion of Hong Kong's shopping and commercial districts.

Booking Hong Kong

The Hong Kong Tourist Association (HKTA; www.hkta.org) provides a great deal of useful information for travelers at no cost. It publishes pamphlets on almost every subject imaginable, many of which you can pick up as you exit passport control at Hong Kong International Airport.

The monthly *Official Hong Kong Guide* contains general information about the city, including listings of festivals, events, and exhibits. The HKTA also publishes a weekly newspaper called *Hong Kong This Week*. It contains news on events and shows, along with the usual ads for shops. It's free at major hotels and in HKTA offices.

Inside the free tourist packet you can pick up at the airport is the A-O-A Map Directory. Maps show both building and street location—helpful for finding addresses that include the building, street, and area names.

Getting There

When it comes to booking your plane tickets, you'll encounter a confusing number of possibilities, deals, routes, and reasons to go with any number of different plans (or planes). (*Note:* Remember that you can often add on a single city for very little extra money.)

TICKET DEALS

Because they buy in bulk, wholesalers often get better prices and pass their savings on to their customers.

Other thoughts:

- If you're flying to Hong Kong from the West Coast, look into a Circle Pacific fare or an All Asia ticket. Many carriers allow you to make your own itinerary, traveling to several cities in Asia at package-tour prices. You do not join a group; you set your own pace, but you get a break on the price because you fly all legs with the same carrier. I've seen a Cathay Pacific deal for $1,100 (when bought online) that offered a choice of some 17 cities.

- Watch for gateway deals. When Cathay added a second daily flight between Hong Kong and San Francisco, they offered excellent prices.

- If you're pricing airfares on several carriers, it is imperative that you understand the quality of the service and what you are getting. Virgin has made quite a splash with its extra perks and great entertainment system, but it offers real value only to those travelers able to pay extra for upper-class service (flat oversize beds!). The non-upper-class seats don't compete with other airlines for comfort or price.

- If you must fly in a coach seat, look for ways to break up the travel. You can get a discounted seat from the U.S. to London or Paris for $300 to $400, and a seat to Hong Kong for $600 to $700, leaving you enough money for a refreshing layover, and a bigger adventure.

- Expand your coach-seat horizons with extended economy, available on some airlines (such as **United** and **EVA**) which gives you 5 to 6 more inches and makes a world of difference for back-of-the-plane prices. With United, if you are a **premium**-class passenger (25,000 miles per year) you are automatically upgraded...for free.

- **Regent Hotels** is coming back to Asia and doing tie-ins between their hotels and their cruise line. Look for deals.

- Package tours often offer the best deals financially, especially if they include airport transfers and some extras. Check them out, especially when you can stay at luxury hotels. Likewise, add-on tours offered by cruise lines sometimes have fabulous prices that include promotional events and benefits.

- Don't outsmart yourself in ticketing. To save money on a research trip I decided to book tickets through my Canadian travel agent because the Canadian dollar was very low—my bank card hit me with so many fees that it cost me an extra $250 for trying to be clever.

- Those 55 and over may qualify for special flight deals for seniors. Cathay advertises "Worry Free" fares that provide fare for two seniors traveling together to Hong Kong and one other city of your choice from a select list. Do check out the competition before you book, however; for a Christmas trip to Thailand, Sarah and Tom priced Cathay's deal and then saved $300 per ticket by booking United Economy Plus. They received frequent-flyer miles, which are not available with Cathay's promotion.

- If you are planning big-time shopping, consider buying your ticket by class of service and excess baggage rules/costs. Find out if you qualify for perks when you are a premium member of a certain airline or what the weight allowances are with the various classes of service. Know if your carrier goes on the weight system or the per-piece system since more and more airlines are now switching over to a weight system, even if you are flying into the U.S. from Asia.

- Consider weight allowance as you book onward travel. Our last research trip was organized as a long-haul round-trip through Hong Kong International. Airport and then we did an AirAsia (www.airasia.com) round-trip to Bangkok, leaving most of our luggage in Hong Kong for the second portion of our trip. We chose not to go to Hanoi because of the cost of the luggage and the logistics of many legs and much weight in the suitcases.

Arriving in Hong Kong

The gorgeous Hong Kong International Airport, designed by Sir Norman Foster, is like a metallic crab sunning itself on Lantau Island. It's modern and easy to use; you whisk along electric carpets, onto trains, and through to the main terminal. If you have arranged car service with your hotel, look for the hotel desks in the center of the arrivals hall. Someone will escort you through the rest of the process, taking your baggage, and meeting you at your car.

CAR SERVICE

Traveling from the airport in the swank car your hotel sends for you is a delightfully elegant way to arrive—and an expensive one. Although public transport is simple and inexpensive, part of the fun of being in Hong Kong is settling into the hotel's Rolls, Daimler, or Mercedes-Benz. Expect to pay $95 to $150 (it varies from hotel to hotel) each way for the luxury, but do try to find it in your budget. Hotels in the Central district—the main shopping and business area—may charge more than those in Kowloon. Ask not for whom the Phantom rolls, it rolls for thee.

AIRPORT BUS & TRAIN

AirBuses run every 15 minutes or so, but another bus option is Executive Coach. The seating is nicer than the first-class cabin of any airline, with tons of legroom for you, your wheelchair, and your carry-on. You can reserve your seat through your hotel or go to the bus desk in the arrivals hall, section A. The fare to Central is HK$140 ($18).

The train (Airport Express) is for those who have little to no luggage. It whooshes right through the airport terminal; you can hop on and be at the main station in Central in 22 minutes. From there, you take a taxi to your hotel. You can buy a tourist package for HK$220 ($29) that includes the one-way Airport Express fare and a 3-day MTR Octopus Card (see "Getting Around," below). For HK$300 ($39), it includes the round-trip fare to the airport. You can even buy the pass duty-free on some airlines. If you don't buy the package, the bus costs HK$154 ($20) each way.

TAXIS ON ARRIVAL

The taxi stand is near the arrivals lounge. A large sign lists approximate fares to different areas of Hong Kong and Kowloon. Taxis are standing by in three different, color-coded lanes for destinations such as Kowloon, Central, or New Territories. They often charge a flat rate of approximately $40— it is a long drive to town. Our most recent taxi from Kowloon to the airport cost $35.

Getting Around
....

Hong Kong is an easy city to navigate because its transportation options are excellent. It's a good city for walking, true, but you'll also want to enjoy its ferries, *kaidos* (bigger ferries), trams, double-decker buses, and superb MTR (Mass Transit Railway).

Most rides on the MTR take less than 20 minutes; you can cross the harbor in approximately 5 minutes.

Crossing the harbor by car or taxi during rush hour is difficult, but it's a breeze on the MTR. The Star Ferry is much changed (see below).

MTR

The MTR stop at Central will get you to most locations in Hong Kong, and the Tsim Sha Tsui (TST) stop is convenient to most locations in Kowloon. See the map in this section.

The MTR is half the fun of getting to great shopping. Three lines connect the New Territories to industrial Kwun Tong, to business Central, to shopping Tsim Sha Tsui, and to the residential eastern part of the island. Each station is color coded, and signs are in English and Chinese.

The longest trip takes less than an hour, and the cost is based on the distance you travel; one-stop journeys usually cost HK$8 ($1.10) to HK$10 ($1.30). Buy your ticket at the station vending machines by looking for your destination and punching in the price code. You will need exact change, which you can get from a machine nearby. Ticket windows sell multiple-journey tickets.

If you're visiting Hong Kong from overseas, the best value is a 1-day unlimited MTR ticket, available at any HKTA office, any MTR station, select Hang Seng banks, MTR Travel Services Centres, and online at www.mtr.com.hk. It costs HK$55 ($7), and must be purchased within 2 weeks of your arrival.

Stored-value cards are called **Octopus Cards,** which cost HK$150 and include a HK$50 deposit plus stored value of HK$100. You can return the card at the end of your trip for the HK$50 refund. Cards are electronic and can be read through your wallet or handbag; just place yours on the pad. Flash it again to depart the station at your destination. To use single-journey tickets, insert and retrieve. You need the ticket to exit the station, at which time it will be "eaten."

The MTR runs between 6am and 1am.

Insider's tip: The Kowloon-Canton Railway (KCR), the railroad line that leads to the Chinese border, has been merged into the MTR.

TAXIS

Taxis in Hong Kong are low-cost compared to big cities in U.S. and Europe. The meter starts at HK$20 ($2.50); after that, the charge is HK$1.50 (25¢) per 200m (656 ft.). Taking the Cross-Harbour Tunnel costs an extra HK$10 ($1.30) each way, making the total additional fees HK$20 ($2.60). I tend to avoid taking a taxi through the Cross-Harbour Tunnel unless I'm loaded down with packages and have had a long, hard day of shopping. Surcharges apply for luggage, waiting time, and radio calls. The Western Tunnel is quicker, but more expensive ($20 each way).

If a taxi is in Central and has a sign saying kowloon, it means that the driver would like a fare going back to Kowloon and will not charge the extra HK$10 ($1.30) tunnel fee if he gets such a fare. It is sometimes hard to find a cab during the 4pm shift change. If a taxi doesn't stop for you on a busy road, it is probably because the driver is not allowed to stop.

Look for a taxi stand where you can pick up a cab. Hotels are always good places to find a taxi. Even if you are not a guest, the doorman will help you. Tip him HK$5 (65¢).

English is still an official language, but it's always nice insurance to have your destination written in Chinese. Hotels have preprinted cards, one side of which tells the driver how to reach the hotel. Get a card ahead of time; otherwise, drivers may put a map book in your hand and ask you to find the address. There is a guidebook called *Hong Kong Taxi* that you can carry with you.

TRAINS

The Kowloon-Canton Railway (KCR) has merged with the MTR, making one smooth ride directly to Shenzhen, increasing routes for local commuters and lowering fares for all. There are now two stations serving Shenzhen, so depending on your destination there and your goals once in town, you need to consider which station to use.

The TST East station allows you to step out of the Peninsula or InterContinental hotel and into a luxury train that whisks you to China in less than an hour. For tips on visits across the border, see p. 170. You can use the Hung Hom station for travel deeper into the Pearl Delta.

FERRIES

The most famous of the Hong Kong ferries is the Star Ferry, "the least expensive tourist attraction in the world," with service from Kowloon to Central and back. The green-and-white ferries have connected the island to the peninsula since 1898, and the 8-minute ride is one of the most scenic in the world. You can see the splendor of Hong Kong Island's architecture and the sprawl of Kowloon's shore.

However, if you know Hong Kong, you may be shocked to learn that the ferry terminal on the Victoria side has moved! I personally don't feel quite the same way about the Star Ferry and don't find the new terminal location to be very convenient. I am eagerly awaiting confirmation of the rumor that the ferry will go back to its original pier in Central within the next 2 years.

That said, the Star Ferry can be a small piece of magic for no more than pocket change. First-class costs HK$2.20 (30¢); tourist class is HK$1.75 (25¢). The difference is minimal except at rush hour, when the upper deck (first-class) is less crowded, or if you want to take pictures: You get a much better view from the upper deck. The Central/Tsim Sha Tsui (TST) service runs daily from 6:30am to 11:30pm.

TRAMS

Watch out crossing the streets of Central, or you're likely to be run over by a double-decker tram. Victoria Island trams have operated for more than 85 years, from far western Kennedy Town to Shau Kei Wan in the east. They travel in a straight line, except for a detour around Happy Valley. The fare is HK$2 (20¢) for adults, half price for seniors and children. You pay as you enter and Octopus Cards are accepted. Many trams do not go the full distance east to west, so note destination signs before getting on. Antique trams are available for tours and charters, as are the regular ones.

The **Peak Tram** (www.thepeak.com.hk) has been in operation for more than 100 years. It is a must for any visitor to

Hong Kong—unless you are afraid of heights. You can catch the tram on Garden Road. A free shuttle bus will take you from the Star Ferry or Central MTR station (Chater Garden exit) to the Peak Tram terminal. The tram runs to the peak every 10 minutes starting at 7am and ending at midnight. The trip takes 8 minutes and costs HK$33 ($5). The best time to make this trip is just before dusk; you can see the island scenery on the trip up, walk around to various viewing points or peek in on some of the expensive mansions and high-rises, watch the spectacular sunset, and then ride down as all the city lights are twinkling.

RICKSHAWS

It's over, folks. Rickshaws are *fini,* kaput, anachronistic, socially incorrect, and gone with the wind. There's a single shaw at the Star Ferry Central Terminal for a photo op.

Sleeping in Hong Kong

I can't think of any other city in the world—and that includes Paris—where your choice of hotel is a more integral part of your stay than in Hong Kong.

Although I'm incredibly picky about hotels, I've found several in Hong Kong that offer the most important factor in a shopping hotel—location—and still have all the luxury I lust for. Asian hotels are famous for their deluxe standards and fabulous service; enjoying these perks is part of the pleasure of staying in Hong Kong.

HOTEL TIPS

I find hotels' official rack rates irritating and refuse to quote them in these pages. Few people pay the official rates, and deals can almost always be made; Hong Kong is deal city.

Rates are on the rise in Hong Kong, however, and rooms can be dear, especially when trade fairs are in town and hotels are full of convention goers. It pays to shop around for rates and for the right time of year to visit since prices change with the seasons. You must also decide if a hotel with club privileges is worth the extra cost to you—this gives you breakfast, tea, snacks and cocktails.

TRICKS OF THE TRADE

Some secrets that might make booking your hotel easier:

- Ask about packages, which may include breakfast, airport transfers, and other items that usually incur an extra charge. Almost every luxury hotel in the world offers a honeymoon package. As long as you don't show up with the kids, you're on your honeymoon. And these days, well, having kids before marriage is actually normal.

- Mileage awards can be used to pay for hotel rooms, to obtain discounts on rooms, or to accrue more mileage for your favorite frequent-flier account.

- Always ask whether the hotel offers weekend or 5-day rates. Almost all hotels discount rooms during the off season or when not a lot of trade shows are in town.

- Check on prices on club floors or lounge floors—these rooms usually cost $75 to $100 a night more but have a ton of perks from free breakfast to free Internet and cocktails. Even at $100 a night extra, you can often save money by spending money.

- There is no more high or low season in Hong Kong. Summer rates are usually the least expensive, but watch out for mainland or Japanese visitors who pay top dollar.

- In fact, mind your Japanese and Chinese holidays, which are usually not on U.S. and U.K. calendars; Hong Kong hotels fill up at these times.

- Check the big chains for promotional rates. Often you can prepay in U.S. dollars and save, or the chain will have a deal in the computer that your travel agent doesn't know about. A Hilton telephone operator once told me about an exceptional value at the Conrad, which at the time saved me about $100. Go online, but also make calls.

HONG KONG'S BEST SHOPPING HOTELS
CENTRAL

I've found three hotels that serve as one because they're in the same location: **Pacific Place,** right above the mall of the same name. They all have entrances within the mall as well as front doors on the street.

Conrad Hotel
88 Queensway, Central (MTR: Admiralty).

This is the hotel that made me fall in love with the Conrad brand, which specializes in hotels all over Asia (although this division of Hilton has spiffy hotels worldwide, even in places like Brussels, where the Conrad is one of the fanciest hotels in town). But I digress. Conrad in Hong Kong is one of the three anchor hotels of the Mall at Pacific Place, which instantly makes it a shopper's delight.

Plus, Conrad gives a little extra in order to woo luxury and business travelers—you get a robe, you get a rubber ducky in your tub, and some stays include airport transfer fees. You can get a price break for booking further in advance and may even pick up a promotion—say, a king-deluxe room with an ocean view and breakfast buffet. U.S. and Canada reservations © 800/445-8667.

Four Seasons Hotel Hong Kong
8 Finance St., Central (MTR: Central).

Four Seasons returned to Hong Kong with this wow-'em hotel in the IFC Tower, overlooking the water, Kowloon, and the new Star Ferry terminal. The IFC Tower also houses a multilevel luxury shopping mall and cinema complex, and the Airport Express train station. The hotel has drop-dead fabu restaurants, direct entry into the mall, and makes the Star Ferry seem viable one more time. Rates begin around $600. U.S. and Canada reservations © 800/819-5053. Local © 852/3196-8888. www.fourseasons.com/hongkong.

WAN CHAI

Grand Hyatt

1 Harbour Rd., Wanchai (MTS: Wanchai).

Attached to the Convention Center, with direct ferry service to TST East, adjacent to a large Chinese Arts & Crafts store, and famous for its restaurants and its spa, this hotel is one of the best in town. The hallways are decorated with dramatic black-and-white photos; most of the rooms have views; and, while the rooms are not gigantic, they are technologically equipped to offer amenities at the push of a button. The pool, garden, and spa transport you to another world, making it impossible to believe you are in downtown Hong Kong.

Rooms with a view of the harbor begin around $450. U.S. and Canada reservations © 800/228-9548. Local © 852/2588-1234. www.hongkong.grand.hyatt.com.

KOWLOON

Intercontinental Hotel Hong Kong

18 Salisbury Rd., Kowloon (MTR: TST).

To me, this will always be the Regent, but locals have adapted to the change and call this hotel the InterConti. In one of the most scenic locations in Hong Kong, the hotel occupies the tip of Kowloon Peninsula. The views from the lobby bar at night are nothing short of spectacular.

The tricks and treats are also incredible—an Alain Ducasse restaurant; Nobu, a club membership that provides for tons of perks, making it a bargain shopper's best buy; and a feng shui spa. Rates here vary enormously; I have heard of $550 during high season, so look for promos. Obviously, harbor views cost more. (But are worth it!) U.S. and Canada reservations © 888/424-6835 or 770/604-2000. Local © 852/2721-1211. www.interconti.com.

The Peninsula Hong Kong
2 Salisbury Rd., Kowloon (MTR: TST).

The Pen, as it is called, is the most famous hotel in Hong Kong, and possibly, in the world. In the ever-changing world of hotel competition, this grande dame keeps ahead with new and imaginative programs. The Peninsula Academy allows you to take exclusive classes, hear lectures, meet with specialists, or eat in the chef's private kitchen. The newer part of the hotel, a tower with superb views, a health club, a pool, and a Philippe Starck–designed restaurant (Felix), provides the modern foil to the old-world 1928 fancy. There's a helicopter airport in Wanchai and a lot of programs for you and your chopper. The 14 Rolls-Royce Phantoms transfer you to or from the airport in grand luxe style, and yes, they hold a ton of luggage.

Not only does the hotel have a complete shopping mall, but also a wonderful health club and E-Spa, which is the most dramatic spa I have seen in my entire career. The new Salon de Ning clublike cocktail lounge provides a twist on Shanghai glamour and the bar/party and dance scene. The fictional Madame Ning was a wealthy, eccentric social maven who supposedly lived in Shanghai in the 1930s. Her travels and lifestyle are yours to enjoy as you sip cocktails in one of several *in time* salons featuring her art, artifacts, and memorabilia. (Try the chrysanthemum tea martini.) U.S. reservations ℂ 866/382-8388. Local ℂ 852/2920-2888. www.peninsula.com.

Dining in Hong Kong

If you think Hong Kong is most famous for shopping, think again. The number-one attraction is culinary pleasures—from five-star restaurants in the most elegant hotels to Chinese eateries off the beaten path. Certain places are so fabulous that you just have to try them to complete your Hong Kong experience. True foodies may even want to book a trip to coincide with the Hong Kong Food Festival in August.

Because this is a small town and food is so important to the culture, Hong Kong has a number of private dining clubs. If you don't know a member, ask your hotel concierge if he can book you a table at either **Kee Club** or **China Club.**

Please note that in the last year or two many of the world's most famous chefs have opened eateries in Hong Kong, including Alain Ducasse, Pierre Gagnaire, Joel Robuchon, and Nobu. Macau, with its big-name Las Vegas hotels, also has a lot of fancy eats and famous toques. Did someone say *bon appétit?*

LEGENDS & LANDMARKS

When I pick a restaurant for this category, I consider the length of time the establishment has been in operation, the quality of its food, its location, and its ambience.

Some places so typify what is special about Hong Kong that I consider them don't-miss experiences. A few (such as Jumbo) are good for the family, for first-timers, or for people who want an entire experience that includes food. In fact, all of the places in this section are legends, landmarks, or both, and are worthy of a memory-making meal.

Gaddi's

The Peninsula Hotel, 2 Salisbury Rd., Kowloon (MTR: TST).

Visitors and locals alike know Gaddi's as the best French restaurant in town, and serious foodies wouldn't consider a trip to Hong Kong complete without a visit. It's much like a private club of local and visiting professionals.

If you are looking for something special, you may want to book lunch or dinner at the chef's private table in the kitchen. You can ask the chef to create a menu for you, or you can pick from the regular menu. If the kitchen table is booked, note that some people request the kitchen menu for lunch in the restaurant. Lunch and dinner are both popular; lunch is less expensive. The house offers a set dinner menu of five courses, each with its own wine. Reservations are a must; call © 852/2315-3171.

Luk Yu Teahouse
24 Stanley St. (MTR: Central).

It's not the teahouse of the August moon, but Luk Yu—a landmark eatery in the center of Central—could be a movie set. Order dim sum from the menu in Chinese, and try not to take pictures, because that's what everyone else is doing. Go for an early lunch (locals eat between 1 and 4pm, so if you're there by noon, you should be able to get a table without much of a wait) or at teatime, when you can get a table easily.

Dim sum is served until 5pm. A perfect location in Central makes this a good stop for shoppers; it's halfway to Hollywood Road and not that far from the Landmark.

Do note that waiters at Luk Yu make it a policy to be rude to Westerners unless they know you. On the other hand, it's rude for you to ask about the recent gangland shoot'em-up. Dim sum will run about $20 per person; full meals cost more. For reservations, call © 2523-5463. Cash only.

Sevva
Prince's Building (MTR: Central).

Old China hands may feel a vibe that is similar to the old Joyce Café (RIP) and be amused to note that this new, hottest place in town is the brainchild of her sister Bonnie Gokson. Certainly these two gals have more style than anyone else we know. The restaurant does a big lunch, brunch, bar, and dinner service with its wraparound views inside the heart of Central—and the fact that different parts of the restaurant have a different style of decor and therefore a different mood.

I had the French Toast Dai Pai Dong style, which is a memory I will never forget. Truly, the earth moved: Satay sauce between the toast, topped with warm maple syrup. © 852/2537-1388. www.sevvahk.com.

Shopping Hong Kong

SHOPPING HOURS

For the most part, stores open at 10am and close at 6:30pm in Central, 7:30pm in Tsim Sha Tsui, and 9pm on Nathan Road in Yau Ma Tei and in Mong Kok. The Seibu store in Mong Kok is open 11am to 11pm. I think that as long as traffic keeps up, the stores are willing to stay open.

Mall stores are open during regular business hours on Sunday. Most shops in the main shopping areas of Tsim Sha Tsui and Causeway Bay are open daily. Those in Central close on Sunday.

Many shops close on major public holidays. Everything closes on Chinese New Year; some stores are closed for 2 days, others for 2 weeks. Do not plan to be in Hong Kong and do any shopping at this time.

Store hours are affected by the following public holidays:

- January 1 (New Year's Day)
- January/February (Chinese New Year)
- March/April (Good Friday, Easter Sunday and Monday)
- June (Dragon Boat Festival)
- August 25 (Liberation Day)
- December 25 (Christmas) and December 26 (Boxing Day)

On public holidays, banks and offices close, and shops may close as well. Factory outlets will definitely not be open. Many holiday dates change from year to year. For specific dates, contact the HKTA (p. 54) before you plan your trip.

Department store hours differ from store to store. The larger ones, like Lane Crawford and Chinese Arts & Crafts, maintain regular business hours: 10am to 5pm. The Japanese department stores in Causeway Bay open between 10 and 10:30am and close between 9 and 9:30pm. They're all closed on different days 1 day of the week, however, which can be confusing. Don't assume because one department store is closed that they all are.

Market hours are pretty standard. Only food markets (sometimes called "wet markets") open very early in the morning. Don't bother arriving in Stanley before 9am. Even 9:30am is slow; many vendors are still opening up. The Jade Market opens at 10am every day, including Sunday, and closes around 3pm.

Insider's tip: I see a movement toward later store openings (11am).

CHRISTMAS IN HONG KONG

Even when I'm in Hong Kong in July, I start thinking about Christmas. It's time to start shopping.

Christmas decorations go up in Kowloon (it's hard to spot the neon amid all the neon) in mid-November, when stores begin their Christmas promotions. Christmas permeates the air; even street markets sell decorations—plastic wreaths, silk flowers, ornaments, and more.

Among the best deals in town at this time of year is the free shipping many department stores offer. It covers shipping to the United Kingdom or to anyplace in the world, depending on the store, for purchases that cost more than a certain amount.

Better yet, Hong Kong is the perfect place to load up on inexpensive presents. What can you find at home that's fabulous for less than $5? Not much! Go to the Jade Market and you'll find plenty.

NEW YEAR IN HONG KONG

I mean Chinese New Year, and when it comes, you may go crazy if you want to shop. Expect most stores to be closed a minimum of 2 to 3 days, but some stores close for weeks. The date of the new year varies because it is based on a lunar calendar; the danger zone falls somewhere between the end of January and mid-February. In 2010, the big day is February 14 (the year of the Tiger); in 2011, it's February 3 (the Rabbit) and in 2012, it's January 23 (the Dragon). Enter the dragon, laughing.

HONG KONG ON SALE

The sales in Hong Kong are the best time to get regular retail merchandise—and designer brands—at the lowest prices. The real bargains in Hong Kong are not in retail stores; the real bargains in Hong Kong may not be in perfect condition. So if you insist on brand-new, clean, undamaged goods, you should feel safe buying them on sale. If you have teens or are on a limited clothing budget, shop Hong Kong during the sale periods. Check the advertisements in the *South China Morning Post* for special sale announcements.

FAKES FOR SALE

While Hong Kong doesn't have a lot of fake Chanel on the streets (it's hidden), there are many items for sale—especially at markets—that appear to be real. But they aren't. They usually hold up in the same way you'd expect a fake to hold up—not well. But for trendy items, you could be very impressed with these look-alikes.

I once bought a canvas-and-leather book bag from a street market for the high (for Hong Kong) price of $20. It had a big, perfect Gap label on the front. It fell apart 36 hours later. Both buckles and one leather strap broke so quickly (in three different incidents) that I am convinced that real Gap labels were sewn onto shoddy canvas bags. Let the buyer beware.

Remember that when you buy fake merchandise, the person who gets cheated is you.

Shopping Neighborhoods

The more I visit Hong Kong, the more comfortable I am with getting away from tourists and the commercial main streets of Central and Kowloon. I define a successful visit to Hong Kong as one in which I've spent at least a little bit of time in the real-people neighborhoods. And I hardly ever go to big malls, unless I'm in a real hurry.

GETTING AROUND THE NEIGHBORHOODS

The MTR will get you almost everywhere, or at least into the main neighborhoods and basic shopping areas. Unless I specifically note otherwise in an address, the MTR stop at Central gets you to most locations in Hong Kong; use the MTR stop at Tsim Sha Tsui (TST) for most shopping in Kowloon.

Excellent bus and ferry service goes to outlying islands where you can roam around upon arrival. Getting to specific addresses in the New Territories can be difficult without a car; consider hiring a taxi or a car (with driver) from your hotel.

A WORD ABOUT ADDRESSES

An address is most often the name of the building and not the street address. I want to stress that when street addresses are written out, they may designate a specific door or portion of a building. So you may see different addresses for the same building, like the **Landmark, Swire House,** or **Prince's Building.** Don't assume it's an error. Simply check your trusty map. If an office building takes up a city block, as many do, shops can list different street addresses on all four sides!

The same is true when cruising the boutiques in a shopping center like the **Landmark:** Often the shop's address will simply be the name of the building. The easiest way to find what you're looking for is to check the directory on the main floor of the mall.

HONG KONG ISLAND NEIGHBORHOODS

The island of Hong Kong, also called Victoria, makes up only a portion of what most tourists refer to as Hong Kong. Read on for the lowdown and the uptown.

CENTRAL

Central is the part of Hong Kong that refers to what we used to call "downtown" when I was growing up. It's the main business and shopping part of town, and the core of Hong Kong Island. Shopping in Central is mostly Westernized and even

Central & Western Districts

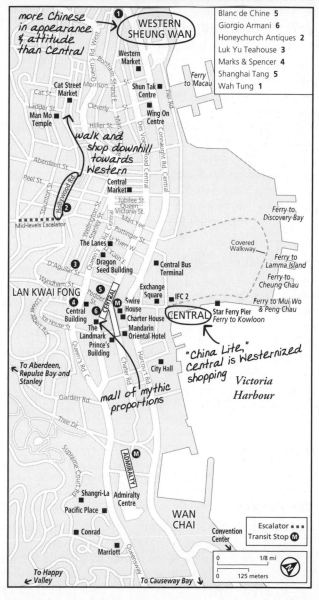

more Chinese in appearance & attitude than Central

WESTERN SHEUNG WAN ➊

Blanc de Chine **5**
Giorgio Armani **6**
Honeychurch Antiques **2**
Luk Yu Teahouse **3**
Marks & Spencer **4**
Shanghai Tang **5**
Wah Tung **1**

Western Market

Queen's Rd. West

Bonham Strand E.

Morrison St.

Ferry to Macau

Cat St. Cat Street Market

Ladder St.

Man Mo Temple ➋

Shun Tak Centre

Cleverly St.

Wing On Centre

Pier Rd.

Connaught Rd. Central

walk and shop downhill towards Western

Hillier St.

Des Voeux Rd. Central

Man St.

Aberdeen St.

Peel St.

Staunton St.

Hollywood Rd.

Central Market

Jubilee St.
Queen Victoria St.

Man Yee

Ferry to Discovery Bay

Mid-levels Escalator

Wellington St.

Stanley St.

Queen's Rd. Central

Pottinger St.

Li Yuen W.

Li Yuen E.

Covered Walkway

Ferry to Lamma Island

The Lanes

D'Aguilar St.

➌

Dragon Seed Building

Central Bus Terminal

Ferry to Cheung Chau

Ferry to Mui Wo & Peng Chau

Wyndham St.

LAN KWAI FONG

Pedder St.

➎ ➍ **CENTRAL**

➏

Central Building

Swire House

Exchange Square

IFC 2

CENTRAL

Star Ferry Pier
Ferry to Kowloon

Ice House Rd.

Albert Rd.

The Landmark
Prince's Building

Charter House

Mandarin Oriental Hotel

To Aberdeen, Repulse Bay and Stanley

Queen's Rd. C.

Charter Rd.

City Hall

"China Lite," Central is Westernized shopping

Victoria Harbour

mall of mythic proportions

Garden Rd.

Harcourt Rd.

Tree Dr.

Supreme Court Rd.

ADMIRALTY Ⓜ

Shangri-La

Pacific Place

Admiralty Centre

WAN CHAI

Conrad

Marriott

Queensway

Convention Center

Escalator ∎∎∎
Transit Stop Ⓜ

To Happy Valley

To Causeway Bay

0   1/8 mi
0   125 meters

glitzy. The **Landmark** (see map, above), a shopping mall of mythic proportions, houses five floors of shopping, including stores in the basement, at street level, on a mezzanine, and in two towers that rise above the main floors. European designers have their shops here or across the street in **Swire House,** the **Prince's Building,** or the **Mandarin Oriental Hotel. Giorgio Armani,** across the street from the **Landmark,** is a knockout and brings a good bit of energy to this corner of Central.

The **Pedder Building** (p. 114) is conveniently located across the street from the Landmark and in every shopper's direct path. There are a handful of factory outlets and jobbers here, as well as the tony **Blanc de Chine. Shanghai Tang** has its flagship here, alongside the outlet building (which has few outlets these days). Use MTR: Central.

The **Lanes:** real people galore and crammed into the center of Central. The **Lanes** are two little alleys (Li Yuen West and Li Yuen East; see map) half a block apart and teeming with people and products. They are lined with storefronts and filled with stalls, so you have to look behind the stalls and poke into nooks and crannies to get the full flavor. One lane partially specializes in handbags (mostly imitations of famous brands and styles, few of good quality), the other, underwear and fabrics. MTR: Central.

The **IFC Mall** houses over 200 upscale international brands plus a cinema and several restaurants. The Four Seasons Hotel is in this mall. Located in the western portion of Central and walking distance by street or bridge to the heart of Central. *Note:* This mall is close to the Star Ferry pier and the Airport Express bus terminal.

WESTERN

The Western District is adjacent to Central and can be reached on foot or by MTR. Take the MTR to Sheung Wan to get to central Western. Because of the newish Western Tunnel, and the lower real estate rentals, more businesses and showrooms are opening in Western. See p. 93 for information about the new Wah Tung showroom.

Going west from Central, the area begins shortly after **Central Market,** at Possession Street, and continues to Kennedy Town, where most of the local working people live. Western includes the famous **Man Wa Lane,** where you can purchase your own personalized chop (p. 93), the **Shun Tak Centre** (where you take the ferry to Macau), and **Bonham Strand East,** where you'll find scores of Chinese herbalists. The farther west you wander, the more exotic the area becomes.

My best way of "doing" Western is to combine it with a trip to Hollywood Road; if you walk downhill from Hollywood Road, you'll end up in Western. Then you can take in the **Western Market** before walking back to Central or hopping on the MTR at Shun Tak station. When visiting the market, don't be discouraged by the junk on the ground floor; the best buys are in the fabric department upstairs. Sarah found top-quality wool ($30/meter), silk ($20/meter), and linen ($10/meter). There's also a good selection of Thai silk for around $10 per meter.

New hotels and retail shops are sprouting on the Kowloon side of this tunnel also, see p. 80.

HOLLYWOOD ROAD

Up above Central, and technically within the Central District, Hollywood Road—Hong Kong's antiques district—is a shopping neighborhood unto itself. It isn't hard to get to, but it is not necessarily on the way to anywhere else you're going, so it's essential that you specifically plan your day to include this outing. You can reach it from the Central or Sheung Wan MTR stop. It's within walking distance if you're wearing sensible shoes and have the feet of a mountain goat; you can also tell your taxi driver "By Fa Gai" (meaning "white flower") and be dropped off in the core of the antiques area, in what used to be the neighborhood where the prostitutes (white flowers) plied their trade.

There are antiques stores elsewhere, but Hollywood Road is still a great place to get to know. The idea is to walk the 3 blocks of Hollywood Road from Wyndham to the Man Mo

Temple. Then you'll hit Cat Street (also called Upper Lascar Row) and the flea market before descending into Western. This lane has antiques shops on the sides and market stalls in the middle featuring merchandise similar to what you'll find at the Jade Market. Prices are high, so be prepared to bargain.

As charming as this area is, I must warn you upfront that much of what is in these shops is imitation, or at least faux. If you are looking to do anything more serious than browse, I suggest you make your first stop **Honeychurch Antiques** (no. 29). Expatriate American owners Glenn and Lucille Vessa are bright, honest, and always willing to help. They know who's who and what's what in their world of dealers and will tell you about their stock and everyone else's. Their look is an eclectic blend of antiques from around the Orient (kind of country chinoiserie); however, they know who has the more formal pieces. In fact, they know who has everything. If you are spending big bucks, it is imperative that you buy from a reputable shop. Ask Glenn and Lucille for guidance.

But wait! **Wah Tung,** the porcelain shop, has a showroom on Hollywood Road (no. 148), but it's hidden upstairs, see p. 93.

WAN CHAI

Wan Chai these days means hot-hot-hot. The area that was once known as the home of Susie Wong and then better known for the Hyatt hotel is now trendy and mostly known for clubs and eats. Stores are popping up on Hennessy Road, in the Wan Chai District but not on Wan Chai Road.

Note that if you are at a convention in the convention center, you have a lot of walking to do to get to any decent shopping. The **Chinese Arts & Crafts** store, China Resources Building, 26 Harbour Rd. (© **2827/852-6667**), is nearest; everything else is a big schlep.

The Star Ferry provides direct access from Kowloon Peninsula: It travels from Tsim Sha Tsui to Wan Chai Pier. Old Wan Chai has been pushed back from the waterfront and will continue to be developed. If you want to see some original architecture and shops, prowl Queen's Road East and the lanes connecting it to Johnston Road. Shopping in the convention center is decidedly unexciting, but if you move on to the Hopewell Building, there is a fabulous **street market** on nearby Fenwick Street—no other tourists in sight, and a great place for taking pictures.

CAUSEWAY BAY

This area is so crowded, so fast paced, so hip, and so much fun that I feel 20 years younger when I wander the streets wondering why I've been such a stick-in-the-mud to stay in more established areas. Causeway Bay features one deluxe hotel (the **Excelsior**) and many tourist package–style hotels. It has several fancy Western malls, a street of outlet stores (Lee Gardens Rd.), some curving little alleys and streets filled with funk and glory, and countless shoppers, pushing their way to low-priced copies of the latest fashions.

This area is far funkier than Central, but it does have **Chanel** and a branch of every other designer, if that's your thing. The MTR stop is Causeway Bay. Note that Causeway Bay is directly across the bay from Tsim Sha Tsui East, so getting through the Cross Harbour Tunnel is a tad easier.

Why do I love Causeway Bay?

- Funky street shopping, with a nod toward fashion, just-starting-out talent, and Japanese designers.
- Jardine's Bazaar, a small warren of street stalls.
- Fashion Walk, a gathering of designer and up-and-coming designer shops in three adjoining buildings.
- Times Square, a relatively new giant mall that has taken the town by storm because it has four floors of local and Western brands. My favorite store there is City Super.
- The Japanese department stores, which are less and less Japanese and more and more global. The two best are **Sogo** and **Mitsokoshi. Seibu,** the Bergdorf Goodman of Japanese department stores, is in the Pacific Place mall.

AP LEI CHAU

Some people think that this neighborhood is part of Aberdeen, but it is a place unto itself, connected to Aberdeen by a bridge. The high-rise **Horizon Plaza** is home to many outlets, including the **Joyce Warehouse** (closed Mon) and the **Lane Crawford Warehouse.** For more furniture, try **Beijing Antiques Shop,** on the 20th floor, which has the kind of furniture many people cross into China to buy; it looks antique but is mostly refinished. Nearby is a Prada outlet, **Space.**

This is mostly a residential area, popular for its water views. Take a taxi and either have the driver wait or get the number of a taxi company so you can arrange a pickup.

STANLEY/REPULSE BAY/OCEAN PARK

It seems to be very "in" to bash **Stanley Market** and say it isn't up to the old standards. I have a love-hate relationship with this tourist trap, which sits in the heart of downtown Stanley (no MTR; take a taxi or bus no. 6). Last trip, I loathed it. I actually had tears streaming down my face. It's very touristy, and I couldn't find anything to buy.

However, Sarah found some great Tommy Bahama buys and when I spoke to some British first-timers a week later, they couldn't stop raving about Stanley. And my Hong Kong shopping friends still claim to find bargains here. Maybe it's a matter of perspective.

Part of the pleasure of a visit to Stanley is the drive across the island, especially the view as you go around some of those coastal curves. If you agree with me about Stanley, simply get back in the taxi, go to Repulse Bay, shop the snazzy stores, eat lunch, and then return to Hong Kong proper.

Stanley is exceedingly crowded on the weekends, delightfully quiet midweek. Note that Stanley is not one of those markets where the early bird gets the worm. The early bird gets to sit and sulk until the shops open around 9:30am. The area has been remodeled and is still popular with locals.

Causeway Bay

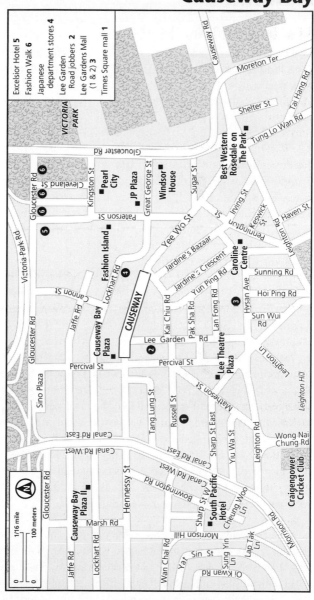

Excelsior Hotel **5**

Fashion Walk **6**

Japanese department stores **4**

Lee Garden Road jobbers **2**

Lee Gardens Mall (1 & 2) **3**

Times Square mall **1**

VICTORIA PARK

Gloucester Rd

Moreton Ter

Causeway Rd

Tai Hang Rd

Shelter St

Tung Lo Wan Rd

Best Western Rosedale on The Park

Haven St

Irving St

Keswick St

Pennington St

Leighton Rd

Pearl City

JP Plaza

Windsor House

Great George St

Sugar St

Kingston St

Cleveland St

Gloucester Rd

Paterson St

Yee Wo St

Jardine's Bazaar

Jardine's Crescent

Caroline Centre

Sunning Rd

Hoi Ping Rd

Sun Wui Rd

Fashion Island

Victoria Park Rd

Cannon St

Lockhart Rd

Yun Ping Rd

Hysan Ave

Lan Fong Rd

Pak Sha Rd

Kai Chiu Rd

CAUSEWAY

Causeway Bay Plaza

Jaffe Rd

Gloucester Rd

Lee Garden Rd

Percival St

Percival St

Lee Theatre Plaza

Leighton Ln

Sino Plaza

Tang Lung St

Russell St

Matheson St

Sharp St East

Yiu Wa St

Leighton Rd

Wong Nai Chung Rd

Canal Rd East

Canal Rd East

Canal Rd West

Canal Rd West

Sharp St East

Leighton Hill

Craigengower Cricket Club

Hennessy St

Bowrington Rd

Sharp St W

South Pacific Hotel

Cheung Woo Ln

Morrison Rd

Lap Tak Ln

Morrison Rd

Causeway Bay Plaza II

Gloucester Rd

Marsh Rd

Jaffe Rd

Lockhart Rd

Wan Chai Rd

Yat Sin St

Sung Yin Ln

Ol Kwan Rd

N

1/16 mile

100 meters

KOWLOON NEIGHBORHOODS

Kowloon is packed with shops, hotels, excitement, and bargains. You can shop its more than 10sq. km (4 sq. miles) for days and still feel that you haven't even made a dent. Like Hong Kong Island, Kowloon is the sum of many distinct neighborhoods.

TSIM SHA TSUI

The tip of Kowloon Peninsula consists of two neighborhoods: Tsim Sha Tsui and Tsim Sha Tsui East. It is home to most of Hong Kong's fine hotels and to Kowloon's serious tourist shopping. The MTR's Tsim Sha Tsui (TST) station is in the heart of things. Use the Jordan Road station when you're traveling a bit farther into Kowloon and working your way out of the tourist neighborhoods.

At the very tip of Tsim Sha Tsui are the Star Ferry Terminal and the Harbour City Complex. This Western-mall, built-up harborfront includes Ocean Terminal, Ocean Galleries, Ocean Centre, the Marco Polo Gateway Hotel, the Marco Polo Hong Kong Hotel, and the Marco Polo Prince Hotel.

The heart of Tsim Sha Tsui is **Nathan Road,** Kowloon's main shopping drag; it's the equivalent of London's Oxford Street. Nathan Road stretches from the waterfront for quite some distance and works its way into the "real people" part of Kowloon in no time at all. The most concentrated shopping is in the area called the **Golden Mile,** which begins on Nathan Road perpendicular to Salisbury Road. Both sides of this busy street are jampacked with stores, arcades, covered alleys, and street vendors. There are also some hotels here, each with a shopping mall and enough neon to make Las Vegas blush.

Nathan Road is the core of Kowloon, but my favorite part of Tsim Sha Tsui is a bit off the beaten path—though directly in sight. In the Golden Mile section of Tsim Sha Tsui, two streets run parallel to Nathan Road and are centered between the Golden Mile and Ocean Terminal: Hankow Road and

The Kowloon Peninsula

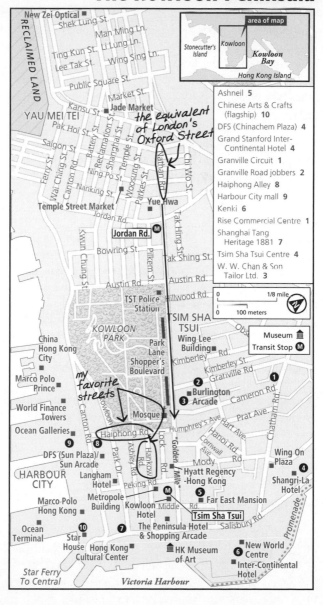

area of map

Stonecutter's Island
Kowloon
Kowloon Bay
Hong Kong Island

New Zei Optical
Shek Lung St.
Man Ming Ln.
Ting Kun St. Li Lung Ln.
Lee Tak St. Wing Sing Ln.
Public Square St.
RECLAIMED LAND
Market St.
Kansu St. Jade Market
YAU MEI TEI
Pak Hoi St.
Saigon St.
Battery St.
Wai Ching St.
Canton Rd.
Ferry St.
Reclamation St.
Shanghai St.
Temple St.
Woosung St.
Parkes St.
Nathan Rd.
Chi Wo St.
Ning Po St.
Nanking St.
Temple Street Market
Yue Hwa
Jordan Rd.
Jordan Rd. M
Kwun Chung St.
Bowring St.
Pilkem St.
Tak Shing St.
Tak Hing St.
Austin Rd.
Austin Rd.
TST Police Station
Hillwood Rd.
TSIM SHA TSUI
KOWLOON PARK
China Hong Kong City
Wing Lee Building
Kimberley Rd.
Kimberley St.
Marco Polo Prince
Park Lane Shopper's Boulevard
Granville Rd.
Burlington Arcade
World Finance Towers
Cameron Rd.
Ocean Galleries
Mosque
Humphrey's Ave. Hart Ave.
Prat Ave.
Hanoi Rd.
Chatham Rd.
Haiphong Rd.
Cornwall Ave.
Lock Rd.
"Golden Mile"
Wing On Plaza
DFS (Sun Plaza)/ Sun Arcade
Hankow Rd.
Ashley Rd.
Mody Rd.
Shangri-La Hotel
HARBOUR CITY
Langham Hotel
Peking Rd.
Hyatt Regency-Hong Kong
Marco Polo Hong Kong
Metropole Building
Kowloon Hotel
Middle Rd.
Far East Mansion
Ocean Terminal
Star House
The Peninsula Hotel & Shopping Arcade
Salisbury Rd.
Tsim Sha Tsui M
Hong Kong Cultural Center
New World Centre
Star Ferry To Central
HK Museum of Art
Inter-Continental Hotel
Victoria Harbour
Promenade

the equivalent of London's Oxford Street

my favorite streets

Ashneil **5**
Chinese Arts & Crafts (flagship) **10**
DFS (Chinachem Plaza) **4**
Grand Stanford Inter-Continental Hotel **4**
Granville Circuit **1**
Granville Road jobbers **2**
Haiphong Alley **8**
Harbour City mall **9**
Kenki **6**
Rise Commercial Centre **1**
Shanghai Tang Heritage 1881 **7**
Tsim Sha Tsui Centre **4**
W. W. Chan & Son Tailor Ltd. **3**

0   1/8 mile
0   100 meters

Museum 🏛
Transit Stop Ⓜ

Haiphong Road. They have some outlets, some jobbers, and several stores that sell DVDs and legal VCDs (video compact discs). Also check out Lock Road, which runs perpendicular to these streets. Once you become an old China hand, you'll note that prices on Nathan Road are for tourists, and you may disdain the whole Golden Mile area.

Near Jordan Road, farther up the peninsula, the atmosphere is more real. Be sure to get to the **Temple Street Market** (p. 123). And you can't miss the **Jade Market.** If you have a true spirit of shopping and adventure, you'll also make sure you get to Fa Yuen Street (see below).

TSIM SHA TSUI EAST

If you have Hong Kong Harbour at your back, Ocean Terminal to your left, and the InterContinental Hong Kong Hotel to your right, you're looking at the heart of Kowloon, or Tsim Sha Tsui. As the Kowloon peninsula curves around the harbor and the land juts away from Kowloon and the InterContinental, the area just east of Tsim Sha Tsui but before Hung Hom and the old airport is known as **Tsim Sha Tsui East.**

Mobbed on weekends by local shoppers, the area's various buildings include **Auto Plaza, Houston Centre,** and the enclosed mall itself, **Tsim Sha Tsui Centre.** There is street-level shopping all along Mody Road, in the various buildings, in the mall, and at street level of the buildings behind the Grand Stafford and Nikko hotels. There is also some shopping in each hotel. My favorite store in this area is **DFS,** which has terrific souvenir, food, and traditional medicine departments.

YAU MA TEI

The most famous shopping site in the area is the well-known **Jade Market** at Kansu and Battery streets; look for the overpass of the highway, and you'll spot the market right below it.

The experience is just short of mind-boggling. Here you can shop from 10am until 2:30pm, going from stall to stall, negotiating for all the jade (p. 43) that you might fancy. There are two tents filled with vendors. You'll never be strong enough to do both tents.

Alongside the Jade Market, on Shanghai Street, is a "wet market"—a real live Chinese **green market** (farmers' market) worthy of exploration with or without a camera. As the street stretches to the south, it has some old-fashioned paper stores.

PRINCE EDWARD & FA YUEN

Even though Fa Yuen is just a street and not a true neighborhood, it's enough of an event that it should be considered a separate destination. It's my favorite new neighborhood in Hong Kong. On a recent visit, I bought so much I truly could not fit through the stairwell to the MTR station.

In a nutshell, Fa Yuen is a market street with fixed stores and after 4pm, a street market too. Fa Yuen has been blossoming for several years now; no doubt it will become too commercial, and a new place will sprout. Until then, what are you waiting for? Bring plenty of cash because most of these stores do not take plastic. Consider bringing airline wheels—or a donkey. It is time to shop 'til you drop, Hong Kong style.

From here, you can wander over to the nearby **Ladies' Market** (see below). It's 2 blocks away on Tung Choi Street and also opens around 4pm. Don't confuse these two shopping venues.

The **Ladies' Market** is mostly a street market with stalls on the road, while Fa Yuen Street consists of traditional retail with actual shops. Look at a map. Also note that the **Bird Market** is in this neighborhood, on Yuen Po Street. To get there, take the MTR to Prince Edward and work your way south. Take a map to help connect the dots.

Prince Edward, Mong Kok & Fa Yuen Street

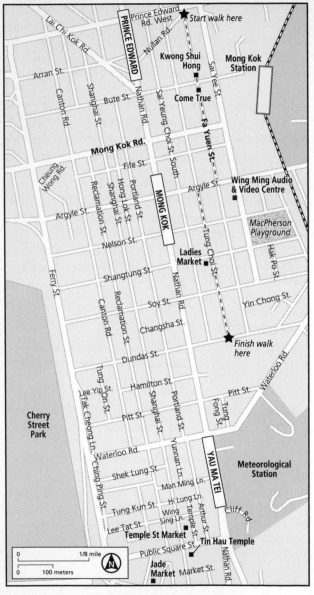

Chapter 5

Hong Kong Resources A to Z

Antiques

Hong Kong is home to many places where you can buy art and antiques. Two important things to remember:

- Internationally famous dealers do business in London, New York, Tokyo, Vancouver, Taipei, Brussels, and other places besides Hong Kong; buy according to reputation and trust, not location.
- The number of fakes and frauds in the art business is infamous and truly frightening, especially in Hong Kong and China.

Buy what you know; if you don't know much, buy what you love, regardless of its real value. Bring your own expert if you are truly serious, or hire one in Hong Kong. If you are considering something pricey, get a second opinion. Many dealers on Hollywood Road will appraise an item from another source for a flat fee.

Bear in mind that the truly wonderful pieces are usually put away. Most dealers have warehouses or back rooms where they keep their best wares; many are open only by appointment.

Consider an "artistic" piece, such as a well-priced fake with an antique look that is known as a reproduction but is priced accordingly.

Arch Angel
53–55 Hollywood Rd., Central (MTR: Central).

I can't tell you how many personal recommendations I have received from readers who love this store. Prices are high, but the name can be trusted. Open daily for furniture, statuary, and tabletop items. © 852/2851-6848.

Honeychurch Antiques
29 Hollywood Rd. (MTR: Central).

Honeychurch Antiques has been my home base on Hollywood Road since the beginning of the Born to Shop series. I know you will be well taken care of by American expat owners Glenn and Lucille Vessa. They have held court for over 25 years and know everything and everyone; stop by and ask whatever pops into your mind; they will help out. Also ask to meet "my" armoire, the one I will let you buy if you remember that I found it first.

The store carries a wide variety of merchandise. The look is sort of Oriental country. There are goods from Japan and other exotic locations besides China. Try both floors in the main shop and a warehouse floor next door (ask to be taken over), with larger pieces of furniture and a few other goodies. Yes, they have blue-and-white; yes, they'll let you smell the opium pipes. If you ask nicely, they will even let you use the bathroom. © 852/2543-2433. www.honeychurch.com.

Arts & Crafts

The Chinese look hasn't been fashionable in years, certainly not since the Beatles took to wearing Mao jackets. Now everything's coming up ethnic so Chinese classics are more chic than ever. You can buy them in markets, at souvenir shops, and at **Chinese Arts & Crafts** (p. 98).

Kenki

New World Center, 20 Salisbury Rd., basement 1, shops 126 & 127, Kowloon (MTR: TST).

This store has a few branches around town—they differ enormously. I always start at the New World Centre, adjacent to the InterContinental Hotel because two different branches are actually there. For a store in Central, right near the main Shanghai Tang, head to Pottinger House, 24 Pottinger St., Central © 852/2523-9993.

BEST BUYS   Kenki sells embroidered shirts and blouses, reversible silk to velvet or cotton and silk Chinese coolie shirts, brocade vests with and without fur—I call it the poor man's Shanghai Tang. Prices are excellent—about $40 for a shirt, $100 for an elaborately embroidered jacket. © 2367-8908. www.kenki.cc.

Bath & Beauty

See "Spas," later in this chapter for more information, and remember that this is a city where the InterContinental Hotel has a 24-hour "bath butler"—all sorts of beauty products for the tub (and shower) are readily available. For brands you may not be familiar with, high-tail it to any of the big malls. For color cosmetics, see p. 96.

I am quite fond of Japanese bath salts. You can buy them in any drug- or grocery store and can tell the scent by the pictures—since the package is entirely in Japanese; I buy mine at City Super (p. 106).

Aesop

52–60 Lyndhurst Terrace, Central (MTR: Central).

This Australian brand of skin care is an excellent line of all-natural products. Unfortunately for travelers, almost everything is packaged in glass, which makes items heavier. You can buy this product in the U.S., but the store is sensational to look at, and this brand is very much in keeping with the new Pacific Rim. It opens at 11am daily. ✆ 852/2544-4489.

Cosmetics Concierge

Lane Crawford Pacific Place, 88 Queensway (MTR: Admiralty).

This complimentary service includes makeovers and image styling, professional consultations, and personalized skin-care advice. The Lane Crawford team of experts will continue to keep you informed of new products suitable for your skin type by e-mail. ✆ 852/2118-3333. www.lanecrawford.com.

Harvey Nichols

The Landmark Mall, 15 Queen's Rd., Central (MTR: Central).

Listed elsewhere in this book (p. 97), Harvey Nicks is great when it comes to cult beauty brands. ✆ 852/3695-3388. www.harveynichols.com.

Jurlique

Landmark Atrium, 16 Des Voeux Rd. (MTR: Central); Times Square mall (MTR: Causeway Bay).

Say "Jur-*leak*," then celebrate Australia and this terrific brand. Lavender hand cream is the most famous of Jurlique's numerous products. I fly with Herbal Recovery Mist in my purse, and I like the silk dust (instead of powder) for really sweaty summer days. www.jurlique.hk.

Lush

Festival Walk, shop 40, (MTR: Causeway Bay); Harbour City, shop 3315 (MTR: TST); Hong Kong International Airport, arrivals hall.

You can almost smell a Lush shop before you see it; asthmatics need not apply. Despite the high prices, the British firm is onto something charming. The deli-counter environment features beauty and bath products, soaps that are sliced like deli cheeses, and bath bombs as large as tennis balls, ready to lob into a hot tub. The concepts and scents are the same throughout the world, but ingredients may be different in some international stores. www.lush.com.

Books

Because English is still used as a second language in Hong Kong, it isn't hard to find books in English. True, they are pricey, but not as expensive as in other cities in China. Also check airport news kiosks for international editions of the latest books—they are soft cover with large print.

Dymocks

IFC2 mall (MTR: Central).

I have good news and bad news here. Since the Star Ferry terminal has moved, my favorite branch of Dymocks is now gone. But plenty of branches of this famous bookstore still exist; about half of the chain's stores are in areas where tourists shop and the others are farther out where locals live. You'll find local guidebooks, cultural information, and new releases as well as fiction by author, international magazines, some stationery items, and plenty of nonfiction in English. Other locations include Peak Galleria, Prince's Building, and Harbour Centre. © 852/2117-0360. www.dymocks.com.hk.

WEB TIPS 🖱 Book events and special promotions are listed on the website.

Page One the Bookshop

Times Square mall, 1 Matheson St., lower level, Causeway Bay (MTR: Causeway Bay).

This is a firm based in Singapore with stores dotted around Southeast Asia. Branches of this chain are often in malls alongside the grocery store City Super. Books are in Chinese and in English, and the magazine selection is huge. The house specialty is art and design. They stock a few nonbook items; the trophy of one of my sprees was an eight-lens camera for $50. They carry office supplies, paper goods, and novelty items, too. Sometimes they host author events in English. Other stores around town are in malls such as Festival Walk, Harbour City, and Century Square. ✆ 852/2506-0381. www.pageonegroup.com.

Swindon Book Co., Ltd.

13–15 Lock Rd. (behind the Peninsula Hotel), Tsim Sha Tsui, Kowloon (MTR: TST).

Although this medium-size store carries everything, most impressive is the selection of art books and books on Chinese culture. It is open 7 days a week and will ship overseas. ✆ 852/2366-8001. www.swindonbooks.com.

Cameras

Forget it. If you're talking serious money, buy at home. And for heaven's sake, avoid those guys on Nathan Road.

Cashmere

Cashmere from the Orient is not of the same quality as that which comes out of Scotland or Italy because of how the yarn is combed and milled. Meanwhile, Iranian cashmere, which is of even lower quality than Chinese, is flooding the market. Price should be related to the ply number (from 1, the lowest quality, to 4); 2 is the usual number available in Hong Kong.

You can find cashmere in many of the outlet stores in the **Pedder Building,** in several stores at the **Peninsula Hotel Shopping Arcade,** at **Stanley Market,** and at the Chinese department stores. Quality will be a big issue here—it affects the hand (feel) as well as the price. Most likely, you can get cashmere at home for prices similar to those in Hong Kong. But wait: Did I tell you about the **Tse Cashmere** outlet sale?

Pearls and Cashmere
The Peninsula Hotel, Salisbury Rd., Kowloon (MTR: TST).

The selection of colors is excellent. Prices are not dirt-cheap but are competitive with low-end prices in the U.S., meaning you get more quality than usual for the price, which is close to $200 per sweater. Some sweaters cost less; the store also carries other items. © 852/2723-8698.

Tse Cashmere
The Landmark 304–305; Central (MTR: Central); Elements mall 2116–2118, Kowloon (MTR: TST).

Tse (say "say") is a luxury brand with expensive merchandise sold at fancy stores around the world. Once a year, usually before Christmas, an outlet sale takes place at an address announced in the *South China Post* newspaper. When I went, the floor was dirty, but the merchandise (organized by size and color) was fabulous. The staff took credit cards and spoke English. Just about everything cost less than $100. It was a heart-stopping shopping moment, especially good for those who need luxury labels in their bargains. © 852/2147-3033 Landmark; 852/2724-6303 Elements. www.tsecashmere.com.

CDs, VCDs & DVDs

CDs and VCDs (video compact discs) are sold on the street, in the usual music stores and chains (such as HMV), and in China, although China specializes in the bootleg DVD.

Note that VCDs are not DVDs—DVDs are more expensive and are said to have better quality, although I have had no problem with the quality of VCDs. DVDs also hold more information, so a movie fits on one disc, as opposed to two (or more) VCDs. But VCDs are legal.

The average price for a VCD in Hong Kong is HK$50 ($7). However, when I last tested, VCDs did not play on a U.S. machine—though they do play on my U.S. laptop. Hong Kong has really cracked down on fake DVDs; most of the stores that sell low-cost movies sell them in VCD format.

Ceramics & Porcelain

Chinese crafts stores carry a selection of china. And yes, assume that blue-and-whites there are fake.

Overjoy
Kwai Hing Industrial Building, 10–18 Chun Pin St., block B, 1st floor, Kwai Chung, New Territories (MTR: Kwai Hing, then taxi).

Located in the heart of Hong Kong's shipping and container district, where there are a few other porcelain showrooms, Overjoy is worth the trouble. Although it's not a replacement for Wah Tung (see below), it is a good source. The selection includes both Western and Chinese patterns. I bought ginger jars for $5, mugs with lids for $10, and lamps for $40. The store offers international shipping (rates are posted) and free delivery to Hong Kong hotels. There is also a showroom in Wan Chai. When you are ready to leave, the staff will give you a small piece of paper asking your taxi driver (in English and Chinese) to take you to the MTR station. Taxis are readily available out front. © 852/2487-0615.

Wah Tung China Company

Main Showroom: 16/F Cheung Fat Building, 7–9 Hill Rd., Western District (no nearby MTR).

Store: 7/F Lee Roy Commercial Building, 57–59 Hollywood Rd. (MTR: Central).

Ohhhhh boy, here's the new reality in Hong Kong—big stores are downsizing, giving up warehouses and moving to oddball neighborhoods. Not that Western is odder than Aberdeen, but the Wah Tung warehouse we knew and loved is gone and a spiffy, new, clean, bright, gorgeous showroom has been opened not far from the mouth of the Western Tunnel.

Everything is in one shop on one floor; there are a variety of salons divided by specialty, such as blue-and-white, monochromatic, smalls, and so forth. As you walk in, there's a table set with gift items priced under $100.

You can call to get someone to come to your hotel for you or you can take a taxi and turn in your receipt at the store to be reimbursed. The location is industrial but worth the trouble. © 852/2873-2272. www.wahtung.com.

Chops

In China a *chop* is a form of signature stamp on which a symbol for a person's name is carved. The chop is dipped in dry dye (not pressed onto an ink pad) and then placed on paper to create a signature stamp, much like a rubber stamp—though chops are not made of rubber.

Although chops vary in size, they are traditionally as big as a chess piece, with a square or round base. Up to four Chinese characters or three Western initials can be inscribed on the base.

Quality varies greatly, depending on the ability of the person who does the carving. We have done enough chop shopping to know that the very best place to get a chop, if you crave atmosphere, lies in **Man Wa Lane,** deep inside the Western District. It's also the worst place because it is so confusing—you may never find your way back to the proper vendor when you need to pick up your finished chop. Nevertheless, Man Wa feels very authentic, and you may enjoy the entire experience.

Every hotel has at least one gift shop that will have your chop engraved. Allow at least 24 hours. Many shops will provide 1-hour service. A variety of dealers at **Stanley Market** offer while-you-wait service.

You may buy the chop a la carte or in a set or gift box. The boxed set comes with your chop and the inkpot in a silk-covered (or faux-silk) box with an adorable clasp; expect to pay about HK$100 ($13) for a boxed set at Stanley Market.

Computers & Electronics

I am nervous about buying computers and most other electronics in Hong Kong—too much can go wrong. On the other hand, my greatest delight has been buying small DVD players to give as gifts in the U.S. They play DVDs, VCDs, and discs from all zones. Well, they play DVD-9 all over the world.

I shop for electronics at **Broadway,** a reputable chain with stores all over Hong Kong, and buy either the brands we all know or Shinco. Make sure the instructions are in English and that voltage is 110–220. You will also have to buy plugs. Another reliable chain is **Fortress,** which has stores in all trading areas. There are computer buildings, streets, and fairs (even a flea market) for locals who know what they are doing. Shop at your own risk.

Broadway
Times Square mall, 7th floor (MTR: Causeway Bay); 28 Soy St. (MTR: Mong Kok); and many other locations.

I've had my share of bad experiences buying electronics in Hong Kong, so it's a pleasure to find a store I can trust. This chain has locations everywhere. I won't shop anywhere else. ✆ 852/2506-0228.

Fortress

5 Peking Rd., Kowloon (MTR: TST), and many other locations.

This is the other trusted name in electronics, with stores all over town. This one is behind the Pen. The downstairs (ground floor) area is smallish; go upstairs. ✆ 852/2311-2318.

Cosmetics Supermarkets

The best buys in this category are noteworthy in terms of availability, not price—check out scents that have been introduced in Europe but not in the U.S. And I am not going to mention a brand just because it's new or hot in Hong Kong, such as Kiehl's (the latest thing), because you can easily get Kiehl's for less money in the U.S.

Many big-name cosmetics companies manufacture for the Far East in and around Hong Kong; often they will have a product with the same name as the one you use at home, but it will be slightly different. They may also have a product or shade that you have never heard of and will never find again anywhere else in the world.

If you just wander through any of the malls, especially **Harbour City,** you will finds tons of little shops selling brands that may interest you—a few local labels, some European brands that don't have good distribution in the U.S., and many Japanese products.

Bonjour

Locations all over town.

This is a chain possibly devised for adolescent girls; I'm not crazy for it, but your 12-year-old might enjoy it. It's a knock-off of the SaSa concept (see below).

Boots

In Watson's (below).

Boots is a British chemist that sells several of its own brands of makeup and treatments, among other things. Some Watson's stores carry the line at in-store boutiques, but there is a growing trend toward free-standing stores for beauty items only (these are not Boots stores as we know them in the U.K.), with an emphasis on well-being products. The line No. 7—a riff on No. 5, as in Chanel—is an excellent color cosmetics selection at a moderate price.

SaSa Cosmetic Company

Locations all over town.

SaSa has emerged as one of the leading discounters in Hong Kong, with branch stores everywhere. Note that all branches are not created equal; some have more stock than others.

Many goods come directly from sources in the U.S., which makes them much cheaper locally—but not cheaper than at home, if you are American. Shop carefully. Also note that some items are closeouts and discontinued lines.

Watson's, the Chemist

24–28 Queen's Rd. (MTR: Central), and many other locations.

There's a Watson's on almost every big, busy block and in every mall in Hong Kong; I stop in all of them because they're not all the same. Selected stores have a Boots department (see above). Watson's is actually a drugstore-cum-general-store that sells many things, including other lines of makeup and treatments.

Department Stores

EUROPEAN-STYLE

Harvey Nichols

The Landmark, 16 Des Voeux Rd. (MTR: Central).

Just when you thought the British had left Hong Kong, London's best department store arrives at the city's fanciest mall. Harvey Nicks has a bit of a Barneys feel to it and is excellent in its selection of cult brands in fashion and makeup. The cafe is a good place for people-watching and getting your cool down pat. Part of the store's cachet is that they carry brands not found elsewhere, even by Joyce (p. 112)—such as Goyard from France. © **852/3695-3388.** Fourth Floor Restaurant © 852/3695-3389.

Lane Crawford

IFC2 mall (MTR: Central); Mall at Pacific Place, 88 Queensway, Central (MTR: Admiralty); Times Square mall (MTR: Causeway Bay).

Lane Crawford is the most prestigious Western-style department store in Hong Kong. It's a jewel to those who work and live here but crave the elegance of old-world charm in a retail setting. Lane Crawford is not huge by American standards, but you'll find all the familiar top-quality brands. It is not really for tourists, but it does offer the guarantee that you are not getting fakes, seconds, or inferior merchandise. Snobs often buy their jewelry and their lifestyle here.

The largest branch, some 8,361sq. m (89,997 sq. ft.) of razzle-dazzle, is in the IFC2 mall. If you stay at the Four Seasons hotel, you are practically adjacent to the IFC2 mall and Lane Crawford and will get to know it as a friend. Though actually, I like the outlet store (p. 102) better.

Also note that Lane Crawford is in the same retail group now as the Joyce Ma stores and City Super. Give these guys a hand—they are the best stores in town. © 852/2118-3388.

LCX
Ocean Terminal, Harbour City, Tsim Sha Tsui, Kowloon (MTR: TST).

The concept is one big warehouse, so it's a department store within a mall—and one that has no walls. Brands have different identity areas, clearly delineated, but you wander from one to the next as if sailing from island to island. A few of them are names you know (Gap, Banana Republic), some are names you have been dying to meet, and others are totally unknown even to the savviest shopper. The space is young and hip, but it's also interesting if you just want to see something very different from an old-fashioned department store or mall.

Marks & Spencer
Harbour City Ocean Galleries, 25–27 Canton Rd., Kowloon (MTR: TST); Mall at Pacific Place, 88 Queensway, Central (MTR: Admiralty); the Landmark, 16 Des Voeux Rd. (MTR: Central); Cityplaza III, 1111 King's Rd., Quarry Bay (MTR: Tai Koo).

I love M&S, but there are no great bargains here. Being in the store, especially the grocery department, is just fun. It also offers a chance to buy Western sizes and larger sizes. Need a brassiere? Need shoes? Can't get a fit elsewhere? This is your source. Just watch out for clothes marked "Asian fit," which probably will not fit you. Women's shoes go up to size 42 (U.S. size 11).

CHINESE STYLE
Chinese Arts & Crafts Stores (H.K.) Ltd.
Flagship: Star House, next to Star Ferry, Canton Rd., Kowloon (MTR: TST); branches throughout town.

This is the most Western of the Chinese department stores. By American standards, the prices are good, although the

David Tang look-alike merchandise is just as expensive as his! Ouch! The stores are clean, easy to use, and tourist friendly, but you pay for these luxuries.

The silk-fabric (yard goods) department is fun, although the prices are cheaper in markets. I've been told this is a reputable place to buy jade. There's no imitation passed off as real here. *Be warned:* Real jade is quite pricey.

The store will ship for you; the sales help has been very pleasant to me—unusual for some Chinese stores. This is a good place for souvenirs. All stores are open basically Monday to Saturday from 10am to 6:30pm; Sunday hours vary with the location.

Yue Hwa Chinese Products Emporium
G40 Park Lane Shopper's Blvd., ground floor (MTR: TST).

This is a real Chinese department store, with many convenient branches. Unfortunately, the newer the store, the more Western it is, which is not my favorite style of Chinese department store. The newer Park Lane store is almost as nice as Macy's. Buy from the "Great Wall of China," as I call the china department; get silk pj's; get silk by the yard.

Ignore the Western goods and buy Chinese. The stores mail to the United States. Hours are daily from 10:30am to 10pm. © 852/2739-3888.

BEST BUYS   I just bought a silk ancestor's coat (in other words, a men's-style dressing gown) on sale for $99 in size XXXL; it is divine.

JAPANESE STYLE
Most of the large **Japanese department stores** are in Causeway Bay and aren't very different from U.S. department stores. Seibu, the most upscale of all Japanese department stores, bucked the trend by opening in the Pacific Place mall. Hard times have forced cutbacks, but the store is still open.

Seibu

The Mall at Pacific Place, 88 Queensway, Central (MTR: Admiralty); Langham Place, Kowloon (MTR: Mong Kok); Nathan Rd., Kowloon (MTR: TST).

Once one of the best department stores in the world, Seibu is now cutting back a tad but still has two very stylish outposts in Honkers. The store has many brands and strives to introduce brands that no one else has. It specializes in the Antwerp Gang, the Belgian designers who get so much coverage in the fashion press. Seibu also opened the first **Diesel StyleLab** in town and was among the first to see the potential in Mong Kok. *Insider's tip:* The two branch stores pale compared to the location in Pacific Place. ℰ **852/2269-1888.**

Designer Goods

Hong Kong gains designer shops everyday; I cannot come to town without being annoyed that so many new ones have opened. Who in the world is shopping at these places? Did any of us come to Hong Kong to buy big-name designer clothes at regular retail prices? Or to buy at prices higher than at home? I mean, *really*.

Every now and then you can get a break on designer goods, but not often. Some Chanel items (such as makeup) are cheaper than in the U.S. or at the airport duty-free shop. Most items, however, are not. If you are interested in a certain designer line, I suggest you shop for it at home and come to Hong Kong with notes in hand. Don't be surprised if designer prices are totally out of line; Ferragamo may just give you heart failure. But wait: I just read an article in a Toronto newspaper by the fashion editor who went to Hong Kong this past summer, hit some sales, found Prada to be half her hometown prices, and felt that designer goods were all but growing on trees. Maybe there's hope yet.

Up-and-Coming Talent

More and more young designers are finding that Hong Kong is a fine place to be discovered. Although many of the young designers in town are not yet represented in boutiques, they are busy designing private-label goods for large stores. You may never have heard their names, but you may dig their designs.

You'll find the latest and wildest designs by hot young talents in the shops that line **Kimberley Road** and **Austin Avenue.** These two streets, in the northern end of Tsim Sha Tsui, have become the SoHo of Hong Kong. The shops' decor is avant-garde; the prices are affordable. Start at the corner of Austin and Nathan roads, walking east. Austin Road turns a corner and becomes Austin Avenue, which turns again and becomes Kimberley Road, heading back toward Nathan Road. Also in this area is the **Rise Commercial Building** on Granville Circuit, a small, hard-to-find alley off Granville Road.

If confused, go for brands or selection in Hong Kong that have not yet come to the U.S. or that you do not know, so that you can be the first on your block to wear a certain style.

Discounts & Deals

Most manufacturing is done outside of Hong Kong, so there are few genuine factory outlets these days. Still, there are some jobbers in the **Pedder Building** (p. 114) and a handful of good sources elsewhere. Changes at **Horizons Plaza** make it worth the trip, and there's usually a line of taxis waiting to whisk you home—a recent improvement.

With the exception of Lok Wah, none of these establishments is near the MTR; take a taxi.

Joyce Warehouse
Horizons Plaza, 2 Li Wing St., 21st floor, Ap Lei Chau.

Joyce has been the most famous name in European luxury brands in Hong Kong for over 25 years. She's had a number of stores and has suffered the usual ups and downs of retail in hard times. All of her stores are now owned by Lane Crawford (see above). Her warehouse and outlet store sells off goods that don't move out of her stores. I saw an Armani blazer for $50 and other designer bargains that left me breathless. Sizes tend to run so small that I get depressed easily.

Kaiser Estates
Phases 1, 2 & 3, Man Yue Rd., Hung Hom.

This is a formerly famous shopping district that I find very boring and somewhat overpriced. A Donna Karan DKNY blazer for $250 is not my idea of a bargain. I did, however, luck into the Adidas outlet sale—shoes at $30 a pair were a good bargain. Most of the outlets are in Phase 1, with a few in Phase 2. Frankly, I think you can give this area a miss, but I got a note from readers who loved it here. Go figure. © 852/2362-1760.

Lane Crawford Warehouse
Horizons Plaza, 2 Li Wing St., 25th floor, Ap Lei Chau.

Better than any other Hong Kong outlet I've recently been to. Armani jackets for under $200, suits for $400. Shoes, accessories, home-style, menswear—gorgeous stuff. Maybe I got lucky, but it sure was more fun than the Joyce Warehouse. The Lane Crawford Warehouse has a greater variety of sizes, and you can buy nice gifts if you find nothing for yourself. © 852/2118-3403.

Lok Wah
Lok Wah Bo, 193 Fa Yuen St. (MTR: Mong Kok); Lok Wah Top World, 175 Fa Yuen St. (MTR: Mong Kok); Lok Wah

Top Place, 53 and 55 Granville Rd., Kowloon (MTR: TST); Lok Wah City, 11 Lee Garden Rd. (MTR: Causeway Bay).

This small chain of jobbers operates stores that sell clothes—often including big-name brands—out of bins. Each major shopping area has a store, which can be your jumping-off point in its neighborhood. I'm not saying it's the best of the jobbers, but I have done well on repeat visits and found a variety of merchandise and sizes at low everyday prices.

Space
Marina Sq. E., 2F Commercial Block, South Horizons, Ap Lei Chau.

Space is the name the Prada Group gives to its warehouses selling all its lines—Prada, Miu Miu, Jil Sander, Helmut Lang, and so on. With all the fake Prada in China, it's hard to suggest that you visit, but this *is* the real thing, and it carries clothes, shoes, and accessories, too. This outlet is in Ap Lei Chau but not in Horizons Plaza (though it is nearby). Ask your hotel concierge to call © 852/2814-9576 for directions, then have him write them in Chinese.

Ethnic Style
....

Costumey Chinese dresses, jackets, and shirts are for sale just about everywhere in Hong Kong, from souvenir stores to **Chinese Arts & Crafts** to the chicest of them all, **Shanghai Tang** (p. 4). However, if you prefer the look that qualifies more as boho chic, you will need a good eye and some luck. The fanciest Asian chic is from **Blanc de Chine** (p. 112) and **Shiatzy Chen** (p. 4). For the wannabes that are quite affordable, try **Kenki** (p. 87).

Fabrics

As a rule, don't think that just because you are close to the silkworms, you can walk away with bargains. Silk is usually about $15 a meter.

Buying fabrics from tailors in the People's Republic of China can be tricky (they may lie about the origin of the goods), but you can trust the fine tailors in Hong Kong to offer European fabrics for suits, shirts, and other clothing. If you don't know your tailor, don't let him sell you European fabric without showing you the bolt or sample book. Low-class tailors have been known to do a switcheroo—or just fib.

The second floor of the **Western Market** (p. 124) is home to a fabric market. You may get a kick out of **Excellent Silk Mill**, 17 Cameron Rd., 2nd Floor, Kowloon (MTR: TST), which takes only cash but has vintage fabrics for sale off the bolt. It's near Nathan and Granville roads.

Shanghai Tang sells gorgeous silks and fabrics, but the prices may kill you. For similar fabrics, try a branch of **Chinese Arts & Crafts.**

Shenzhen, across the border (see chapter 6), is a good place to shop for silk; there is an entire fabric market located in the main shopping mall at the border. **Li Yuen West,** in the Lanes (p. 122), is more convenient.

Furs

Just when you thought it was safe to go out into the cold, fur is back. Fun fur—cheap, funky, colorful, and possibly fashion forward—is the latest trend and can be found in Hong Kong in the winter. There's also a fair amount of fake fur around, even in markets. Trusted names in real fur include **Mari Furs** and **Prestige Furs,** both in the Peninsula Hotel arcade, and **Siberian Furs** on Chatham Road in Kowloon.

Glasses

....

The days of truly inexpensive eyeglasses are over, but many people do find considerable savings in Hong Kong.

Eye'n-1
1 Lan Fong Rd. (MTR: Causeway Bay).

With an optometrist in the shop and more designer frames than you can imagine, this is one of the hipper spots for eyewear in a very trendy neighborhood. © 852/2882-2948.

New Fei Optical Supply Ltd.
Lucky Horse Industrial Building, 64 Tong Mi Rd., 1–7 Bute St., 12th floor, Kowloon (MTR: Prince Edward, then shuttle bus or taxi).

This source comes from my friend Louis, who is chief concierge at the InterConti and wears glasses (I had LASIK surgery). Louis knows everything and everyone. This is one of the best sources he has ever given me.

It's a factory in an industrial part of town. You pick your frames, you have your eyes tested, and you wait 10 minutes. If your prescription is more complicated, you may wait a half-hour while they make your glasses.

You can buy reading glasses, eyeglasses, or sunglasses; children have their own selection. There are thousands of frames, many from big-name Euro designers. The eye test is free. The setup is sort of supermarket style, then you sit at a table with a mirror and try on frames all day. Cold drinks are served.

I have had about a dozen pairs of glasses made here in the past few years. Prices average about $100 per pair. Note that you will not only need your Rx but something called the PD (pupillary distance measurements). If you are having glasses made for someone who is not with you, make sure you have the PD!

You can take the shuttle bus or a taxi from the MTR; the area is industrial but not frightening. To arrange for the shuttle bus before you head out, have a hotel staff member call ✆ 852/2398-2088. Avoid weekends if you can; some 400 people a day pass through on Saturday and Sunday. Hours are daily from 10:30am to 8pm.

Grocery Stores

The best grocery stores in Hong Kong are more like department stores. Indeed, one of my favorite stores in town is called **City Super**—it sells everything. **Marks & Spencer** stores sell some packaged (not fresh) foodstuffs; the local grocery store chains, **Wellcome** and **Park 'N Shop**, have small branches all over.

City Super
Harbour City, level 3 (MTR: TST); IFC2 mall (MTR: Central); Times Square, basement, Causeway Bay (MTR: Causeway Bay).

I'm not sure if I am more in love with the wide selection of Japanese bath products, the gadgets department, the international foodstuffs, or simply the people who shop here—but this is a great business and a really fun concept. It's the modern version of the general store.

GrEAT
Mall at Pacific Place, 88 Queensway, downstairs from Seibu, Central (MTR: Admiralty).

I don't like GrEAT as much as City Super because it's more of a gourmet grocery and less of a department store. But baby, what a grocery store. There's a fancy food court and all sorts of international grocery and gourmet products. Branch stores are opening in Kowloon. ✆ 852/2918-9986.

Needs
New World Centre, Salisbury Rd., Kowloon (MTR: TST).

Every time I check into the InterConti next-door, I make this my next stop. I'm not saying you should make a special trip here (as I would suggest for any branch of City Super), but the Kmart-type establishment is a great grocery store. You can also buy health and beauty aids, electronics, and more.

Super Wellcome
Causeway Bay (MTR: Causeway Bay).

Wellcome is a well-known grocery chain; this location is almost a superstore in the heart of crowded Causeway Bay, near the big hotels there. You can buy snacks and browse in a fun, modern supermarket.

Handbags

Ashneil
Far East Mansions, 5–6 Middle Rd., shop 114 (up the stairs), Tsim Sha Tsui, Kowloon (MTR: TST).

My heart goes pitter-patter every time I walk into this closet-size store. I've never seen so many bags that I couldn't live without. As Ashneil himself says, "the quality has to be good; we have no logos."

These bags are not copies—they do not have designer logos or anything illegal. They just coincidentally look a lot like the handbags in the fashion magazines. These bags are not cheap, but they cost less than the designer versions. The company does private trunk shows across America, but you have to sign up to be invited while you are in Hong Kong. It is also possible to choose and pay for your bags in Hong Kong and have them sent from the U.S.—you save space in your luggage and don't worry about Customs or duties.

Ashneil is off Nathan Road, a half block from the Inter-Conti, right behind the Sheraton. However, the building is what you might call funky, so first-timers may feel nervous. Don't be. Walk up one flight of stairs to the first floor and follow the signs to room 114.

Maylin
Peninsula Hotel Shopping Arcade, Salisbury Rd., Kowloon (MTR: TST).

Big changes in this store! It's expanded, remodeled, and totally changed the stock so there's nary a Birkin to be seen. Insiders always knew this as a great source for well-made Hermès-like styles, but no more! It has expanded the shoe department, still takes custom orders for shoes and bags, and specializes now in woven-leather handbags that are very, very good looking and fairly priced, beginning around $250. Think major Italian brand you wish you could afford.

Sam Wo
41–47 Queen's Rd., basement, Central (MTR: Central).

Sam Wo is an old source who has been on and off these pages for years. I am very conflicted about sending you here because it takes a very good eye in order to score. When I look at all the bags, they seem to jump off the wall and race toward me. I get dizzy, and the sans-logo bags look cheap. However, when I see a single bag worn by a stylish woman, I am always shocked when she tells me her treasure came from Sam Wo. For the same sort of thing, I like Shenzhen better. If you can't get to Shenzhen, you may have a ball here.

Expect to pay about $75 to $100 for a decent designer copy. Some bags are leather, some are PVC—they will tell you which is which if you can't tell the dif. Sam Wo has two shops: a tiny, stall-like location in the Lanes (p. 122) and a larger basement store, which has a door in the Lanes but an official Queen's Road address.

Home-Style

GOD

48 Hollywood Rd. (MTR: Central); Silvercord, 30 Canton Rd., basement, shop B02, Kowloon (MTR: TST); Leighton Centre, Sharp St. E. (MTR: Causeway Bay).

The name means Goods of Desire, thank you. This store is also listed below for its home items, but I shop here for accessories (like wallets) and gift items. Locals, however, load up on furniture, home-style, and more. © 852/2784-5555. www.god.com.hk.

KOU

Fung House, 20 Connaught Rd., Central (MTR: Central).

The offerings at KOU are more lifestyle than home-style, and everything here is within the range of one woman's vision. It feels so well done that you could truly move right in. Great for wedding gifts. The store opens at 11am. © 852/2530-2234. www.kouconcept.com.

Jade

Books have been written on jade, and there is a small section about it in chapter 4. The news here is that I now have a contact in the Jade Market, so you can ask for Erica and have her guide you to the more honest dealers and help with your negotiations. She runs her business, **Jade Butterfly**, out of booth no. 63. If you want to call from your hotel before you head over, her mobile is © 852/9042-3872.

Jewelry & Gemstones

The jewelry and gemstone businesses are separate and converge only at the wholesale level, where you will never be admitted without a bona fide dealer. If you are serious about buying stones, you should be introduced to the wholesale dealers. This requires personal contact from a dealer in Hong Kong or from a friend who is Chinese and living in Hong Kong. It is a very tight business. Don't expect to just walk into a shop off the street and see the best stones or get the best prices.

There is risk in every purchase, but if you are dealing with a reputable jeweler, that risk is minimized. Reputation is everything. If you are looking for good pearls, diamonds, opals, jade, or ivory, educate yourself. Take the time to learn before you leap.

If you are into creating your own necklaces, you need to meet Jenny. You pick and buy the beads from her, tell her what you want, and she will string them and deliver to your hotel. **Jenny Gems Company,** Nos. 364–65 and 410 Jade Market, Yau Ma Tei (MTR: Jordan Rd.). jennystore@hotmail.com.

Leading Co. Jewel & Watch
New World Centre, 18–24 Salisbury Rd., no. L066 (MTR: TST).

This is the jeweler that my friend Richard has been using for years: James Ma. I have never had anything made here but have enjoyed the bling that Richard's friends and family have shown me. The shop is adjacent to the InterContinental Hotel. © **852/2369-9727.**

Pan Am Pearls
9 Lock Rd., Kowloon (MTR: TST).

I sometimes buy faux pearls here, and I consider this as one of my single best sources in Hong Kong. The faux pearls I've bought here are about the best I've seen at these prices. I have seen fluctuations in quality according to stock, and I have yet to match the quality of the double-strand, 8-millimeter set that cost me $40, several years ago. A strand of pearls runs about $20; the staff will string together several strands into a single necklace with a new clasp as you wait. Baroque pearls are also available.

The Showroom
Central Building, Pedder St., 12th floor (MTR: Central).

I run with an expatriate crowd in Hong Kong that seems to do everything in groups; everyone knows everyone and shares the same resources. Many of those resources have become regulars in these pages. According to my sources, the place for jewelry these days is a small place simply called the Showroom, where a woman named Claire Wadsworth holds court. Good work at excellent prices is the general opinion, backed up by many I trust.

Leather Goods

Hong Kong is a big handbag and shoe destination for several reasons:

- If you go to Shenzhen, you might buy a dozen handbags—fakes but also inspirations; see p. 148.
- Almost all American and European designer brands have shops in Hong Kong; you will find brands you've never heard of and models your neighbors haven't got.
- If you go for quality but don't need a brand name, you will be floored by the number of Kelly, Birkin, and Bollido bags in Hong Kong, usually in the $100-to-$300 price range. Hotel arcades (p. 118) are a good source for these items. Note that Hermès has just gone the Chanel route and begun to prosecute, so there are fewer Hermès copies out there.

- The major malls and hotel shopping centers usually have stores representing European brands that often don't have distribution in the U.S.

Local Heroes

Blanc de Chine

Pedder Building, 12 Pedder St; the Landmark, Central (MTR: Central).

The original showroom in the Pedder Building is still open, but the brand-new boutique across the street in the Landmark is quite sleek and spiffy. Blanc de Chine is one of the best stores in Hong Kong: chic Chinese clothes for men and women, and home-style...sort of Armani goes classic Asian. Expect to pay about $500 for a blazer. © 852/2524-7875.

Joyce

2106 Canton Rd., Kowloon (MTR: TST); 3 other locations.

Joyce is my personal saint. She is the most brilliant and successful woman in Hong Kong retail; joining up with a big-time holding company has ended her financial woes and she continues as a beacon of good taste and great ideas. Her main store is just as eye-catching and fabulous as any other Joyce project. For information about the Joyce Warehouse in Ap Lei Chau, see p. 102. © 852/2367-8128.

Malls

Hong Kong is totally overrun with shopping centers. It's as though a contagious disease has spread to all architects, who now feel compelled to equip hotels and office buildings with three floors of retail shops.

CENTRAL
IFC2
1 Harbourview St. (MTR: Central).

Hot damn, this is the new center of the world. It's the tallest building in town, the location of the new Four Seasons hotel, and home to a very nice mall, complete with a **City Super.** It's also where the Star Ferry now comes to port. The package is rounded out by a cinema, an MTR station, and an Airport Express stop as well as a great view to Kowloon. Just about every major store has a branch here; **Lane Crawford's** new flagship is here. And, yup, **Starbucks,** too. © 852/2295-3308.

The Landmark
16 Des Voeux Rd. (MTR: Central).

The most famous of the Central malls, the Landmark has the reputation and the big names in luxury retail, and it stays ahead of the game by adding new stores and concepts. The latest innovations are a **Mandarin Oriental** boutique hotel and the first Asian branch of the London department store **Harvey Nichols.** I suggest this mall as a jumping-off place for Westerners who want to see something but aren't quite ready for Kowloon. After a quick survey, you'll probably find that everything is gorgeous but very expensive, and that you are ready to move on. A few cafes here offer lunch. © 852/2525-4142.

The Mall at Pacific Place
88 Queensway, Central (MTR: Admiralty).

If you are staying in one of the many hotels built next to the mall, this place is a natural for you. If you are in a hurry, you may want to come by because you can pack a lot in. Note that the official name of this place is the Mall at Pacific Place, but everyone calls it **Pacific Place.** Technically speaking, Pacific Place includes the office tower above the mall and the fancy hotels grouped around the tower (Marriott, Conrad, Island Shangri-La). It also includes a branch of every store you want to visit, and you can do it here in Western fashion—it's not quaint, but it's handy. You'll have plenty of choices for lunch (or dinner) and a good opportunity to have a look-see at some big hotels. © **852/2844-8900.**

Pedder Building
12 Pedder St. (MTR: Central).

Well, the Pedder Building is looking downright spiffy. My bet is that rents have risen, which explains why almost all the old favorites have moved out. Although it's across the street from the **Landmark,** it offers the opposite in shopping appeal—outlet stores on one side and the famed **Shanghai Tang** at street level. Most of the outlets in the Pedder Building have dried up. There are two reliable destinations: **Shopper's Safari** and **Blanc de Chine** (p. 112). Note that Blanc de Chine is not discount or inexpensive or anything other than Armani with an Oriental twist.

Prince's Building
Chater Rd. (MTR: Central).

This office building with five levels of shopping has so many big names now that it competes with the **Landmark** and the **Central Building,** both of which are across the street. The Prince's Building connects by bridge to the Mandarin Oriental Hotel (don't miss shopping there, either) and may be more fun than the Landmark. It is not mind-boggling like the Landmark, so you can shop and enjoy yourself, and it houses many other big names in international deluxe brands.

CAUSEWAY BAY
Fashion Walk
Gloucester Rd., Causeway Bay (MTR: Causeway Bay).

Not technically a mall, Fashion Walk is a shopping concept. The street level of several adjacent buildings—three of them in sort of a triangle—houses up-and-coming designers, cutting-edge designers, Japanese designers, hopeful designers, and the likes of Vivienne Tam. There are also several cafes. On the Victoria Park side of the Excelsior Hotel, this destination is extremely refreshing because the stores are unique and you aren't inside a mall too much of the time.

Lee Gardens 1 & 2

Leighton Centre and Hennessy Centre, 111 Leighton Rd. (MTR: Causeway Bay).

This mall has so many fancy designer shops that you'll forget you are in Causeway Bay. The two buildings lie perpendicular to each other: Lee Gardens 1 is on Hysan Avenue, and Lee Gardens 2 is between Yun Ping Road and Jardine's Crescent. The two malls have brands such as Anya Hindmarch, Shiatzy Chen, Chanel, Hermès, Vuitton, Paul Smith, Prada, Cartier, Loewe, Gucci, Bottega Veneta, Etro, and so forth. You get the picture. Philippe Starck designed the Jean-Paul Gaultier shop.

Times Square

1 Matheson Rd. (MTR: Causeway Bay).

This mall is divided by category of goods, which simplifies life for someone shopping for a specific item; it combines Western chains and big names with local dealers and small firms. There are four floors of restaurants. This is a destination, not merely a mall, and it attracts a lot of young people. My favorite shop is **City Super,** a grocery store and department store in one (enter through Lane Crawford).

ABERDEEN

Horizon Plaza

2 Lee Wing St., Ap Lei Chau (no nearby MTR).

This is not a mall, but it functions like one. The high-rise tower houses many furniture showrooms, wholesale sources, outlet stores, carpet stores, and gift sources. It's worth the trip because of the selection.

The **Joyce Warehouse** is in this building; I've never done well with Joyce in outlet stores, but hey, you never know. The

Lane Crawford outlet is here; I found it great. **Tequila Kola** is sort of a large version of Pier 1 Imports: It carries tabletop accessories, bed linens, curtains, and small decorative items, but it's known for furniture. That makes it more of a source for locals—unless you want to ship (which you can) or are just looking for ideas. The large space holds a number of room sets. The tenants change frequently, but there are so many of them that you can still have fun. Each store keeps its own hours. There's a free directory at the welcome desk. Taxis wait out front.

TST

1881 Heritage

2A Canton Rd., Tsim Sha Tsui, Kowloon (MTR: Tsim Sha Tsui).

This is a fancy new Las Vegas–style mall, heavy with high-end jewelers and big Shanghai Tang. Still evolving. © 852/2388-7786.

Harbour City

Canton Rd., Kowloon (MTR: TST).

The shopping complex that occupies most of Tsim Sha Tsui's western shore is generally known as Harbour City. It includes **Ocean Terminal, Ocean Centre,** and **Ocean Galleries** along with the **Hong Kong Hotel,** the **Marco Polo Hotel,** and the **Prince Hotel.** There are four levels of shopping, and if you can successfully negotiate your way from end to end, you won't even have to come up for air. All luxury brands have stores here, as do most chains. © 852/2118-8666.

New World Centre

18–24 Salisbury Rd., Kowloon (MTR: TST).

The New World Centre is yet another massive, multilevel, spick-and-span, concrete-floor shopping center filled with little shops, 1-hour photo stands, and ice-cream vendors. It has a cute Japanese department store (**Tokyu**—open Fri–Wed 10am–9pm) at street level, but really, don't waste your time on my account. If you are a guest at the adjoining Inter-Conti—or any nearby hotel—the grocery store, **Needs,** is a lot of fun and sells all sorts of things besides groceries.

Park Lane Shopper's Boulevard

181 Nathan Rd., Kowloon (MTR: TST).

This architecturally unique strip mall will certainly catch your eye (and maybe your credit card) as you stroll the infamous Nathan Road. There's also an **American Express.** © 852/2508-1234.

KOWLOON

APM

Millennium City 5, 418 Kwun Tong Rd., Kowloon (MTR: Kwun Tong).

This is a convenience mall for those who live out here, and—oh my!—what a lifestyle. This is a fun evening of sociology—go for a meal (huge food court and many restaurants), shop, and take in a movie. This mall really gets going at night, with the action keeping up almost until midnight. © 852/2267-0500.

Elements

1 Austin Rd. W., Kowloon (MTR: Kowloon).

This megacomplex has a 12-theater cinema, ThreeSixty; Hong Kong's largest organic supermarket; and even a skating rink. It's divided into five shopping zones: Metal, Fire, Wood, Earth and Water (for example, "metal" houses jewelry stores, including Tiffany, Bulgari, and Chaumet). © 852/2735-5234.

Festival Walk

88 Tat Chee Ave., Kowloon Tong (MTR: Kowloon Tong).

This is the local go-to mall for young people and foodies, with more than 200 shops, 30 restaurants, plus a food court. It's not that well-known by tourists, which makes it all the more attractive. © 852/2844-2223.

MONG KOK
Langham Place
8 Argyle St. (MTR: Mong Kok).

With 300 stores, this is the hot new place in town for the younger crowd, as well as an attempt by the city to rejuvenate the area. Part of the mall is the snazzy new Langham Place Hotel. There are also the usual cineplex and food court. This mall is not a destination for tourists, so it's a great place to get a look at the future—Mong Kok is arriving, the young people from China are arriving, and the trendy clothes and concepts are already here. And it's not at all downmarket or funky: There's a branch of the posh Japanese department store **Seibu** here as well as a huge branch of **Muji.**

HOTEL ARCADES/HOTEL MALLS
The fanciest hotels have the most trustworthy shops. Certainly the shops in the **Peninsula** are the most expensive and most exclusive. But that doesn't mean there's anything wrong with the shops in the **Holiday Inn,** which happen to be touristy but fine if you want a TT (tourist trap).

The InterContinental Hotel
18 Salisbury Rd., Kowloon (MTR: TST).

As the hotel arcade/shopping center/mall sweepstakes heats up, this small mall offers one of every big name (including **Chanel**) *and* adjoins the New World Centre. This is not a destination mall but a convenience for hotel guests. Most interesting is the **Shanghai Tang** in the hotel lobby.

The Peninsula Hotel
Salisbury Rd., Kowloon (MTR: TST).

Small shops fill the eastern and western wings of the hotel, with more on the mezzanine and still more in the basement. Every big name in the world has a shop here. A free handout lists all the stores in the arcade, so don't miss out.

Markets

· ·

Markets offer a real slice of life and one of the few less-than-glamorous looks at the real China. Some are not pretty or fancy. If you are squeamish, avoid the food markets that sell live chickens or ducks and slaughter them on the spot.

Merchandise markets are busy and hectic. Each has its own clientele and its own personality. There are no spacious aisles or racks of organized clothing. Some markets exist only at certain hours of the day or night. At a preappointed time, people appear from nowhere, pushing carts laden with merchandise. They set up shop along the street and sell their goods until the crowds start to dissipate, at which time they disappear into the night.

Most markets have no specific street address but are known by the streets that bound them or that intersect in the middle of the market area. Most cabdrivers know where the markets are by name. However, it is always a good idea to have your concierge write the name of the market and location in Chinese. You probably won't need it, but it can't hurt. Buses, trolleys, and the MTR usually serve the markets as well. Take a hotel business card with you so you'll have the address in Chinese. The following markets are open daily.

Bird Market

Yuen Po St. Bird Garden (next to the Mong Kok stadium) (MTR: Prince Edward).

The Bird Market is really just an alley that sells birds and bird supplies, but it's also an experience you will never forget. The sound of the chirping is overwhelming. I just want to know if the noise is made by birds chirping or grasshoppers chirping. The vendors sell bird supplies (including grasshoppers); you will be surprised at how many bird cages you suddenly want. You won't buy much here, but it is fun. Forget it during outbreaks of bird flu.

Cat Street Market

Cat St./Upper Lascar Row. (just below Hollywood Rd.)
(MTR: Central).

Cat Street Market is Hong Kong's answer to a flea market:
Vendors sell used merchandise of the tag-sale variety from
blankets and a few stalls on a 2-block stretch of pedestrian
pavement just below Hollywood Road. One guy sells only
used typewriters and used sewing machines. A few dealers sell
old jade, which I like. There's also new "jade" similar to what
you'll find at the Jade Market. One vendor has Chinese sunglasses from the 1930s. The shops behind and around the
market specialize in formal antiques; some of these stores are
reputable and even famous. Most Hong Kong street maps
show this lane as Upper Lascar Row (the official name).

Fa Yuen Market (Flower Market)

Fa Yuen St., Kowloon (MTR: Prince Edward).

This is not the Ladies' Market, although the two very different markets are close enough to be a single destination. For
walking directions, see p. 83. Some people call this the Flower
Market only because a few vendors sell fruit and flowers in
baskets. A nearby flower market sells flowers, plants, and
plastic greenery. You're here for the fun fashions, however,
and will be walking toward Argyle Street. With Prince
Edward to your rear, walk toward Kowloon.

The jobbers on Fa Yuen Street (p. 83) are open during the
day when the market is closed. But at about 4pm, the street
becomes a pedestrian mall, filled with fruits and veggies,
handbags, and brassieres. The jobbers remain open, so this is
a mad case of too many bins, not enough money.

You will not see many tourists in these parts; the rummag-
ing through bins may not be to everyone's liking. This is my
favorite kind of shopping, and I always find deals. You'll see
men's, women's and children's clothing as well as plus sizes in
various jobbers' stores on both sides of Fa Yuen running for

about 3 blocks. Cash only. ATMs are not that easy to find, so be prepared.

Jade Market

Kansu and Battery sts., Yau Ma Tei, Kowloon (MTR: Jordan Rd. and then walk a bit or take a taxi).

The market is in two free-standing tents under the highway overpass at Kansu and Battery streets.

The Jade Market is an official market organized by the Hong Kong and Kowloon Jade Merchants Workers' and Hawkers' Union Association. Each merchant inside the fence is licensed to sell jade and should display his or her license above the stall. It is a good idea when buying to note the number next to your purchase, just in case you have a problem later on and the jade turns out to be plastic.

If you are not willing to bargain here, don't buy. The merchants in the Jade Market expect to lower their price by 20% to 40%, depending on your bargaining skill and their need to sell. Market hours are 10am to 3pm, although many of the vendors close up at 2pm. Go early rather than late.

Ladies' Market (Mong Kok Market)

Argyle St. and Nathan Rd. (MTR: Mong Kok).

The market sets up a short distance away from the Mong Kok MTR station; it begins around 4pm and goes into the evening, until about 10pm or so. It really gets going after work and seems to be a date spot. Watch your handbag.

The streets have the feeling of a carnival, with lots of people parading by the stands, stopping to examine shirts, socks, sewing sets, buttons, and bras. There are some toys and sunglasses—mostly lots of trinkets, clothing, everyday goods, and the usual ringing alarm clocks, fake designer goods, electrical doodads that flash and whirr—no live snakes or chickens. It's very different from Fa Yuen Street, so visit them both, if at all possible.

The Lanes

Li Yuen East and Li Yuen West, Central (MTR: Central).

The Lanes are twin alleys, about 50m (164 ft.) apart from each other, darting between Queen's Road and Des Voeux Road in Central. I had given up on them for several years, but a friend asked me to reconsider. I had a ball. Furthermore, the women I took here all liked it a lot.

The general layout of each lane is the same—stores along the thoroughfare, and a center aisle of stalls. One lane specializes in Chinese arts and crafts, T-shirts, fabric off the bolt, and blinking electronic toys that make annoying sounds. This is also a good place for reading glasses that fold up into a slim tube.

The other lane specializes in handbags and padded bras. (Could I make this up?) Bra Lane also has several jobbers; I personally have never met a jobber I could walk past. On my last foray, I bought a pair of Nautica khakis for $10 and a T-shirt for $4.

The stores and stalls are crowded and active; you are pestered and pursued and pressured to buy. Haggle until dusk. Who needs a trip to mainland China when you can shop here? Also note that this is an excellent neighborhood to snoop around in—1 block from Shanghai Tang and the Landmark, yet in another world. Queen's Road has many branches of favorite stores, even the Chinese department store **Yue Hwa**. And there are lots of banks with ATMs.

Luen Wo Market

Luen Wo, New Territories (KCR from TST East to Fanling, then bus 78 or taxi).

This is an authentic local food market quite near the border with China. The market and the merchandise are not enormously different from what you'd see in town, so the trip may not be worth your time. On the other hand, if you crave a peek into the real China or a world gone by, this is your Sunday adventure. The market fills a square city block. The shoppers are far more rural looking than those you might find in downtown Central. You go here for the total experience, for the fact that it's real. You might want to give it a miss if there have been avian flu outbreaks.

Mid-Levels Market
20 Borrett Rd., Mid-Levels (take escalator).

This is more of a Sunday-stroll, easygoing-neighborhood kind of thing but it offers a little bit of everything. It is held the second Sunday of each month only, from 10am to 5pm.

Stanley Market
Stanley Main St., Stanley Village, Hong Kong (bus 6 from Exchange Sq. in Central or 20 from Star Ferry).

Any tourist coming to Hong Kong knows about Stanley: Shopping legends abound about bargains in this village-cum-market-cum-tourist-trap. Some people love Stanley; they are mostly first-timers. Stanley has become so touristy that I can barely cope—and I go there often, just to make sure I am up-to-date. I found no retail stock and no fake designer merchandise (oh, woe!). All I found were tourist goods—white linens, Chinese pajamas, knickknacks, and cheap gifts. Not bad if you want that sort of thing, but I wanted deals. But wait. Sarah found Tommy Bahama trousers and shirts for her husband, Tom, for $10 each. Actually, I bought three "van Gogh" oil paintings for $6.50 each. The market is open daily from 10am to 7pm. A taxi will cost about $15 each way; the bus from Star Ferry takes about an hour.

Temple Street Market
Temple St. and Jordan Rd., Kowloon (MTR: Jordan Rd.).

This night market has grown a lot over the years, and as it spreads, the charm is diluted, making it yet just another street market. You have to know where the Chinese opera singers and the fortunetellers are in order to find them.

Exit the MTR onto Nathan Road. With the harbor to your back, it's the left side. Walk north on Nathan Road for 2 or 3 blocks. Keep looking to your left. You are searching for a tiny entryway, a small alley crammed with people. This is where the opera singers do their thing on little patios. When you spot the alley, turn left into the crowd.

This alley is only about 45m (148 ft.) long. When you emerge from the alley, you will be on Temple Street, at the corner of a real temple. Walk forward 1 block, keeping the sidewalk that borders the grounds of the temple yard on your right. On this sidewalk you'll see a long row of fortunetellers, each with his (they're all men) own gimmick. One or two may speak English. The market itself begins thereafter.

Western Market
323 Des Voeux Rd., Central (MTR: Sheung Wan).

Once upon a time, Western Market was a dump. Then along came a developer who turned the space into a festival market. It has a branch of **Fook Ming Tong,** the fancy tea broker; there are toy soldiers and plenty for kids to see and buy. Many of the cloth merchants who were disenfranchised when Cloth Alley was destroyed have taken space on the second floor of Western Market. Flags fly, banners flap, people shop. The space has a lot of energy and a number of unique stalls that sell merchandise I haven't seen anywhere else in town. True to its name, this market is much farther west than the rest of Central's basic shopping areas.

Men's Shirts: Made-to-Order

There are a lot of choices to be made: the fit of the body, the type of collar and cuffs, the fabric, and the possible use of contrast fabric. Prices usually depend on the fabric: 100% cotton costs more than a poly blend; Sea Island cotton costs more than regular cotton. Expect to pay about $75 for a Sea

Island custom-made cotton shirt, although such a shirt can cost more, depending on the maker. For custom shirts, two fittings are necessary—one for the measurements and one with the garment.

Many shirt houses have a minimum order; most tailors make shirts as well as suits. If you are buying the shirt and the suit from the same tailor, there is usually no minimum shirt order. Most shirt houses also make pajamas and boxer shorts.

Ascot Chang Co. Ltd.

The Peninsula Hotel, Salisbury Rd., Kowloon (MTR: TST); InterContinental Hotel, 18 Salisbury Rd., Kowloon (MTR: TST); Prince's Building, Chater Rd. (MTR: Central).

Perhaps the best known of the internationally famous shirt dealers, Ascot Chang advertises heavily in the U.S. and stresses its quality and devotion to fit. This shirt maker has many branches in Hong Kong and Kowloon. The shops are filled with wonderful fabrics imported from Switzerland and France. Prices are competitive with **David's** (see below); mail order is available once your measurements have been taken. Shirts run between $40 and $125, depending on the fabric and style. Top of the line. Ascot Chang also has a shop in Manhattan. www.ascotchang.com.

WEB TIPS You can order custom shirts online; be very careful and precise with measurements as goods cannot be returned.

David's Shirts

Mandarin Oriental Hotel, 5 Connaught Rd. (MTR: Central); Wing Lee Building, 33 Kimberley Rd., ground floor, Kowloon (MTR: TST).

David's is one of the most popular custom-shirt shops in Hong Kong. It's less glitzy than **Ascot Chang** (see above) but just as famous to those in the know. David's also has a branch in New York City. The main shop in Hong Kong is in Kowloon on Kimberley Road. But there are more convenient branches, mostly in hotels like the Regent and the Mandarin Oriental.

David's will copy any shirt you like; just bring it with you and plan to leave it. The shop also has a framed illustration of collar and cuff styles you can choose from. Mail order is not only possible but common with repeat customers. If you cannot get to Hong Kong, ask for a current swatch and price list. Return a shirt that fits you perfectly and a check, along with fabric and collar and cuff choices. Approximately 4 to 6 weeks later, a box of new shirts will arrive.

Men's Suits: Made-to-Order

Probably the most-famous Hong Kong fantasy is that made-to-order suits grow on trees or that they are easily and inexpensively obtained with a snap of the fingers and a few hundred dollars. No way. Remember the first law of Hong Kong custom-made suits: A bargain is not a bargain if it doesn't fit. Furthermore, the whole point of a bespoke suit is psychological—you must feel (and look) like a king in it. Its impact derives from the fact that it was made for your body, so it moves with you as no off-the-rack garment can.

- Start your search for a tailor the minute you arrive. Leave yourself time for three fittings while in Hong Kong. The first will be for measurements and choice of fabrics; the second will involve a partially finished suit with only one sleeve in place; the third will be to detail the finished garment. Good tailors usually have everything wrapped up by the third fitting.
- If at all possible, choose your tailor before you leave home and fax ahead for an appointment so you can meet shortly after arrival in Hong Kong. For the two best men's tailors in Hong Kong, see below. After you check in to your hotel, the tailor should be your first stop. You may want to choose your hotel based on the convenience to your tailor.

- Most tailors carry a full line of imported fabrics from Italy, England, and France. If your tailor is not one of the top two, ask whether the thread is imported also. If it is not, ask to see the quality, and test it for durability. Remember all those horror stories you have heard about suits falling apart? It wasn't the fabric, it was the thread. You do not need to worry about quality at the two biggies.
- Well-made suits from a Hong Kong tailor are not inexpensive. Imported fabrics run about $50 to $100 per yard, and an average-size suit will take 3½ yards. Silk-wool blends and cashmeres cost more. The total price for a top-quality, killer suit runs $800 on up. You could do better in some cases with an off-the-rack suit in the U.S., but the quality would not be the same. Your suit should be the equal of a $3,000 Savile Row suit in London.
- The tailor will want a 50% deposit to start the work. You may be able to pay with a check in U.S. dollars or pounds sterling. Ask ahead of time.
- If you are having the tailor ship the suits to you, remember to figure in the Customs charges and shipping. On average, air freight costs $20 per suit. Shirts can be shipped for $30 per dozen. U.S. Customs charges about $75 in duty on a single new suit. Once you have established an account with a tailor or a shirt maker and he or she has your measurements on file, you can simply get fabric swatches sent to you and do your shopping through the mail—or in a local hotel, if your tailor visits major U.S. cities.
- Check to see if the tailor you have chosen travels to the U.S. to visit customers. Chances are, if you live in a major city (New York, Washington, San Francisco, Los Angeles, or Chicago), he or she will. Most of the tailors I recommend either come in person once a year or send a representative with fabric books and order forms. At that time, new measurements can be taken in case you have lost or gained weight.

THE BIG NAMES: HONG KONG'S FINEST TAILORS

A-Man Hing Cheong Co. Ltd.

Mandarin Oriental Hotel, 5 Connaught Rd. (MTR: Central).

Fondly referred to as "Ah-men," this shop turns out quite a few garments for the rich-tourist-and-businessman trade and, therefore, has become adept at relating to the European-cut suit. The tailors don't even blink twice when you ask for an extra pair of trousers. They just smile and ask for more money. The prices here are on the higher side, with a suit beginning around $650.

A-Man will also do custom shirts for approximately $50 to $150. © 852/2522-3336. Fax 852/2523-4707.

W. W. Chan & Sons Tailor Ltd.

Burlington House, 92–94 Nathan Rd., 2nd floor, Kowloon (MTR: TST).

Peter Chan carries on a family business, which he has built and expanded over the years. He also has two shops in Shanghai (p. 259) and is personally based there. In Hong Kong, men want to see Eric and women want to see Danny. The average price for a suit is $800 to $1,000; mink-cashmere blends can cost more. The W. W. Chan showroom is decidedly more relaxed than other big-time contenders' spaces. The showroom is neat, clean, modern, and even spacious, which is hard to find in Hong Kong. But the location in Kowloon and the approach to the actual showroom are not so swank; businessmen who are used to wall-to-wall carpet may need a moment to adjust. © 852/2366-2634.

Pharmacies

Fanda

G/F Mirador Mansion, 60A Nathan Rd., Kowloon (MTR: TST).

© 852/2368-8638.

Marvel Medicine

G/F, 12A Peking Rd., Kowloon (MTR: TST).

✆ **852/2737-2260.** marvelmedicine@yahoo.com.hk.

Resale

This is somewhat of a new category in Hong Kong (and Kowloon). It follows a major trend in London, Paris, and New York: Many socialites take their year-old designer clothes and accessories to resale shops, which sell them to the public for less than full cost. Ah, the consummate Hong Kong Hobson's choice: to buy used or fake? Used is more expensive.

France Station

80 Russell St. (MTR: Causeway Bay).

Heads up—this will be on the final. The resale shops related to the next listing (Paris Station) are all named after cities, so Milan Station is part of that family. This store, however, is part of a different group, with a name chosen to confuse or blend with the concept. This store's main specialty is designer bags.

Paris Station

Metropole Building, 12 Hankow Rd., Kowloon (MTR: TST).

This is one shop in a growing chain—other stores have names such as Milan Station and so on. Paris Station sells designer handbags and accessories. It's around the corner from the Kowloon Hotel and behind the Pen, so you're going to be in the area anyway. There are no bargains, but it's fun to poke around.

VIP Station

61 Granville Rd. (MTR: TST East).

I think this is a third chain getting into the action—its business cards list another store near Times Square. I like this one because after you've been bin shopping at the jobbers on

Granville Road, it's fun to finish up here. Mostly designer handbags in good condition, but pricey.

Souvenirs

It's not hard to find gifts or souvenirs in Hong Kong—they are everywhere. Actually giving the gifts to your friends will be harder; I always want to keep everything for myself. I included some gift suggestions in chapter 1. Below are a few stores that specifically sell great gifts.

City Super
Times Square mall, Causeway Bay (MTR: Causeway Bay); Harbour City, Kowloon (MTR: TST); IFC2 mall (MTR: Central).

I listed City Super under "Grocery Stores," but it is really a department store of goodies with a complete section of dry goods separate from the foodstuffs. Tons of inexpensive novelty items—especially beauty supplies and bath items—make great souvenirs and gifts. I bought many in packaging that I could not even understand.

DFS (Duty Free Shoppers)
DFS Galleria at Sun Plaza, 28 Canton Rd., Kowloon (MTR: TST); DFS Galleria at Chinachem Plaza, 77 Mody Rd. (MTR: TST East).

This is a department store meant mostly for Japanese shoppers but handy to all. I don't like it for normal designer shopping only because it bores me. When it comes to souvenirs, however, DFS may have the best in town.

A department in each store sells Chinese meds, foods, and souvenirs—I'd head there, ignoring the Burberry and Chanel. Don't miss the key chains, including one that allows you to insert your own photo into the body of a Chinese warlord.

DFS sells in bulk units, with prices discounted according to how much you buy. It has shuttle bus service that makes a loop from a few major hotels to the stores, and will deliver your purchases to your hotel so you can continue shopping with free hands.

Spas

Most of the swank hotels in Hong Kong have had spas for quite some time, and they have all refurbished their spas to take on the competition. Especially with the problems caused by jet lag—or the general need for detoxification—a trip here is no longer complete without some sort of treatment.

Note: All of the spas listed in this section require a reservation. Most hotels let nonguests test the spa waters.

The latest trend is foot treatments. Hawkers on the street will hand you brochures or try to lure you into alleys for a treatment. One of the nicest evenings I spent in town was an early dinner with friends and then a trip (for all four of us) to a foot spa.

E-SPA at the Peninsula
Peninsula Hotel, Salisbury Rd., Kowloon (MTR: TST).

I have been to many spas in my time, but I gotta tell you: This isn't a spa—this is paradise. I'm talking about the architecture, the cocooning feel, the cozy little room where you sip tea and stare at the wild blue yonder, and the steam room. Yes, the treatments are excellent, too. I always come for the cure to my jet lag and spring for ESPA products to carry along on my travels; they're just good, and I'm worth it. Pick your treatment from the spa menu online and book ahead of your arrival. © **852/2315-3271.** www.peninsula.com.

I-Spa
InterContinental Hotel, 18 Salisbury Rd., 3rd floor, Tsim Sha Tsui, Kowloon (MTR: TST).

Not to be confused with the E-SPA brand of spa products, I-Spa will cure whatever else ails you. I always do a spa treatment after my long-haul flight and tried Ancient Rituals of the Orient recently. It was amazing, right down to the part when my neck and arms were stretched against tension and sprung free from their pins and needles and jet-lag woes. The treatment was so successful in helping me get acclimated to local time that I also booked a treatment for my evening of departure. This time I did a face treatment that actually aerated my skin. It wasn't so relaxing, but it was therapeutic. I could see the difference immediately after the treatment and felt it was a smart thing to do before spending 12 hours in a tin can flying across the world.

Note: If you book a Born to Shop & Spa Tour, you have an I-Spa treatment included in the package (see www.suzy gershman.com). © 852/2721-1211, ext. 81.

Plateau
Grand Hyatt Hotel, 1 Harbour Rd. (MTR: Wan Chai).

While Hyatt hotels are internationally renowned for spa facilities, no other Hyatt has anything quite like this. A new addition includes a 23-room section of the hotel that is dedicated as a "spa lifestyle program." The city's most incredible spa, constantly voted one of the best in the world by various travel magazines, is where I discovered the June Jacobs brand of spa treatments, which you can also buy in the U.S. © 852/2588-1234.

FOOT SPAS/REFLEXOLOGY
Foot spas are everywhere. I am always reluctant to try just any old place (I am still Dr. Kalter's daughter), so the ones I list here were suggested by friends and tested by my tootsies. Wherever you go, if there is no disinfectant process before you begin, grab your shoes walk out.

Big Bucket Foot
Hoi Kung Court, 264 Gloucester Rd., shops 1 and 2 (MTR: Causeway Bay).

I will always have a soft spot for this place because it was my first foot spa and because I first thought it was a shoe store for large sizes. It's half a block from the Excelsior Hotel and not too swish—but it is clean. Your feet soak in a big bucket, hence the name. The 90-minute treatment costs about $20; I tipped HK$20 ($2.60) afterward. I did a treatment before leaving for the airport on departure eve and swear it helped me. ✆ 852/2572-8611.

Heng Lam Fong
Star House, 3 Salisbury Rd., 18th floor, Kowloon (MTR: TST).

When I told Louis, the chief concierge at the InterConti, that I was researching reputable foot and reflexology treatments, he suggested this establishment. Located right at the Star Ferry, it provides traditional Chinese medicine as well as reflexology and massage treatments. The staff's English can be spotty. ✆ 852/2376-3648.

Tai Pan Foot Soaked Bath
18 Middle Rd., Tsim Sha Tsui, Kowloon (MTR: TST).

This is a fancy, clean, and swank place, as befits its address right behind the Pen. You take off your shoes and socks and put them in a locker, soak your feet to disinfect them, and then settle into a first-class airline seat for a treatment that will have you floating. Prices begin at $20. ✆ 852/2301-3820.

Tea

Some of the best tea in China is sold in Hong Kong. In fact, it's sold everywhere, and it makes a great gift. The packaging seems to be the main attraction—to me, anyway—but there are many tastes you won't find at home, and they're far more exotic than Lipton Yellow Label. (Not that I'm knocking Lipton; their Yellow Label makes excellent iced tea.)

The listings below include individual brands and retail chains. Don't forget that every supermarket has a large selection.

Bojenmi

Chinese supermarkets such as Needs, New World Centre, Kowloon (MTR: TST).

The red-and-white Bojenmi brand box has an illustration of a girl playing the lute. I find that the tea smells like dead fish and tastes worse. But I have several friends in Hong Kong who swear by it. They claim you get used to it and then eventually like it, and that in 6 months, your cholesterol numbers will drop and life will be much healthier. So I am doing my three cups a day. But I am nursing the same tea bag through the three cups because it tastes better when it's weak.

Chinese Healing Tea

Locations in major MTR concourses, including TST (near exit B), Central (exit A), and Admiralty (exit A).

About a dozen of these little shops—all clean and white and spiffy—operate in MTR stations. They're selling their packaging, their hype, and their marketing skills. The shops have tea, jellied tea, and a line of health products made from tea. You can taste brewed teas. I can't tell you whether any of the teas work, but for $10 you can get a cute gift package.

Fook Ming Tong

Western Market, 323 Des Voeux Rd., Central (MTR: Sheung Wan); Ocean Terminal, Harbour City, Tsim Sha Tsui, Kowloon (MTR: TST); IFC2 mall (MTR: Central); and many other locations.

This is the leading chain of tourist-oriented (excuse me) tea shops, selling tea and teapots. The shops are adorable, the selection is exotic, and there is nothing too unusual about it. The packaging is so perfect that you will be comfortable and willing to buy all your gifts here.

Ying Kee Tea Co.

151 Queen's Rd., Central (MTR: Central); 28 Hankow Rd., shop G8, TST, Kowloon (MTR: TST); and other locations.

This is a small chain with a store in just about every major shopping district in Hong Kong.

Teens & 'Tweens

All of Causeway Bay—the area behind the Excelsior Hotel and between Times Square mall and Lee Gardens—is a hive of teen, 'tween, young, and hip fashion. It's mobbed but exhilarating. Try to avoid the hours when the kids get off work in the evenings, unless you want to observe the phenom rather than shop.

The Alley

New Territories (MTR: Lai Chi Kok).

A garmento friend from the U.S. brought me here—I never would have found it on my own! It's possible that "The Alley" is the name given to it by Americans who work this space looking for hot new ideas—there are no signs that say the alley. Do we care? This is a trade building with a ground-level floor filled with stall after stall of shops selling teen and 'tween fashions at *grrreat* prices. It's an amazing social phenom just to be here and watch it going on swirling around you, but it's not for princesses. You walk down a center aisle that gives you the feeling of being in an alley, hence the name. It is indoors; it is truly incredible.

To get here, take the B2 exit from the MTR, walk away from the green and yellow towers, and turn right at the Hong Kong Industrial Center. Enter through parts B/C.

Sun Arcade
78 Canton Rd., Kowloon (MTR: TST).

This small mall is underground, as is the fashion—which is mostly Japanese. Sizes are small, but the clothes are so fabulous that creativity freaks will be drooling. The crowds are also fun. Located beneath DFS.

Watches

As they say on the street, "Copy watch, lady?" Indeed, you can buy a fake Rolex or save money on a real Rolex. The trick is finding the right watch at the right price. You can pay anything from $50 to $10,000 and still not know what you have bought. Furthermore, the savings seem to be on high-end merchandise, so, yes, you can save $3,000 on a $15,000 Rolex—but did you really want a $15,000 Rolex in the first place?

Some things to be aware of before you buy:

- Check to see that the whole watch and not just the movement was made by the manufacturer. A common practice in Hong Kong is to sell a Swiss watch face and movement with a Hong Kong–made bracelet. The bracelet is probably silver with gold plating. This can work to your advantage if you do not want to spend $5,000 for a solid-gold watch but want the look. A reputable dealer will tell you that this is what you are buying and will price the watch accordingly. These watches cost $150 to $400.

- Check the serial number on the inside movement against the serial number on your guarantee.

- If you do not receive a worldwide guarantee, don't buy the watch.

- Do the same careful checking at brand-name dealers that you would do at a no-name shop. We know of someone who bought a brand-name watch from a reputable dealer, got the watch home, and had problems. When she turned to the brand's U.S. dealer, she learned that, yes, indeed, she had bought one of their watches, but the movement was 5 years old. She had bought a current body with a used movement!

If you are simply looking for something unusual and fun, try **City Chain,** a huge chain with a branch in every mall and shopping district. It carries Seiko, Bulova, and Zenith, among other name brands, as well as fashion watches like Smash (a takeoff of Swatch).

Copy watches are sold in every market and on the streets of Nathan Road. Far better copies are for sale in Shenzhen, although quality varies and the whole process can be overwhelming. Expect a Triple-A quality (the best fake possible) version of a Cartier watch to cost about $150. Prices for watches in Shenzhen begin at $10.

Women's Attire: Made-to-Order

I started going to **W. W. Chan** for the simple reason that Peter Chan made my husband's clothes. Of the top two tailors, only W. W. Chan has a women's division.

Women are charged a flat rate for the making of the garment (no matter what size or how complicated); you pay for the fabric by the yard or provide your own. See p. 128 for the W. W. Chan address and coordinates. To make an appointment or send a message directly to Danny Chen, who makes my clothes, e-mail danny@wwchan.com.

Chapter 6
Pearl River Delta: Shenzhen, Canton & Macau

Welcome to the PRD

I do not have any professional training on the political, economic, or cultural situation in the People's Republic of China. All I can tell you is what I've seen, what I feel, and how important I think it is that anyone who travels knows about the amazing things that are going on there.

You can get a small taste of China with a day trip, overnight visit, or weekend in the nearby **Pearl River Delta,** or PRD. This is one of the fastest-growing areas in China, and once you really get into it, you can participate in the new China. The main shopping cities are Shenzhen, Canton (Guangzhou), and Macau; the entire area is part of the Guangdong Province. Do not confuse Guangzhou (say "Gwan-*joe*"), the city, with Guangdong, the province. To me, Macau is the new Las Vegas, not the new China.

With Hong Kong as your base, you can do a circle tour, plan a series of days out or nights away, or even arrive through one of the area's flashy new airports—which often offer less-expensive flights than those that go directly to Hong Kong. All sorts of adventures are out there, waiting for those who dare to do something a little bit different; who are wise enough to be curious about the new China.

LOCAL LINGO

Once you cross into China, you can expect the ability to speak or understand English to plummet. One morning I asked for "two eggs, poached" and got two eggs, toast. They sound amazingly similar when you think about it. Learn to speak Chinese or get a grip.

TOURIST GUIDES

Because very few American tourists go into the PRD, few tourist guides cover the area. For specific information, often in Chinese and English (very helpful when dealing with taxi drivers), check bookstores in Hong Kong, which carry several locally printed guidebooks. Shop carefully—many guide books are out-of-date. A well-connected concierge in Hong Kong may have some contacts for you, people living in the PRD or people from HKG who will go with you as guide. This is not Indian Territory, but if you want a guide, you can find one.

Welcome to Shenzhen

There is talk by politicos that by the year 2013, Shenzhen and Hong Kong will be united into one giant metroplex. As crazy as this sounds (to me, anyway), insiders say that this idea makes a lot of sense. Time will tell.

I've seen Shenzhen (sometimes abbreviated SZ) described as "the new Hong Kong," which sort of puts Shanghai in an awkward position. To me, Shenzhen is the new Shenzhen. It was once a fishing village without history or locals, and now it is a card-carrying part of the new China: a massive city of wide boulevards, apartments that rival those in Shanghai, theme parks, shopping malls, and factories. While I used to come on just a day trip, or maybe an overnight to ease the shopping burdens, I've now discovered how amazing this huge city has become and love it for a weekend getaway or a

3 to 4 day exploration that broadens understanding of this brave new world that China has created.

In the past, a day trip or a first-timer's excursion to Shenzhen (say *Shum*-sum in Cantonese) meant visiting one building—a sort of giant mall where the merchants sell a lot of copy merchandise. I have been doing this for years and now that fakes are so boring and my watches have stopped ticking and my own vision is expanded, I think very little of this particular building, the **LoWu Commercial Center (LWCC)**. I will, of course, tell you all about it, but there is so much more to Shenzhen that my job is to open your eyes and lead you to the truth about one of China's most successful economic zones.

The day trip to Shenzhen, especially for a Shenzhen virgin, is as good as a trip to the far side of the moon. The difference from Hong Kong is shocking. The true Shenzhen, past LoWu, is mind-boggling and even LoWu as a one-off adventure is mind-boggling. Copy watch, lady?

I must say right upfront that I do not condone fake merchandise. For the most part, I think you get what you pay for—fake is fake. It won't last, it usually looks cheap, and it tarnishes your reputation. But then, I am referring to fake handbags, shoes, ties, and, well, fashion. I have something totally different to say about fake art—see p. 150.

In the years that I have been doing this day trip, it has gotten enormously easier—partly because anything is easier after you've done it once and partly because China has made crossing the border easier and the system more efficient. They have also opened a second border into Shenzhen, which is clean and neat and easy to use.

- Look at a map and decide if you want to enter Shenzhen through LoWu or Lok Ma Chau. If you do not have a HKG resident card, you may want to enter through Lok Ma Chau and then connect to the local Mass Transit Railway (MTR) and the LoWu stop—if indeed, your day trip intention is to spend most of your time at the LWCC.

Serious Shopper Notes

- Consider taking a rolling suitcase for all your purchases. Especially if you have no hotel room, you could have an uncomfortable load to schlep. Note that there is a luggage check counter on the level beneath the entry level plaza to the LWCC.
- Wear comfortable shoes.
- Wimps and wusses need not apply—this is a tiring day or even weekend because there is an overwhelming amount to see and do.
- Have plenty of cash and patience. Note that prices are now in RMB; if you want to pay in Hong Kong dollars, not yuan, there is a 6% to 10% surcharge. There are ATMs and exchange booths all over the immigration center at LoWu and currency exchange booths and machines at Lok Ma Chau.
- HKG authorities are anti-fake-DVD. If they catch you, you will surrender your DVDs and pay a fine.

- No matter where you leave HKG and enter China, there are two serious steps involved. You must leave Hong Kong's New Territories and walk across a river and then enter China. Or enter China and then walk across the river. Either way, a river runs through it. Paperwork and lines are involved in both portions of this procedure. It usually goes more quickly at Lok Ma Chau but LoWu is next door to the LWCC so you have to figure it out at best guess.
- The new Tsim Sha Tsui (TST) East train station in HKG makes it possible to jump onboard right in front of the InterContinental Hotel in Kowloon, and *vroom vroom*—you are soon walking across the border at LoWu into China. You may need to go through the Hung Hom station to get to Lok Ma Chau. This is a situation in transition.
- The new organization at the immigration center makes the lines go more quickly, the transition more smooth, and

the wait less annoying. You MUST have a visa to enter the People's Republic of China (PRC) and you cannot get it at the border.

RUSH HOUR

Most stores in Shenzhen don't open until 10am, giving you plenty of time to arrive. Some local businesses open at 9am but these are not the ones you will visit unless you are staying more than a day (see below). Avoid travel at peak times when the workforce crowds trains and immigration lines.

Rush hour is 7 to 9am heading inbound, and 5 to 8pm heading outbound. Try to leave Shenzhen by 4pm if you are on a day trip. Avoid holidays and weekends if possible.

Seriously consider staying over at least 1 night.

STAY AWHILE

A day trip to Shenzhen is an amazing experience: This is power shopping to the max and it will leave you exhausted, but giggling. If you return to HKG on the same day, you'll sink into your hotel spa with a whimper and wake up the next day mad at yourself for not buying more. The experience is easier if you stay overnight. You can avoid rush-hour traffic, and you have a chance to get a grip on your mental health.

Now that I have spent more time in Shenzhen, I say stay at least 3 nights—there's so much more to see, do, and buy than LWCC. If you limit yourself to just the LWCC, you will not have experienced this city and its magic.

Shenzhen is filled with modern malls, a downtown area that is humming with commerce, a growing number of luxury hotels (all with spas), many tailors, a modern convention center, a gorgeous international airport, a wholesale gift building (or three) where you can shop, an optical mart, and, of course, some branches of the BestBite chain of donuts—where you can test green tea, black sesame, mango crème, and seaweed flavored donuts. Take that, Krispy Kreme!

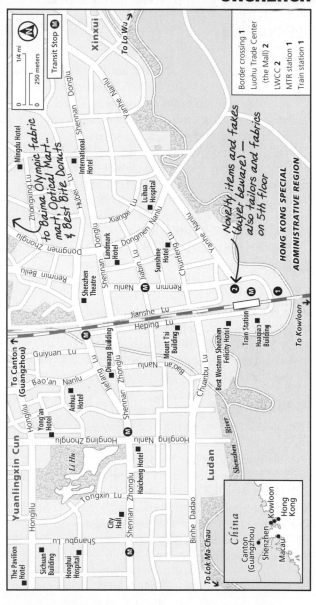

Shenzhen

To Wu ↑

Xinxui

To Lo Wu ↗

Mingdu Hotel ■

Zhongxing Lu to Baima Olympic fabric mart, Optical Mart & Best Bite Donuts

Dongmen Zhonglu

Renmin Beilu

Donglu

International Hotel ■

Shennan

Yatie Nanlu

Hubei

Luihua Hospital ■

Xiangxi Lu

Shennan
Landmark
Hotel ■

Dongmen Nanlu

Jiabin Lu

Chunfeng Lu

Sunshine
Hotel ■

Shenzhen
Theatre ■

Renmin Nanlu Ⓜ

Yanhe Nanlu

**To Canton
(Guangzhou)** ←

Guiyuan Lu

Ⓜ

Jianshe Lu

Heping Lu

Novelty items and fakes (buyer beware) — also tailors and fabrics on 5th floor

2

Ⓜ **1**

HONG KONG SPECIAL

ADMINISTRATIVE REGION

Diwang Building

Mount Tai
Building ■

Train Station ■

Best Western Shenzhen
Felicity Hotel ■

Huaqiao ■
Building

To Kowloon →

Bao'an Nanlu

Jietang Zhonglu

Anhua
Hotel ■

Yong'an
Hotel ■

Honglilu

Bao'an Nanlu

Chuanbu Lu

Hongjing Nanlu

Hongjing Zhonglu

Shennan

Ⓜ

Li Hu

Tongxin Lu

Haicheng Hotel ■

Ludan

Shenzhen River

The Pavilion
Hotel ■

Sichuan
Building ■

Honghui
Hospital ■

Shangbu Lu

City Hall ■

Shennan Zhonglu

Ⓜ

Binhe Dadao

To Lok Ma Chau ↙

Yuanlingxin Cun

China

Canton
(Guangzhou)

Shenzhen
Kowloon

Macau

Hong
Kong

| Border crossing **1** |
| Luohu Trade Center (the Mall) **2** |
| LWCC **2** |
| MTR station **1** |
| Train station **1** |

Ⓝ

0 ——— 1/4 mi
0 ——— 250 meters

Ⓜ Transit Stop

GETTING THERE
BY TRAIN

From Hong Kong, take the MTR from Tsim Sha Tsui East or Hung Hom in Kowloon. The train costs about HK$75 ($9.35) for first-class, which consists of a plush, reserved seat. Rush hours are crowded; at other times, standard service is fine and you should get a seat. But you may also have to stand.

The train is easy to use and well marked. The place to stand while waiting for the first-class compartment is designated on the platform. Please read the destination message on the front of the train before you get on, as the train will branch different directions for either LoWu or Lok Ma Chau.

Trains leave so often that you don't need a schedule or a reservation—buy a ticket and wait for the next train. The ride is 34km (21 miles) and takes about a half-hour.

BY PLANE

More and more insiders tell me that one of the best ways to save money on a trip to HKG is to use the Shenzhen International Airport, Ba'An. You can fly from major Chinese cities, such as Shanghai or Beijing. The new airport is to the west of the city.

FORMALITIES

Because you are crossing the border into mainland China, it's not a breeze. Also note that due to the current political situation, the rules are in flux. As we go to press, U.K. and U.S. passport holders may not get visas at the border. You can get a visa in Hong Kong within 24 hours—your hotel concierge will charge approximately $150 for 24-hour service and a $50 service charge. There are less-expensive ways to do it in HKG, but they aren't as easy. See "Getting a Visa," on p. 18 for more information.

Once you have the visa, this is the drill:

1. Get off the train. Follow the crowds. Stand in the line marked "Foreigners." Exit the Separate Administrative Region (SAR) by going through the formalities here.
2. Walk down a corridor and over a river into a second building and officially enter China with more lines, (again marked "Foreigners"), more paperwork, and your visa.
3. Change money, exit the immigration center. If you arrive via the LoWu border, you are 100m (328 ft.) from the LWCC. If you arrive via Lok Ma Chau but want to go to LoWu, follow the signs to the MTR and alight at LoWu. If you are going to a hotel in Shenzhen, ask for car service to meet you or grab at taxi at either station.

Going back, it's the same thing. Allow about 1 hour each way for the formalities; it can take 3 hours. It can also take 30 minutes, but that's rare.

> ### Traveler's Tip
> If you arrive at Lok Ma Chau, once you cross the river into China, you are in Futian at the Futian Crossing Station. The t is hard, not soft. From HKG, don't tell anyone you are going to Futian because they might think you are mispronouncing FoShan and will send you to another place entirely. Trust me on this.

GETTING AROUND

Shenzhen is quite large and has many neighborhoods. If you are just going to the LWCC, you will walk and never learn more. Those who are staying or exploring can get a taxi in the train station or hop into the new Metro: It is quite extensive, yet easy to use. Stations are marked with colors and in Pinyin.

The LWCC shopping district is not downtown but in a commercial strip near the border crossing that is designated in addresses as "Lo Wu District." Many international hotels are in this area also, although you may not want to walk if you have a lot of bags or luggage.

Note that streets and buildings are not usually marked in English, although this is changing and the big shopping buildings closest to the border now have signs you can read. Once you get oriented, so to speak, you will not need to read much—but you may find that my inability to give you more specific addresses is annoying.

Taxis are cheap, but don't expect your driver to speak English. Have all destinations written in Chinese and in hand.

Wherever you are staying, if you are going any place in Shenzhen besides LWCC, ask your concierge for a map.baidu, the Chinese version of MapQuest. This printout (www.map.baidu.com) will have a map as well as directions, all in Chinese. You mark what it is in your own handwriting because you will not know otherwise, and then when appropriate, you give this map to the taxi driver.

Our most recent trip to Shenzhen allowed us to test the fanciest new hotel in town, the Ritz-Carlton (p. 147) where you can get map printouts in the lounge or at the concierge desk. For reinforcement, the doorman will tell your taxi driver, in Chinese, where you are going.

CALLING AROUND
Shenzhen is in China and uses the 86 country code. The city code is 0755. If you are using a Chinese SIM card, drop the zero when you call locally.

MONEY MATTERS
In all other parts of Shenzhen, you now use Chinese currency, yuan (also called RMB). There are some 15 offices of major international banks in Shenzhen, as well as scads of ATMs.

SLEEPING IN SHENZHEN
InterContinental Shenzhen
9009 Shennan Rd., Nanshan District.

Brand new and modern, this is the latest guy to enter the fray of name-brand hotels fighting for a place in this Chinese border town of businessmen and shopping samurais. The hotel is located on the far side of downtown and has the usual pool, fitness center, and, of course, a 24-hour lounge, one of InterConti's specialties—and the reason you want to book a club floor room. Rates begin around $150 per night.

This hotel is not convenient for shoppers, but that is its beauty. You are forced to drive through town to get here, and that is an education in itself. The hotel itself is owned by the man who owns the theme park next door, Splendid China, so the hotel also has a theme, having to do with Spain and our friend Chris Columbus. I swear that outside the balcony of my spacious room is not only an exact replica of the *Santa Maria* but also the Eiffel Tower.

The hotel is gorgeous—truly a resort setting. It is perfect for romantic getaways or as somewhere to take the kids. It also offers that elusive magic we all travel to find. When I took a taxi out one evening (to a great mall for new Chinese yuppies called MixC), I passed by Splendid China with its thousands of tiny red lanterns all lit up in the night. Local © 755/3399-3388. www.interconti.com.

Ritz-Carlton Shenzhen
116 Fuhai San Rd., Futian District (MTR: Hui ZhanZhongxin).

Most critics agree that this is now the fanciest and best hotel in Shenzhen, although the Four Seasons was not open as we went to press. We don't care because our hearts were won with the stunning building, the easy location (across the street from the new convention center), and the tip to use the Lok Ma Chau border crossing, not far from the hotel.

Aside from the glories of the hotel, and the view from the Club Lounge, there's a giant modern mall (Central Walk) around the corner with everything from Zara to French supermarket chain Carrefour. Also Starbucks and McDonald's, of course.

Our room was a huge junior suite, with a deluxe bathroom and a tub with ae window that overlooks the wide boulevards below.

LoWu for You

The LWCC is five stories high, with escalators that zigzag through an atrium, leading to each floor. There are restaurants and toilets on all floors, usually in the corners. There are some vendors on the roof also, but you may want to avoid this as it's a bit scuzzy. There are elevators to one side (marked for handicap access) and there are lower-level/basement floors that lead to the Metro line, the bus station, and the taxi lines.

LWCC sells just about everything, although it is known for copyright violations. Do not buy fake DVDs as you could get in hot water for bringing them back into Hong Kong. There have been crackdowns on other fakes, so vendors ask you to look at a booklet, choose what you want to see, and wait for the items to be retrieved by a runner. This takes time.

Only after you have the merchandise that you want do you begin to bargain. This takes more time. It's very tiring and emotional; it's also easy to get lost and frustrated. This building is amazing in terms of what's for sale, how low the prices are, and the sheer number of foot treatments you can enjoy. Oh yes, don't forget the Peking duck at Laurel Restaurant.

I go mostly for gifts, and I do load up, but I really try to avoid fakes. I like snazzy, unusual novelty items. The floors are more or less organized by categories of goods, but this is not a rule—so you will find jewelry on floors other than in the jewelry mart, and so forth.

The designer copy handbags are often in the ceiling hidden from police because there are constant crackdowns on fake merchandise. They cost $75 to $100 and rival the ones I bought in Hong Kong for $250.

Best of all was the fact that the concierge had placed framed photos of our hometowns in the room, San Francisco for Sarah and Provence for me (where I own a house). How's that for attention to detail? Local phone ℭ 0755/2222-2222. www.ritzcarlton.com.

Note that a "fake" has a logo on it, and an "inspiration" of a classic is a style without any attempt to fake the hardware or logo—such as bags inspired by the Birkin and Kelly styles. Inspirations are 100% legal. Some copies, especially in watches, are graded by quality. A top-rated (triple-A), Cartier-style watch can cost $150 after hard negotiating.

There is a fabric mart and a row of tailor shops, although it takes several visits to have garments made, making this impractical for the day-tripper. The better shops are on the fifth floor; see p. 156 for our report on the tailors tested.

The merchandise available in the LWCC very much depends on fashion trends and police crackdowns. On one recent trip, the latest fad was Goyard handbags, which were selling for about $40 to $50 each. Prada merchandise was scarce. Franck Muller watches were "in"; Cartier watches are classics.

Many stores had stacks of robin's egg blue boxes (fake Tiffany & Co.), though many of these boxes were actually the wrong color—too green. There were fake Hermès ties and scarves, some in fake orange boxes. Most of the fake stuff does not look or feel real. I've been through a juicy couture phase (thankfully over now) and have recently discovered a second "pleats please" kind of resource in addition to the one that I've visited for years. New = Shop 5018. (The 5 means it's the fifth floor.) MTR: LoWu.

Web tip: Before you leave home, go to **www.tt88time.com** and **www.orolus.com**. Trusty Time will show you fake watches, and Orolus has real watches. Printouts will help you shop and bargain.

SHENZEN NEIGHBORHOODS

LoWu: Also written as Luohu. This is a large business district near the LoWu border; shoppers know it mostly for the wonders of the LWCC (see "LoWo for You," below) when in reality this is an entire district of town, very large and filled with malls and shopping miracles.

There are plenty of other things to see and buy within the LoWu District, so don't think the LWCC is the beginning and end of the world. There are also a lot of hotels here. Note that the Dongmen pedestrian shopping area is also in LoWu, see below. There are a number of Metro stops that serve the district.

Dongmen: This is essentially the old-fashioned market portion of town converted into a quasipedestrain area filled with teens and 'tweens and donuts. This is not East Gate (above). This is home to the **Optical Mart** and many other trade buildings that are open to the public.

This area is a lot of fun, but very confusing because it is not on a grid. It's filled with shopping ops, fast-food joints, and, of course, a giant **McDonald's**. Also **BestBite** (p. 153).

Guidebooks make this area seem like a breeze to shop. We found it both complicated and more spread out than we thought. If you are looking for specific addresses, have them printed out in Chinese. Otherwise, wander; enjoy the atmosphere, which is very exciting because it's local and hot and active; and don't worry about finding the shoe market—the shoes won't fit anyway. Store hours in this area are basically 10am to 10pm; if you can do this in the evening, after work hours, say 7pm, it's crowded but much fun. MTR: Lao Jie.

Nanshan: This is one of the western-most suburbs with a lot of shopping, malls, and furniture showrooms, and yes— Wal-Mart—for expats and well-off locals. It's also gorgeous out here and there are theme parks and resorts, as well as the InterContinental Hotel.

Dafeng Art Village: Perhaps you noticed this on your shopping stroll through Stanley Market, but there are vendors who sell copies of art masterpieces. They cost $10 to $30 depending on the artist and your bargaining skills. These paintings mostly come from Shenzhen, and you can indeed visit the Dafeng Art Village.

I bought several "van Gogh" paintings on unstretched canvas, complete with white borders. I had them stretched onto frames, allowing the borders to show, then I took my paints,

my glue gun, some stickers, and assorted tchotchkes and created my own statement over Mr. van Gogh's. This makes the
work "original" (very original, that's for sure) and therefore
more acceptable to me as a work of art and not a simple forg-
ery. I mean, get real: Who am I to attempt to pull off a real
masterpiece in my home?

But wait, it gets better—if you go to the Dafeng Art Village
with a photo of yourself, you can have yourself painted into a
masterpiece. The most common is *The Last Supper*. Mona
Lisa is also popular. Hey, don't ask me—I don't make up the
news. I'm just the messenger. This village is 45 to 60 minutes
east of Shenzhen and is not on the way to Guangzhou or
Donguan. No MTR. It is marked on the taxi card of the Ritz-
Carlton hotel.

Hua Giang Bei Electronics City
Hua Giang Rd., Futian District (MTR: Hua Giang Lu).

I am the least techno-savvy person in the world and I hate
gadgets because I can't make them work for me. Nonetheless,
this district of stores is just flat-out amazing. There is a handful of large atrium-style modern malls, chockablock with gear
and gadgets.

We found old faithful, **Gome**—the Chinese version of Best
Buy—to be boring compared to the other choices. It is great
for phones, if you care.

The best buildings are **SEG** and **Hua Giang Electronics
Mart** (www.hqew.com/en). These buildings are across the
street from each other. Both stores are open 9am to 6pm. This
is easy to do on the MTR and enormous fun.

For a cool hunter, there may be no better place this side of
Tokyo. I found a plastic (think LIVESTRONG) bracelet with
a USB port closure that is a flash drive for $10.

Note: I spent a fair amount of time inquiring after and
pricing electronic memo tablets, which convert your handwriting to computer files. Prices in the U.S. are comparable to
those in Shenzhen with the benefit of instructions in English
and warranties you can trust. On the other hand, there was a

nonwireless model for $65 that lists in the U.S. for $150. You better know your stuff before you get carried away...or plugged in.

WEB TIP 🖰 The Gome (say Go-may) site is in Chinese (www. gome.com.cn).

Jade & Jewelry Street
Tian Bei 4 St., LoWu District (no nearby MTR).

Sarah has correctly dubbed this the DVD street for jade—it is very similar to our favorite lane in Shanghai with low-slung buildings and a pleasant middle-class atmosphere. In Shanghai all the stores sell DVDs; here, they sell jade or jewelry. There are some high-rise minitowers with names like Diamond Building or Pearl City; for the most part, we can't read what the names are. The big anchor on the corner is Bolin Jewel City, although we went into the jade buildings on Tian Bei and had plenty of fun. We'd have had more fun if we were rich.

This is nothing like the Jade Market in Hong Kong but a very fancy jewelry mart with some high prices, even though they are "wholesale" and in some cases, you can bargain.

You just wander from building to building, floor to floor, dealer to dealer. Try to avoid lunch time as the smell is, well, nauseating from so many different meals being eaten out of so many different Styrofoam containers. The street is only about 2 blocks long; the first jewelry building is no. 2, **Gold City Jewellery.**

We have also dubbed this street the Gump's of China— we are certain we found their sources. Take a look at the silk tassels with jade dangles and know why we travel and shop to save.

Now then, the "4" in the address seems to apply to the section of the road, it is not a building number. Stores are open 9am to 6pm; get your hotel concierge to write or print out the address. It's all easy once you are there as the area is clean, modern, and feels safe. And yes, there are plenty of ATMs.

LOCAL HEROES
Baima Olympic Fabric Mart
Dongmen Zhong Rd. (no nearby MTR).

Some people say you can walk here from Dongmen pedestrian area; frankly—we couldn't figure it out. Take a taxi instead, as well as your shopping tote because this is where you will load up maybe on fabrics, but mostly on trims and gems. Crafty shoppers will go stark, raving, greedy nuts here—fistfuls of diamonds are pennies. With six you get zippers. (Kidding.)

This is one of those market/malls with an atrium and escalators leading up and beyond. The five floors, or portions thereof, are by category of goods so there's more than yard goods. Prices seem to get lower as you go upward.

Frankly, Chinese made fabric is not of a quality that is worth the price of the weight in your luggage, but the doodads are fabulous, sensational, and low cost. Please note, I had an allergic reaction to the sizing in the fabric—the scent of which fills the air and your lungs. Still, I wouldn't have missed this for the world.

BestBite
Dongmen Pedestrian St. (MTR: Lao Jie).

I beg you to walk into the Krispy Kreme of China and taste test the local version of a donut...or a dozen. They are sort of cakelike bagels made in two halves with frosting on top. Flavors have been created per local tastes. See p. 142 for examples, or go to www.bestbitedonuts.com. From our perspective, they were all too sweet; few tasted like the actual flavor (for example, I love green tea ice cream but this green tea donut had no original flavor). © 0755/8239-7089.

Light Industrial Products Center
Meiyuan Rd., Sun Gang District (no nearby MTR).

Just past the Asia Medicine Building, rests the local version of the D&D (Design & Décor) that is just plain mind-boggling.

Well, everything in Shenzhen is mind-boggling…you just have to see this to believe it and come with a lot of cash.

The building seems to be the wholesale source for much of the gift merchandise sold at LoWu. We'd bought Cheongsam-shaped picture frames at LoWu for $20 each—so cute you could die—and found them for half that in the gift building.

Part of the fun is to see showroom after showroom of trends, such as bizarre and/or elaborate telephone handsets, made to please either Marie Antoinette or fit inside a celadon ginger jar lamp. © 755/8249-7912.

Hua Qiang Bei
Hua Giang Rd. (MTR: Hua Giang Lu).

Similar to Tokyo's Akihabara District, this neighborhood is the IT and electronics center of Shenzhen. It's clean and modern and so much fun you will flip out. There are many malls devoted to assorted stalls; each floor often devoted to a specific electronic mode, such as phones, cameras, computers, and so forth. Yes, some DVDs but more programs.

Insider's tip: Rosetta Stone CDs cost about $250 for a Level 1 set in the U.S. In Shenzhen, in any of these malls, expect to pay $10 to $15. Mandarin, anyone?

Mix-c mall
1881 Bao'An Rd. LoWu District (MTR: Da Juyuan).

I love, love, love this mall—it is fancy schmancy and yet represents the new China so it does have some local stores. There are also big European brands, which you can ignore. Try to come in the evening. It's open 9am to 10pm. This is in the LoWu district, so it may not be next-door to your hotel, but it is worth the $4 taxi ride. © 755/8266-8266.

Moi Supermarket
Moi Department Store, basement level, Hua Giang Rd. (no nearby MTR).

View from the Bridge

I had two pairs of glasses made as an experiment, using the same Rx. The pair made here cost $40 ($20 for the frame; $20 for lenses) and the control pair, made at one of the best opticians in the world (New Fei in Hong Kong, see p. 105), cost $125. Both pairs were tried and tested in the U.S. and passed with flying colors. However, at New Fei I was able to communicate and therefore was given a lot of expertise—for this Rx, don't pick a frame with a curve, and so forth.

Moi is a nice, somewhat upmarket department store; you may be attracted to it from the street when you see the two-story Starbucks. The basement has a fun supermarket for those who think that no trip anywhere is worthwhile without a visit to the market. This is in the heart of the electronics district, see p. 164.

Optical Mart
Dongmen Pedestrain St., 6th floor, LoWu District (no nearby MTR).

There is good news and there is amusing news. This optical mart is small and not much to look at compared to others we have been to. It is well located and while you are waiting for your glasses to be made (usually 1 hr.), you can go to BestBite (see above). Sadly for you and me, few people here speak more than one word of English. That one word is *hello* and is not *astigmatism*.

If you are into mime (aren't we all?), you should have no problem getting a great pair of glasses for $20 to $40. They will measure your PD (pupil distance) but if you are getting glasses for someone else, make certain you have this measurement with you.

Tea World
Dexing Building (next to McDonald's, 2nd floor). (no nearby MTR)

If all the fakes and crazies are making you, uh, crazy at LoWu, there's an easy escape into a nearby tea mart, just across the plaza headed toward the Shangri La Hotel. (*Note:* Always use the Shangri La Hotel and the LoWu Train Station as your two visual anchors to know which direction you are headed. A pedestrian plaza connects them; the street is below.) A Chinese tea tasting is yours for the asking.

LOCAL TAILORS

It's not that we want to cheat the system, but we decided that in order to really understand what was going on at the fabric mart and tailoring floor (5th floor) of LWCC, we'd better bring along our own expert. Peter Chan, of W. W. Chan & Son Tailor Ltd. in Hong Long and Shanghai came with us, did some translating and bargaining for us, and inspected the work before and after.

Also please note that we had very good luck in Hanoi, where we paid $12 to have a simple linen dress made (fabric is extra). We wanted to see if price and workmanship compared.

The basics: In Hanoi, I had a simple, tunic kind of dress from Oska (a German designer) copied. The original cost $480. In Shenzhen, I had Flax trousers copied ($114 for original)—this is also a simple pattern. Sarah had a complicated designer jacket copied and then I had six pairs of trousers copied from some ready-made ones that would register as medium in the complicated range.

Ya Qi Western Style Clothes
LWCC, 5th floor, no. 19, Shenzhen.

This tailor had been tried and tested by Pam, one of the passengers on a recent Born to Shop tour. The tailor remembered Pam. I handed over a pair of trousers, and the tailor took me into the fabric mart portion of the 5th floor of LWCC to

Runxin Linen Shop where I chose six different linens, each just under $10 a meter. When I came back for the trousers 2 days later, with Peter Chan, Peter immediately noticed that the buttonholes had not been made. We had to wait 90 minutes more for buttonholes, but the pants were pressed and beautiful. The total price for six pairs of pants was just under $20 per pair. No deposit was taken for the tailor work but the fabric was bought in yuan in cash. © 0755/8234-5363.

Mei/Sunlight Custom Tailor
IWCC, 5th floor, no. 70, Shenzhen.

First, a little background. I have a set of girlfriends in Hong Kong who are the movers and shakers of the city and I have known and trusted them for over 20 years. Chief among them is Lynn Grebsted, PR maven extraordinaire, who knows everyone and everything. She is British and has a Western-style body—tall, with a bosom and not an Asian fit customer. She insisted that her tailor Mei be included in the blind test. Mei, she said, is a gem.

Insider's tip: Mei's stall—and many other tailor stalls—is located in another part of the 5th floor from the fabric mart and Ya Qi (above). Ask for Electric City, 5th floor.

Peter inspected Mei's work before Sarah took the plunge and announced that her women's clothing was well-made but the men's was not. Sarah produced a designer jacket that is unstructured, but has many seams and insets. She chose a Chinese wool from the swatch book—picking the best possible wool at the highest available cost. Peter and Mei had a lot of conversation in Chinese; some amount of English was spoken with Sarah. Total price for this job was $75, including fabric and jacket. The job was paid for in advance in full in yuan.

When we returned, the stall was filled with a crowd and we waited patiently—finally adapting the Chinese pushy style and asking if we could see the jacket while waiting our turn. The jacket emerged from behind a curtain and was a perfect copy in terms of pattern pieces. The stitching was not good and the fabric—so promising from a swatch—seemed cheap and sad. We spent about 15 minutes discussing the faults with Peter and trying to decide what to do. I asked Peter what this same jacket would have cost at his tailor shop for women (Irene Fashions) and he laughed and said you couldn't compare since he uses only Italian fabric and everything is made by hand. To copy such a jacket in good fabric, he would have charged $500. This at least helps put the Shenzhen jacket into perspective.

When it was our turn with Mei, she admitted to the faulty stitching in a pleasant fashion and said she would fix it, but needed time. We had no time. We decided that the copy was well-done, but the fault lay in the use of the Chinese fabric and that it would have been better to bring along fabric from Europe. We also think that Lynn is well-known and that Mei caters to her as a regular and as someone very famous. We were just strangers, business was brisk with regulars, and we did not fare as well as Lynn would have. © 0755/8234-316.

Kuang Jian Ming
LWCC, 5th floor, Shenzhen.

If I could read any more of this guy's personal info on his card, I'd give you more info. Alas, this is one of the tailors in the same row as Mei (above) and I chose him based solely on the fact that a tout—the woman sitting at the sewing machine next to him—said he was "Shanghai Tailor" and I thought that showed great marketing skills. On his part, he looked extremely bored and refused to hustle clients. My goal was to find a total unknown and just see how it went.

I had with me my own fabrics and a pair of Flax elastic waist pants that had no pockets. I said I wanted three pairs of the trousers, but with pockets. He drew a sketch, marked the pockets with arrows and Chinese letters, quoted me $8 per pair and we made a deal.

I also gave him the infamous Oska dress and some brocade-poly dress-up piece of glitz that I had bought for $10 a yard in the nearby fabric mart (same floor, farther over). It was $15 for the dress. (Same dress, $12 in Hanoi.)

English was limited; Peter was with Sarah. Everything was drawn and mimed. I paid a $15 deposit. When I returned, everything was ready, including excess fabric and one piece of linen on which the pattern was chalked, but the tailor explained (I think) there wasn't enough fabric.

This guy was great. The dress was sensational. The only problem with the linen pants was my fault—they were bunchy at the waist because of my choice of fabric. On the other hand, I gave this guy the easiest of the three assignments. ☏ 0755/2549-4330.

Welcome to Canton

Canton is one of those famous names in trade and shopping that seems to stick, long after it has been replaced by the politically correct Guangzhou.

Canton is one of the original 19th-century treaty ports and has been a center of commerce ever since. Now it stands midway between Shenzhen and Macau in the circular loop of the PRD. It is headquarters for those who are adopting a Chinese child (the U.S. consulate is here), home of the most famous trade fair in China (which still uses the name Canton in its official title), and one of the most interesting cities in the new China. I am not easily overwhelmed, but I admit it, Guangzhou intimidates me.

While Guangzhou is only 2 hours from HKG by train, this is not a day trip from Hong Kong (if you can help it) and can be a lot more raw than the other trips suggested in this chapter. The city is enormous; most of it is very ugly. Traffic is horrible and you need to know where you are going to get to the good parts—which are also scattered about town. Shenzhen is much prettier and easier. Shenzhen, however, doesn't have Ben. Read on, read on.

LOCAL CODE

The city is often written as GZ; the telephone code for the city is 20. China is 86.

GETTING THERE
BY TRAIN

From Hong Kong: Fast train from Hung Hom. It's a 2-hour journey; Guangzhou is 121km (75 miles) north of Hong Kong. You will arrive at the **East Railway Station** in Guangzhou.

BY FERRY

From Hong Kong, there are four trips daily between Kowloon and Guangzhou, with departures from Hong Kong beginning at 7:30am and ending at 7:45pm. For the schedule from Guangzhou, call © **020/8222-2555.**

BY AIR

Guangzhou has a great airport, Baiyun International, that is meant to rival Hong Kong's. It has been created to handle some 80 million passengers a year in the upcoming years and will be the area's largest air hub. There are now nonstop flights from Paris on Air France, flights from the U.S. (often through Tokyo) on a variety of carriers (including Delta/Northwest), and a host of Chinese flights. Although you probably won't fly from Hong Kong, daily service is available on Dragonair (www.dragonair.com).

BY BUS

The first time I went to Guangzhou, I went via Macau and Zhuhai. Since there was no train or ferry service, I took the bus, which was easy. You go to the Barrier Gate, cross into China, then cross the street and go down the escalator to the bus station. Buses leave every 15 minutes and cost about $5 one-way. The trip takes 2 hours unless traffic is bad. It's modern highway all the way. If your bus looks full or smoky, consider waiting for the next one. There is a bathroom stop after 1 hour, but there's no toilet on the bus. The bus will drop you at a Western-style hotel in Guangzhou where you can get a taxi to your own hotel.

Canton (Guangzhou)

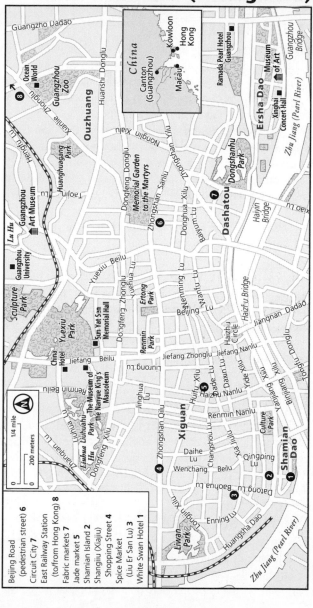

China
Canton (Guangzhou)
Macau
Kowloon
Hong Kong

Guangzho Dadao
Ocean World
Guangzhou Zoo
Ouzhuang
Huanshi Donglu
Xianlie Zhonglu
Guangzhou Dadao
Hengfu Lu

Ramada Pearl Hotel Guangzhou
Ersha Dao
🏛 Museum of Art
Xinghai Concert Hall
Guangzhou Bridge
Zhu Jiang (Pearl River)

Huanghuagang Park
Taojin
Guangzhou Art Museum 🏛
Lu Hu
Guangzhou University
Sculpture Park

Dongfeng Donglu
Nonglin Xialu
Zhongshan Sanlu
Memorial Garden to the Martyrs
6

Dongshanhu Park
Dashatou
7
Donghua Xilu
Baiyun Lu

Haiyin Bridge
Haizhu Xilu Lu

Yuexiu Beilu
Yuexiu Park
Sun Yat Sen Memorial Hall
Dongfeng Zhonglu
Yuexiu Lu
Ertong Park

Beijing Lu
Renmin Park
Bei'enming Lu
Huanshi Lu

Haizhu Bridge
Jiangnan Dadao

China Hotel
Jiefang Beilu
Renmin Beilu
Dongfeng Xilu
Liuhua Hu
Liuhua Park
The Museum of the Nanyue King's Mausoleum
Jinghua Lu
Jiefang Zhonglu Jiefang Nanlu
Liurong Lu

Zhanqian Lu
Zhongshan Qilu
Xiguan
4
Huifu Xilu
Haizhu Nanlu
Renmin Nanlu
Yide Xilu
Yanjiang Xilu
5
Shamian Dao
1
Culture Park
Binjiang
Tongfu Donglu

Daihe Lu
Wenchang
Beilu
Changshou
Xilu
Qingping Lu
2

Dongfeng Xilu
Baohua Lu
3
Liwan Park
Enning Lu
Longjin Xilu
Huangsha Dao
Zhu Jiang (Pearl River)

N
0 — 1/4 mile
0 — 200 meters

White Swan Hotel 1
Spice Market (Liu Er San Lu) 3
Shopping Street 4
Shangjiu (Xiajiu)
Shamian Island 2
Jade market 5
Fabric markets 7
East Railway Station (to/from Hong Kong) 8
Circuit City 7
Beijing Road (pedestrian street) 6

GETTING AROUND

Taxis are inexpensive; the flag falls at ¥7 (slightly more than $1). I took taxis to far-flung areas that were over and under many freeways and way past where Grandma lives. The most I ever paid for a taxi was $5; you can go crosstown for $3. Traffic is horrible and will run up the meter.

If you take the bus from Macau, get off at the China Hotel (Marriott) and take a taxi to your chosen hotel. Taxis are easy to hail in the streets or at hotels.

Private pickup and drop-off or shuttle transfers from the airport or train station can usually be arranged with your hotel.

There are two subway lines; both are relatively easy to use. But taxis are so cheap, why bother?

THE LAY OF THE LAND

Guangzhou is a huge city and getting bigger as I type. For some reason, it reminds me of Caracas. I found it far more frightening than Beijing. Don't begin to think you can get a grasp on it in a day or two. Or in your lifetime. Stick to market areas and Shamian Island.

A WARNING

Even old China hands are warned not to go into Canton's fresh-food markets. The stories I have heard still haunt me. Also, don't look too carefully at those cages in front of restaurants. Just high-tail it (excuse the expression) out of there. And while we're at it, in these days of epidemic and pandemic, stay away from bird markets.

SHOPPING NEIGHBORHOODS

You can get to Bar Street on your own. My list of shopping neighborhoods are near the main hotels and easy to find.

Shamian Island: This is my personal favorite part of the city; I have brought people here on a day trip just to see what colonial China was like more than 100 years ago. I haven't really figured out where the land ends and the island begins, but there's water right up to the **White Swan Hotel.**

Behind the hotel is a strip of residential peace and quiet and greenery with sufficient tourist traps to keep you happy for a few hours. It's clean, safe, easy, and charming. There is a real Starbucks—as well as other coffee joints and cutie-pie restaurants. Don't ask me why, but many of the shops offer to do laundry. There are Internet cafes, crafts stores, and numerous TTs (tourist traps). A TT shop that I like a lot is **E-Gallery,** 61 Shamian Main St., which has a smaller branch around the corner closer to the White Swan in the strip of TTs there. My best find was the artist atelier **Ben's Gallery,** which sells many traditional prints and schlockola artworks but also features original work by Ben, which I consider a must have. I bought two canvases from him, for $250 to $400 each. Ben's Gallery is located in the back end of the White Swan Hotel.

Insider's tip: Ben is now so popular that his paintings arc copied at the Dafeng Art Village in Shenzhen.

Shangiiu Shopping Street: Note that this Cantonese name is Xiajiu in Mandarin; same street, different dialect. This is one of the "new China" phenom streets and is especially fun in the evenings after people get off work. It's a pedestrian street where the locals go out for their promenade; many of the stores are malls and malls of tiny booths.

Beijing Road: This is a different pedestrian street, not that different in feel from the Shangiiu/Xiajiu Shopping Street mentioned above, although farther from the White Swan Hotel. Here you'll find a famous local department store called Good Buy. I wasn't impressed by it because it is attempting to be a Western department store, but what do I know?

Jade Market: Adjoining some streets and alleys selling antiques, this market is a warren of fun and possible good buys. Prices are seriously lower than in Hong Kong. From the street, there is merely a modern arcade of shops selling jade, beads, and semiprecious stones. Head inward to discover an entire village of lanes, with antiques shops to the rear. There is construction nearby, so check the location before you head out. For do-it-yourselfers, this alone is worth the trip just to load up on beads and gewgaws.

Spice Market (Liu Er San Lu): There are no dead or live birds, snakes, or dogs in this market. It's just heaps of gorgeous spices and beautiful textures and colors, all within walking distance of the White Swan Hotel. This is not for those who can't walk up and down many stairs because you have to take a walkway over a freeway. Don't fret: Street vendors sell illegal DVDs on the walkway.

Circuit City: There is an entire street of buildings called the **Haiyin Electronics District.** It is 1 block from the fabric markets, so you can do the whole thing in one swoop. The fabric markets feature home and fashion fabrics, although I was not particularly knocked out. The fabric market in Shanghai is far superior.

The electronics stores, however, are downright amazing. I spent hours here and feasted at McDonald's, which is conveniently located in the main shopping mall. Most of the DVD stores have video CDs on display. In most cases, you have to ask for English DVDs, then follow someone into a corridor. You'll pay about $2 per DVD.

SLEEPING IN CANTON
Garden Hotel
368 Huanshi Dong Lu.

This is one of the top hotels in town; I have not stayed here. It's modern and has over 1,000 rooms in a sky-high tower. As the name suggests, it is built around a garden. Many people like it here because it's in a busy neighborhood and there is shopping nearby. Rates are slightly less than the White Swan Hotel, about $175 a night for a double room. Call ✆ 020/8333-8989 or visit www.thegardenhotel.com.cn.

Ritz-Carlton Guangzhou
3 Xing An Rd., Tian He District

This is a brand-new, fancy-pants hotel meant to knock the competition into the dust. It is inside a 40-story modern tower in the part of town called Pearl River New City. Better still, they may still be offering opening promotional rates, which are around $200 per night, breakfast included. This is a Residences Hotel, the first Ritz-Carlton has in China, so you can live here if you want. © 020/3813-6898.

White Swan Hotel
Shamian Island.

This hotel is so famous that it doesn't have a real street address. Indeed, it's at the end of a street, on a dead end against the point where two rivers merge, so it affords incredible water views. This is a member of Leading Hotels of the World. It's a modern building with a shopping mall, many restaurants, and what locals consider the best dim sum in southern China.

The concierge team is great; they made all my train bookings for me and arranged the free shuttle to the train station when I was ready to return to Hong Kong. They hand out maps of the island as well as the city and have an extensive taxi card that lists the prime sites in town.

There is a Bank of China with an ATM outside the back-door of the hotel. The neighborhood behind the hotel is filled with tourist shops; they all sell pink baby clothes because of the high percentage of girls adopted here.

Aside from the immediate tourist shopping district behind the hotel, there is a nearby spice market (no dogs), and you are within walking distance (or a $2 taxi ride) of one of the main pedestrian shopping districts. There is shuttle bus service to the airport and the two train stations. For travel to Hong Kong, you want East Station.

Rates vary with room, view, and season; they begin at around $200 per night. Reservations through Leading Hotels of the World (© **800/223-6800** in the U.S.). Local © 020/8188-6968. www.whiteswanhotel.com.

Welcome to Macau

The new Macau is even newer than the new China. Most of the old, good, funky stuff has been destroyed—except for the street where they make the antiques.

The Chinese took possession in 1999, and the Las Vegas casinos arrived in 2004. Real estate is booming and architecture is looming, yet a resort feel prevails. Macau remains a luxury getaway destination where you can do a little shopping or gambling. Or a lot. Most of the major Las Vegas hotels have opened resorts; there is even a **Cirque du Soleil** (*Zaia*) at the Venetian (booking hot line: © **853/2882-8818;** www.cirquedusoleil.com).

Macau is a simple day trip from Hong Kong, or a weekend away. It has a new international airport, so you can also make it a main destination. This makes the most sense if you are going past the gates into the PRC and on to Guangzhou (Canton). On the other hand, shoppers who are shopping for pricey branded merchandise prefer Macau over Hong Kong because there is a $3 per $100 difference in the exchange rate. When you are spending $10,000 on an item, this adds up.

WHY MACAU?

As often as I go to Hong Kong, I rarely go to Macau—yet once I get to Macau, I kick myself for not having taken the time or trouble to visit. The colonial Portuguese architecture adjacent to modern high-rises gives you a glimpse of something very different from what you see in Hong Kong. The names on the shops and the Portuguese place names make the destination seem exotic. The atmosphere is laid-back; the casinos offer a little bit of Las Vegas.

Macau's shopping is not great, but it is less expensive than Hong Kong's. And if you need a Chanel fix, you need go no further than the **Wynn.** The Vegas-style resorts are mostly on Cotai, not in the old-fashioned downtown area/city center.

If you are looking for furniture, waste no time in getting here. There are plenty of showrooms with rustic and/or antique styles—right in the city center as well as across the border (see below).

If you are interested in food, many come for the Portuguese-inspired home cooking. If you are in Hong Kong for only 3 days, don't burden your schedule, but if you have time, this trip expands your visual horizons.

Insider's tip: The major furniture factories are on the Chinese side of Macau (Zhuhai) and are easy to shop as long as you have a visa…and a truck (p. 177).

PHONING MACAU

If you're in Hong Kong and want to telephone or fax Macau for restaurant reservations, or whatever, the area code is 853. The area code for Hong Kong is 852.

THE LAY OF THE LAND

A 64km (40-mile) sea lane connects Macau to Hong Kong; it feels a million miles away. Macau itself is not an island but the tip of a peninsula attached to mainland China. You can walk to the gate. You cannot walk through the gate without a visa. On the other side is the economic free zone of Zhuhai.

The "downtown" shopping and gambling area is in the older part of town, or what is left of it. The main drag's official name is Avenida Almeida Ribiero, but it goes by its Chinese name: San Ma Lo. The really fun stuff to browse is up the hill toward St. Paul's Cathedral, but the main drag has stores and banks and my new favorite, the Pawnshop Museum.

The area alongside the ferry terminal has become hot real estate. You pass two malls before you reach the nearby luxe **Mandarin Oriental Hotel.** If you arrive by ferry, you'll need a bus or taxi to get into town; you will also need a taxi to get to various destinations. Your hotel or casino may provide a free shuttle bus. Most resorts are across the bay in Cotai.

GETTING THERE

Your choices are simple: one if by air and two if by sea. Assuming you're not flying into Macau's international airport or crossing the hills from China, you are most likely coming from Hong Kong (near Central) and through **Shun Tak Centre,** or from the Kowloon side, at **China Hongkong City.**

You may also arrive from Shenzhen and from She Kou, both on the PRC side of the bay. The She Kou ferry is famous and takes you into the western portion of Shenzhen.

Shun Tak Centre is the name of the modern, two-tower ferry terminal in Hong Kong's Western District. The MTR stop is Sheung Wan, which is the end of the line. The building and terminals are several floors up in the never-ending lobby space; ride several escalators and read a lot of signs.

China Hongkong City is in Kowloon on Canton Road, almost part of the mall complexes Harbour City and Ocean Terminal.

You will have your choice of kinds of "boats"—ferries, catamarans, and JETFOILS. Sometimes one gets there a little faster than the other, but figure at least 1 hour...maybe more. Ferry service will cease in bad weather.

Fares fluctuate; variables include the day of the week, the time of day (night costs more), and the class of service (first-class costs more). There's even some VIP service, limited to a handful of lucky few.

GETTING THERE QUICKLY

You can take a helicopter to the Ferry Terminal; it's a 16-minute journey. You can also take a chopper from Shenzhen. For information, call © **852/2108-4838** in Hong Kong or visit http://api.airmacau.com.mo/en or www.skyshuttlehk.com.

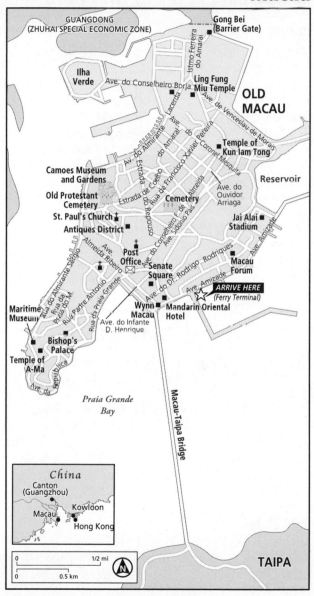

Macau

GUANGDONG
(ZHUHAI SPECIAL ECONOMIC ZONE)

Gong Bei
(Barrier Gate)

Ilha
Verde

Ave. do Conselheiro Borja

Istmo Ferreira do Amaral

Ling Fung
Miu Temple

Ave. de Venceslau de Morais

OLD
MACAU

Ave. do Almirante Lacerda

Ave. do Almirante Amaral

Estrada do Repouso

Ave. do Coelho do Amaral

Rua de Francisco Xavier Pereira

Rua de Coronel Mesquita

Temple of
Kun Iam Tong

Camoes Museum
and Gardens

Rua de Coelho e. de Almeida

Cemetery

Ave. do
Ouvidor
Arriaga

Reservoir

Old Protestant
Cemetery

St. Paul's Church

Antiques District

Ave. do Conselheiro F. de Almeida

Ave. Sidónio Pais

Jai Alai
Stadium

Ave. Amizade

Post
Office

Senate
Square

Ave. do Dr. Rodrigo Rodrigues

Macau
Forum

Rua do Almirante Sérgio

Rua da Praia do M.

Rua da Praia Grande

Rua Padre Antonio

Ave. Almeida Ribeiro

Ave. Amizade

ARRIVE HERE
(Ferry Terminal)

Wynn
Macau

Mandarin Oriental
Hotel

Maritime
Museum

Ave. do Infante
D. Henrique

Bishop's
Palace

Temple of
A-Ma

Rua da República

Ave. da

*Praia Grande
Bay*

Macau-Taipa Bridge

China

Canton
(Guangzhou)

Kowloon

Macau

Hong Kong

0		1/2 mi
0	0.5 km	

N

TAIPA

TRAVEL TIPS

Weekend prices are higher. Crowds are denser. And don't travel on Chinese holidays if you can help it.

If you plan to cross the border and go into China, there are a variety of visas available. Your options may also be based on what kind of passport you hold. There seems to be some prejudice against U.K. passport holders; they pay the most and have extreme limits put on their travels.

You can get your visa in Hong Kong before you leave, or in Macau. You can apply for a visa at the Barrier Gate (Gong Bei). For travel details, visit www.macautourism.gov.mo.

ARRIVING IN MACAU

You'll walk along a little gangway, enter a building, follow a walkway, and go through security. You are now in Portuguese Macau, and Portuguese is an official language. However, when I spoke Portuguese to our taxi driver, he thought I was nuts. Better luck to you and yours.

Once you're outside the terminal, you'll note that there are bus stops and many lanes for cars, taxis, and tourist buses. It's a little confusing, partly because so much is going on. Persevere—your shuttle bus is waiting for you. Mandarin Oriental guests can report to the hotel's service desk inside the terminal and will be escorted to the waiting shuttle.

Also note that you are nextdoor to the New Yoahan Shopping Centre, which is actually a Western-style department store with a fairly good grocery store. It also has a food court and clean bathrooms. Perhaps leave time for this adventure as you depart.

MONEY MATTERS

Macau has its own currency, the pataca (symbol MOP$). Storekeepers will accept Hong Kong dollars but will give change in local currency. The two currencies are more or less at parity: HK$1 = MOP$1.

GETTING AROUND

The taxi flag falls at MOP$10 ($1.35). Although taxi drivers have a destination chart in three languages, I promise you will not find a driver who speaks Portuguese. Use the Chinese chart or carry one from your hotel.

SHOPPING MACAU

The main reason people come to Macau to shop is simple: The prices are lower than in Hong Kong, and the specialty is antiques and "antiques." Yes, they make 'em right here. These copies are so good that you will never buy another antique again, for fear that it just came out of the backroom of a shop in Macau.

Every local from Hong Kong has his or her own private sources in Macau. Indeed, Macau is the kind of place where you need an inside track. There's no doubt that the really good stuff is hidden. And may be illegal.

The shopping must be considered fun shopping, unless you have brought along a curator from a museum or Sotheby's and really know your faux from your *foo*. If you give it the light touch, you're going to have a ball.

SHOPPING MACAU HOTELS

Metro Macau spreads over several islands, and most of the resort hotels are across a bridge. If you've come for the Euro big brands, they are located in the fancy Vegas-style hotels such as **Wynn Macao,** and the **Venetian.** Hotels are still opening— **Sofitel** (www.accor.com) just opened and **Ritz-Carlton** (www. ritzcarlton.com) is about to open. And the beat goes on. Prices on designer merchandise in these hotels reflect the difficulty shipping in merchandise to China and the nature of the high-roller Chinese customers. No bargains.

SLEEPING IN MACAU

There are resorts galore as well as a few charming little boutique hotels; I like to stay "in town" and return, year after year, to the Mandarin Oriental which is between the ferry pier and the "downtown" historical center.

Mandarin Oriental (Grand Lapa Hotel)
956 Av. da Amizade, Macau.

The most famous and fancy hotel in town, the Mandarin Oriental (now called the Grand Lapa after a sale of 50% of its interests to the Sociedade de Turismo e Diversoes de Macau, or STDM) has a country-club atmosphere and amenities in a location between the ferry station and the heart of town. There's big-name designer shopping and several great places to eat. My favorite is the Thai restaurant. Did I mention the spa?

Rooms begin at $300, but there are deals, especially during the week. Note that, naturally, a harbor-view room costs more than one with a city view. U.S. reservations © 800/555-4288. Local © 853/567-888. www.mandarinoriental.com/macau.

MACAU IN A DAY

If you go to Macau as a day trip, you are not going to gamble. Because addresses are hard to find in Macau, and many place names aren't clearly marked, the way for me to show you the best of downtown Macau's shopping area is to take you by the hand. If you are visiting Macau on a day trip, leave Hong Kong early so that you hit St. Paul's Cathedral by 10am. Wander for a few hours and find lunch. Book the 4pm JETFOIL back to Hong Kong.

• Tell your taxi driver "Igresia São Paolo" (St. Paul's Church), or be able to point to it on a map. A *Macau Mapa Turistica* is available free in Shun Tak Centre; yes despite the surrender from Portugal, many things are still in Portuguese. This particular map has a picture of the church. St. Paul's was built in the early 1600s and burned to the ground in 1835, leaving only the facade, which is in more or less perfect condition. Not only is this quite a sight, but it's also the leading tourist haunt in town and signals the beginning of the shopping.

- The church is up a small hill, with two levels of stairs lead-ing to a small square. If you go down both levels of the stairs, you will be at the major tourist-trap area and flea market heaven where dealers sell mostly new antiques... although you always hear stories of so-and-so who just bought a valuable teapot at one of these stalls.

- Before you go lickety-split down all the stairs to the stalls, note that at the bottom of the first staircase is a small alley to the right. Follow it for a block alongside the church until its end, just past the building: There you will find a tiny shrine.

- Not that it's well marked, but the name of this alley is **Rua da Ressurreciao.** It's lined with tourist traps, porcelain shops, antiques stores, and even a ginseng parlor. Don't expect any bargains in these shops, and by all means know your stuff, but begin your shopping spree here. I must say that most of these stores are rather fetching: plates in the windows, red lanterns flapping in the breeze, maybe even a few carved dragons over the doorway. They all take credit cards, and you may have a ball.

- After you've done this alley, work your way around the vendors at the main "square" in front of the church steps. Film, soft drinks, and souvenirs are sold here; there are no particular bargains.

- Normally people head into town by walking down the hill to the market and shopping as they go. The way to do this is to head down the Rua de São Paolo to the Rua da Palha, passing shops as you go. This walkway leads directly to the marketplace and the Senate Square, which is the heart of downtown. There are a few cute shops this way, and I have even bought from some of them.

- But I'm sending you down the hill the sneaky, nontouristy way. If you have the time, you may want to go down my way and then walk back up the main way so you can see the whole hill (and shop, of course). Also note that if you're with people and decide to split up, you can always meet back at the church stairway flea-market area at an appointed time; this is a good place to get a taxi later on. Yes, I said flea market.

- The big red stall is not a toilet; it's a postal box. You can mail postcards here.

- Now turn right, look to the left for an alley called **Calcada do Amparo.** Enter here and begin to walk downhill. It's not going to be charming for a block or so, and you'll wonder where the hell you are and why all the tourists went in the other direction. Trust me, you're headed into the back alleys of the furniture and antiques area, as you will soon discover. You are wearing good walking shoes, I hope. This is the Tercena neighborhood, by the way.

- The reason I haven't given you shop names and addresses should now be abundantly clear—there's no way of really even knowing where you are when you walk down this hill. In about 2 blocks, your alley will dead-end at a small street called **Rua Nossa Senhora do Amparo,** which may or may not be marked. These little alleys are called walkways or *travessas* and may have names (look for **Travessa do Fagao**).

- Get your bearings: You're now halfway to the main downtown square of Macau, on a small street that branches off from Rua do Mercadores, the main small shopping street that connects the main big shopping street to the area above at the top of the hill.

- This will make sense when you're standing there in the street, or if you look at a map. But don't look at a map too carefully because part of the fun of the whole experience is wandering around, getting lost and found, and feeling like what you have discovered is yours alone.

- When you are back on the Rua Nossa Senhora do Amparo, you'll find a ton of little dusty antiques shops. Some have names and some don't. They start opening around 11am; don't come too early. I wouldn't begin to vouch for the integrity of any of the shops here. I can only assure you that you'll have the time of your life.

- When you have finished shopping the antiques trade, work your way laterally across Rua das Estalagens to Rua do

Mercadores. If you turn right, you w
of short blocks to Avenida de Almeid
drag. I suggest instead that you keep m
that you run smack into the market.

- The market is called **Mercado de São Doming**
  outdoor fruit-and-veggie portion tucked int
  alleys, an indoor livestock portion, and a dry-goo
  tion. Wander through as much as you can take, and
  yourself at the main fountain and a square (Senate S
  which instinct will tell you is the main square. *Note:* There
  are still garment factories in Macau, and you will sometimes find name-brand merchandise.
- If instinct isn't enough, look for the Leal Senado, which is
  the Senate building. You have arrived in the heart of town.
- The address of the tourist office (in case you need help, a
  place to meet up with the people you came with, or someone who speaks English and can teach you how to use the
  phone or write something for you in Chinese) is 9 Largo
  do Senado.
- If you've chosen to spend a weekend night, surely you're
  up for the Night Market, which is similar to the Temple
  Street Market in Kowloon—complete with Chinese opera
  singers. Head to the **Cinema Alegria** to find the market, or
  ask your concierge to write it out for you in Chinese. The
  market is not far from the harbor and can be reached
  directly by bus. Taxis are cheap, so I went by taxi. Prices
  on junk and clothes without labels tend to be less than in
  Hong Kong; there are amazing amounts of baby clothes.

GONG BEI

Gong Bei is the Barrier Gate. I won't bore you with what it
used to be like. Let's go with what it is now: fascinating but
neither charming nor old-fashioned. This is big business, with
millions of souls in transit. From the Macau side, your taxi
will drop you at what looks like a modern office tower. Follow the crowds. In two steps, you exit Macau and then ente
China. You must have a visa to enter China.

his case, do not follow the crowds. Look for the immi-
n gates marked foreign passports. They are usually at
ar right, if your back is to the front door.

nce you enter China, you wander through a lobby and
tside, where a million watch salesmen will descend upon
ou. Ignore them and cross the street. To get to the bus station, take the escalators right in front of you down one level.
Buy your ticket, and then go down another level into the bus
station.

If you want a taxi for exploring the area (and going to
furniture warehouses), head to the far side of the plaza *before*
you go down the escalators.

COTAI BARRIER

There is a second border into the PRC, over in Cotai where
Las Vegas has set up shop. Well, Las Vegas is nearby.

FISHERMAN'S WHARF

I don't like Fisherman's Wharf in San Francisco, and now that
there's one in Macau, I am amused and amazed. This new
waterfront development in the outer harbor was designed by
the venerable Stanley Ho, who must have had something other
than casinos in mind until the boys from Vegas came calling. It
is technically called the area's first theme park, with restaurants, a hotel on the way (with casino, of course), and family
entertainment. And, oh yeah—did I mention the medley of
architecture from all over the world, 150 stores, a volcano
that erupts nightly, or the Roman amphitheater? I can just
hear Tony Bennett now crooning about where he left his heart.

ABOUT ZHUHAI

Okay, so I'm running from A to Z in one sentence—who
could resist? Just so you know, Zhuhai is the city across the
Barrier Gate from Macau. It is one of those newfangled, fancy
conomic zones that are progressive and exciting for the Chi-
se while possibly unknown to the average tourist. This one

has a fancy airport and Formula 1 racetrack, neither of which are much written about.

I like the idea of living here—I saw some gorgeous high-rise luxury apartment buildings with sea views. But I digress. The reason most people come here to shop is the furniture warehouses. And yes, the warehouses will arrange international shipping.

If you are interested in only the furniture part (that is, Zhuhai) and don't really care abut Macau or the Barrier Gate, you can take a ferry directly from Hong Kong to Zhuhai and back. Rush hour ends at 5pm, and there are not too many ferries back to Hong Kong after that, so watch the hour or have a backup plan.

The furniture warehouses spread across their own district; you will need a taxi that waits for you. Make sure you have all the information written in Chinese. Change money at the border crossing.

Chapter 7

Weekend in Vietnam: Hanoi & Ho Chi Minh City

So Long, Hong Kong

Some 60% of Americans visiting Vietnam get there through Hong Kong, so here is your guide to one of the most fun shopping destinations you will ever encounter. Worried about changing money again? You can use U.S. dollars in Vietnam. Worried that you don't get much to show for your money these days? Welcome to Vietnam, where money and value go hand in hand and the shopping ops keep on coming.

It's no secret that Vietnam is gorgeous and charming and has great prices. I happen to prefer Hanoi to Ho Chi Minh City (HCMC; formerly Saigon) but maybe it's because I know it so much better. If I lived in a U.S. city with an easy nonstop air connection to HCMC, I'd probably be singing "The Song of the South." As it is, I find Hanoi an easy weekend away from Hong Kong. This chapter is mostly devoted to Hanoi, because of my expertise there—but don't freak, I have the basics of HCMC written up also.

I think part of the beauty of your trip to Hong Kong is not only the opportunity to enjoy Hong Kong but also your proximity to a bevy of Asian destinations that you can visit for a few days with a simple connection from Hong Kong International Airport.

He Ain't Heavy

Many intra-Asia airlines—not just between Hong Kong and Vietnam—have very strict baggage and weight allowances, so you want to construct your weekend away so that you go back out through Hong Kong with at least one overnight in HKG to retrieve the big bags and do your last-minute shopping.

If you prefer a getaway weekend to Bangkok, be sure to find *Born to Shop Bangkok & Beyond* at www.amazon.com; it's small but handy and also covers other hot spots in Thailand.

AIRPORT REMINDERS

To keep this weekend as simple as possible, may I suggest that you leave behind your big-time luggage and weight allowance and go small. It's easy to get to the Hong Kong airport on the train (or the executive coach bus), so you can check your big suitcases at your hotel when you depart, take a smaller piece with wheels on the train, fly to Vietnam and then head back to Hong Kong. The less weight you take to Vietnam, the more shopping you can do without paying for excess weight.

Why Vietnam, Why Now?

I know a helluva lot of people who went to a lot of trouble to not visit Vietnam—but that was 40 years ago and times, as well as politics, change. I'm not going to talk politics or even emotions here—instead I will report as objectively as I can as your Shopping Goddess. This much is true: Vietnam is one of the few countries in the world where you can buy wonderful, sophisticated merchandise for very, very low prices. If the thrill of the chase has gone out of a lot of your travels, you will have a meltdown when you see how much there is to buy here and for how little money.

Frankly, I have found that Hong Kong has gotten very expensive. There's still lots to buy there (after all, that's what this book is all about), but by going to Vietnam for a few days, you see totally different merchandise, you find true killer bargains, and you get a new view of the world.

A SHORT HISTORY

I will not go into politics past or present here; I will not mention that I think we owe Jane Fonda an apology for how she was treated years ago—all she did was suggest we stop bombing these people. Nonetheless, Jane Fonda to one side, this is a thousand-year-old culture that has been fought over for its natural minerals and wealth for centuries. Just take a look at this recent history:

1873: The French move in.

World War II: Japanese occupation with French administration.

1945: War of Independence begins.

1954: French fall at Dien Ben Phu.

1965: American War begins.

1976: United Nations reunites the two parts of Vietnam.

1986: Doi Moi begins, private ownership allowed—stores bloom and serious shopping begins.

FINANCIAL MATTERS

The official currency of Vietnam is the dong, which trades at about 17,500 to $1. However, U.S. dollars are accepted almost every place and are often preferred. Few stores accept credit cards. There are some ATMs in banks at major intersections in downtown areas. To keep things simple, bring cash with you and plenty of $1 and $5 bills.

ENTERING VIETNAM

You will need a visa to enter Vietnam. The 1-day visa—mostly for those on cruise ships—is $65; the 30-day visa costs $130. **Zierer Visa Service** (p. 19) is the provider I often use.

Because we have offices in the San Francisco area, Editorial Director Sarah Lahey can take our passports and the required two photos directly to the Vietnamese Consulate. If your city does not have an embassy or a consulate, there are other ways to get a visa. You pay a combination of two fees if you do it yourself, for the visa ($45–$65) and for the official stamp ($25–$50). Fees are dependent on length of stay and number of entries. If you use a service, there will be an additional fee.

You can also go online, download the paperwork, and submit it to the **Vietnamese Embassy** (© **202/861-2293; www.vietnamembassy-usa.org**); or employ any number of "services," beginning at $40. For details, call the embassy or visit its website.

There is a relatively new process called **Visa on Arrival**. This is not as simple as it sounds; you don't just show up and say "Hey, ya'll." You use a service to fax your application and paperwork. You bring your copy with you and when you arrive at the airport, you go to the immigration desk and get your visa at that time. If they don't have a copy of the paperwork you have in your hand, you are screwed. Look at www.vietnamstay.com.

SPELLING MATTERS

Because Vietnamese is an Asian language (the language is *Kihn*), a Pinyin-like system (called *Quoc Ngu*) must be used to Romanize the sounds. As a result, there are various accepted spellings and writings for the same words. *Vietnam* can be spelled as one word or two (*Viet Nam*), and *Hanoi* is sometimes *Ha Noi*. (The Sai Gon River is obviously where Saigon (now Ho Chi Minh City) got its name.)

LINGO LESSONS

I know, I know, this is another Asian language that you think is totally beyond you, even though it is written with the same alphabet we use and is not in kanji. You don't know the pronunciation rules, you look at the jumble of letters and sounds, and your eyes glaze over. Wait! I bring news!

Much of Vietnam was colonized by the same Portuguese who came in the black ships (remember *Shogun?*) and the spelling of words today is based on a system created in the 16th century by a Portuguese monk. Some 30% of this language is therefore related to Portuguese, which is a romance language.

If you speak some French or Spanish, and if you get creative with your circular thinking, you can practice by reading signs. See that one over there? Banh. Sound it out...sounds like *pain,* which is bread in French. *Voilà.* You're getting it. Sound out everything. It will help.

RENTING A CAR

You're kidding, right? If you want a car and driver; your hotel will arrange it.

CALLING AROUND

The country code for Vietnam is 84, and the city code for Hanoi is 4. The city code for HCMC is 8. If you are calling from within either city, you dial 04 (or 08) and then the number. If you are calling from outside Vietnam, drop the zero.

You can buy a sim card to gain a local phone number if you need one or you can use a phone card from the hotel to make international calls. The system for making international cards (outbound) is a little different here, so ask the hotel operator or concierge. With my sim card, I had to dial 171, then 00, then 1 and the U.S. phone number.

BEST BUYS

Ceramics: I went nuts buying ceramics—vases, place settings, everything. I bought in stores, I bought in the country, I bought in a market. I bought big time. The problem is that shipping increases the cost and packing adds to weight and worries.

Ceramics from northern Vietnam are superior to others because of the qualities of the local clay. Various villages specialize in different styles; see p. 203 for information on an excursion to Bat Trang, a ceramics village outside Hanoi.

Chopsticks: I am not talking "with six you get egg roll" chopsticks—I am talking about an art form. Fancier stores sell chopsticks by the set ($2–$5 per set), but you can buy them in sets for 10 people for $6 at the market. Do not put them in the dishwasher once you get home; wipe with an oiled cloth, please.

Commie Art: In a somewhat recent artistic phenom, posters created to rally the workers in soviet and socialist states have become collectible. In fact, the real thing is hard to find—the Chinese have a fair trade in fake Communist worker posters, many of which are stunning. One of the newest art trends in Vietnam is this same poster, which has its own distinct style—some similarities and some unique qualities. There are three or four galleries in Hanoi alone; the best posters have a tag attached to them that translate the slogan, such as "Workers for a Better Wheat State."

Contemporary Art: I rarely report on art because taste is so personal. I was shocked and amazed by the number of art galleries, however, and the quality of the wares and diversity of styles. Many of the artists are highly collectible and have regular shows in Hong Kong and Europe; some galleries have a branch in Hanoi and another in Paris. Hanoi has more galleries than HCMC. Art for living artists ranges from $300 to $6,000 unless you are talking about street stuff.

Embroidery: What appears to be European-style embroidery, as if the handiwork of French nuns, is actually a local craft. The range is from incredibly elegant and obviously hand stitched, to somewhat tacky, machine-made pieces, such as laundry bags that say *linge* (laundry in French). There are also total works of art, such as Renoir masterpieces or local scenes, stitched in embroidery. I've never seen a really good one of these and they are made by machine, but they can be amazing. Look for the Mona Lisa.

Ethnic Fashion: These items are fashionably ethnic and funky without being costumey. You can buy the traditional dress style, called an *ao dais*—what I call a Madame Nu dress, but that dates me. And just so you know, I asked the computer where Madame Nu is now and it gave me a link to Tussaud's Wax Works. Hmmm. But back to the clothes—yes, yes, yes: There are crinkle skirts and wraparound trousers, embroidered shoes, and all sorts of items that could turn up on the pages of *Vogue*.

Foodstuff: I always go to the grocery stores, although much foodstuff can be bought in the U.S. from Asian markets and specialty stores, either in person or online. And no, fish sauce is not made from fish.

Horn: It's not tortoise shell; it's buffalo horn. Among the best buys: a set of salad servers in horn for $12.

Lacquer: In most cases, this will be the most-sophisticated, drop-dead-chic lacquer you have ever seen. Major home-style stores in Europe and the U.S. are already overcharging for it.

Buyer Beware

Most stores have designs inspired by the likes of Monet and Hundertwasser, so you have to look past that to the eggshell crackle format, the metallics, and monochromes. Pack with care; the lacquer does chip, crack, and/or break in luggage.

Lanterns: Assorted lantern styles are available, but the most popular—and chic—is the style called Indochine, a sort of tulip-bulb shape in various sizes made of silk and usually finished off with a tassel. Prices begin at around $7. You can get the plug-in lamp type (you may have to change the electrical current if you schlep the lamp back to the U.S.) or the hangs-over-a-light-bulb kind. People with real style will add a smarter tassel to make this lantern enviable.

Place mats: Don't look at me as if I am some sort of moron. Would I really be wasting your time if I was talking about plain old bamboo or woven or average place mats? The kind of place mats that I went nuts over were only in a handful of home decor stores where some craftsperson had taken the cheapie and easy-to-find local place mats and added on fringe or beads or passementerie that was so extraordinary that you felt touched by genius. Also table runners. Prices are high—about $25 to $35 for a table runner. The styles are endless. Try the stores near the church in Hanoi.

Quilts: Here's some good news—after you go nuts for the silk, hand-stitched bed quilts in Vietnam...the ones that cost about $100 to $130, know that you can often find the same ones already in the U.S. at Tuesday Morning, the discount chain, for $199. On the other hand, the most readily available quilts are always simple silk ones. I had one made of men's suiting on one side and shirting on the other for $85. I had a baby quilt made for $50 that I thought was a handsome gift for people I wanted to honor. The quilts are amazing. Most can be made in 24 hours if you want custom.

Shoes: Believe it or not, shoes must be made here because there are tons of them. I actually even found a size 41 (American size 10)! I bought some embroidery raffia mules on a princess heel for $36.

Silk: Aside from the usual, you'll see silk duvet covers and hand-stitched silk quilts. I bought several shirts in silk and in linen; I liked the style so much that I then had the shirt made in English cotton (complete with monogram on the cuff) in Hong Kong. Vietnamese silk is thinner than that of other Asian countries and may not wear as well.

Tailoring: I measure all experiences by my favorite tailor who charges me $12 to make a simple day dress, copied from an Oska dress that cost me $380. Custom quilts are about $85.

Velvet: Hmmm, maybe it's silk velvet and that's why it's so plush. I'm talking velvet skirts, tops, coats, and jackets, all in the same slouchy boho style we love in fabulous, funky colors. This is not costumey; this is real fashion and affordable.

There's No Sense to It

Despite the fact that Bangkok is farther away from Hong Kong than Vietnam, flights between Hong Kong International Airport and Bangkok's Suvarnabhumi Airport are usually far less expensive. A handful of low-cost carriers operate from Bangkok, so you can even get to Vietnam from Bangkok for less than from Hong Kong. As we go to press, our favorite low-cost Asian carrier AirAsia has no service to Vietnam.

SEASONALLY YOURS

Prices and packages are related to the seasons, as in most destinations. Summers are hot and humid; you can get bargain prices in August. Fall and early winter are high season—Hanoi does big Christmas and New Year's business with Europeans while HCMC gets an international mix. By January things slow down for Tet, the lunar new year, and then the rains start.

About that rain: Because this is a long, skinny, north-south country, there are two different weather/monsoon seasons. For the most part, the rain begins by mid-March and is worst in May. Best months to visit are June to the end of February. I've visited in August when things are hot and humid but there was no rain; I've been there in October and November when weather was summerlike but pleasant—no rain.

TWO FOR ONE

A lot of visitors are curious about the differences between **Hanoi** and **HCMC** or figure if they've come this far, they want to see them both. Fair enough. There is regular air service with several flights a day between Hanoi and HCMC. You probably want to stay longer than a weekend to fit in two cities, but 3 nights in Hanoi and 2 nights in HCMC should give you a taste. You'll probably want to see some of the cities in between the two biggies, such as **Hue** (say "Way") and **Hoi An,** home of the tailor market. There are also assorted deluxe resorts along the coastal waters up and down Vietnam.

When booking air from HKG, you should be able to get a three-leg trip—Hong Kong to Hanoi, Hanoi to HCMC, and HCMC back to Hong Kong. If you're wild and crazy and ignore my advice about leaving your luggage in Hong Kong, you can even fly from HCMC on to Bangkok or Tokyo.

TRAVEL WITHIN VIETNAM

This is a long, skinny, noodle country with a lot of coastline, a lot of tropical weather, and a lot of interesting cultural and shopping sites. Hanoi and HCMC are about 2,735km (1,700 miles) apart, which makes for an overnight and long train ride—but they have very nice trains. You can also make stops along the way like Hue and Da Nang (get to Hoi An from Da Nang). You can also fly to some cities via Vietnam Airlines.

BOOKING OUT FROM VIETNAM

Vietnam Airlines (www.vietnamairlines.com.vn) controls this market. They offer some really good deals if you use Vietnam as your hub. Note that most of the offers are from HCMC, which is significantly farther south than Hanoi. But, uh-oh, sometimes the deals make no sense whatsoever, like a package from Hanoi to Bangkok for $199 from Hanoi and $229 from HCMC—HCMC is closer to Thailand than Hanoi. Look for a program called Fee & Easy, which offers a 3-day, 2-night package—cities on offer include Singapore, Phnom Penh, Siem Reap, and Guangzhou (p. 159).

Welcome to Hanoi

Don't be surprised if you see the city's name written out the proper Pinyin way as two words: *Ha Noi*. This is a charming city built around three main lakes—West Lake, the largest, is rumoured to be where John McCain was shot down. Now it's home to a gorgeous residential area and some luxury hotels. Downtown has more luxury hotels and a whole lot of very sophisticated shopping. It's tropical and it's hot, man. C'mon baby, light my fire. Stores and restaurants are cash only, for the most part.

Hanoi, known as the City of the Dragon, is celebrating its 1,000-year birthday in October 2010. The basic downtown shopping area, called the District of the 36 Guilds, was organized in the 15th century. The word *hang* means guild and so the streets are named specifically for what they sell (Hang Bac is known for *bac*, or silver).

GETTING THERE

The flight from Hong Kong is about 2 hours. The time zone in Hanoi is 1 hour behind Hong Kong, which may make you think the flight is 1 hour long or 3 hours long. Although various partners do code share (Cathay, for example), all flights are operated by Vietnam Airlines (© 415/677-8909; www.vietnamairlines.com).

BOOKING HANOI

As a general rule, flights from Hong Kong to Vietnam are expensive. Tickets purchased in Hong Kong cost $750, so I buy tickets elsewhere. I've bought my tickets in Paris for $450 and through my regular Chinese travel agent in California (p. 25) for about the same amount.

I went online to www.kayak.com for fares—this was really upsetting. At first I thought the prices quoted were in Hong Kong dollars, which would have been lovely (divide by seven)…alas, airfare was $600 to $700 round trip on China Southern Airlines. The more-expensive flights were during convenient hours; the flights at $599 got into Hanoi after 10pm. I cross-checked via www.farecompare.com and found the same flight for $598.

Peter Chan, Born to Shop regional editor Asia, and his wife, Louisa, went with me one time—on the exact same flights—but bought a late-summer promotional package that included airfare, transfers, and a 2-night hotel stay (as well as other perks) at the Sofitel Metropole for $650 each. They bought their package in Hong Kong. Obviously, it pays to shop around.

Online I found a similar package through www.asiatravel.com—these prices are in Hong Kong dollars and you have a choice of hotels. The travel is on Cathay Pacific; the package does not include departure taxes.

Maybe the part that was the most disturbing is that fares from the U.S. were about $1,200. Go figure.

ARRIVING IN HANOI

The Noi Bai International Airport is brand new, modern, and gorgeous; entry is as easy as chopsticks.

Your hotel can arrange a pickup for you; package tours probably include transfers. You can easily take a taxi into town. Travel time is about 45 minutes; the fare is $13 to $18.

THE LAY OF THE LAND

The main "downtown" shopping area is called the District of the 36 Guilds and consists of small streets and alleys that make up a village of shopping ops. This area is just north of Lake Hoan Kiem, locally referred to simply as "the lake." If you are looking at a shopping address or a business card, it is not unusual for it to say "Hoan Kiem District" after the street address—this is so you know it's right in the thick of things.

The Opera House (called "the opera") is southeast of the lake, and most of the so-called luxury hotels are in the area between the opera and the southern shore of the lake. You can walk to the shopping district or take a taxi for very little money. The two best-known hotels here are the **Metropole** and the **Hilton.** Note that the latter is not called the Hanoi Hilton for obvious reasons but the Hanoi Opera Hilton Hotel.

Hotel Nikko Hanoi, representing a luxury Japanese chain of hotels, is closer to the southwestern section of the lake.

A third district for luxury hotels—but not that much shopping—lies on the far side of the lake in the opposite direction from the Nikko. The two anchors here are the **Sheraton Hotel Hanoi** and the new **InterContinental Hanoi,** which is more of a resort than a plain-old hotel.

Although most hotels have some shopping in them, you'll want to shop downtown. You will need to use a map because I can honestly report being lost several times. Good luck trying to find someone who speaks English...or French. In some cases, you may have to flag a taxi and go back to your hotel and start over. Have your hotel's taxi card with you at all times, and study the map in this chapter.

Hanoi

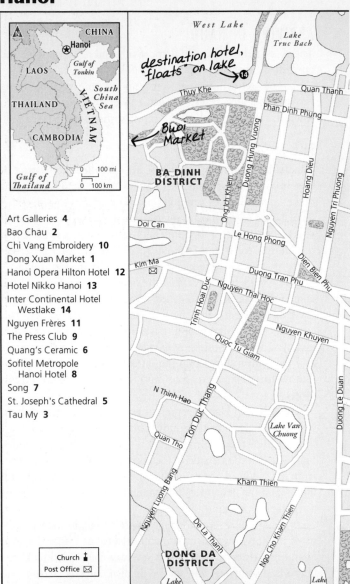

West Lake

Lake Truc Bach

destination hotel, "floats" on lake → 14

CHINA

Hanoi

LAOS

Gulf of Tonkin

THAILAND

VIETNAM

South China Sea

CAMBODIA

Gulf of Thailand

0 100 mi
0 100 km

Buoi Market ←

BA DINH DISTRICT

Thuy Khe

Quan Thanh

Phan Dinh Phung

Duong Hung Vuong

Hoang Dieu

Nguyen Tri Phuong

Doi Can

Le Hong Phong

Kim Ma

Dien Bien Phu

Duong Tran Phu

Trinh Hoai Duc

Nguyen Thai Hoc

Quoc Tu Giam

Nguyen Khuyen

Duong Le Duan

N Thinh Hao

Ton Duc Thang

Lake Van Chuong

Quan Tho

Nguyen Luong Bang

Kham Thien

De La Thanh

Ngo Cho Kham Thien

DONG DA DISTRICT

Lake Xa Dan

Lake Ba Mau

Church ✝
Post Office ✉

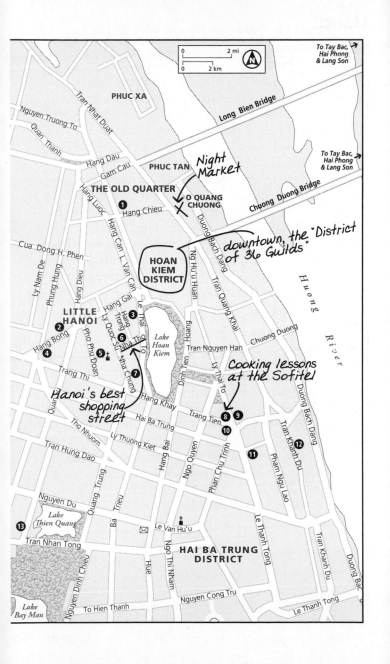

GETTING AROUND

Only the downtown luxury hotels are within walking distance of the best shopping districts of Hanoi. Taxis are plentiful and inexpensive—a ride anywhere in the central shopping area costs $2. Pedicabs are cute but more expensive than taxis (and not air-conditioned)—expect to pay about $3 from your centrally located hotel to the shopping district.

Most luxury hotels have their own car service for transfers, day trips, and hourly rental. A car and driver costs about $30 an hour. We used a driver from the Hilton on one trip; his English was great and he took us everywhere in an air-conditioned Benz. We got a van for a group from the InterConti Westlake and each of us (10 people) paid $25 a day. Since the InterConti Westlake is a bit out of town, we learned what the proper metered fare was and could fight with cabdrivers who tried to cheat us (the answer is $5, by the way).

Hanoi Opera Hilton
1 Le Thanh Tong St., Hanoi.

This relatively new hotel stands next door to the Opera House, at the edge of the shopping district. It offers gold packages as well as the usual Hilton breaks and promotions. From the opera side, the hotel appears to have a colonial look to it; from the arrivals side, it's just modern and a bit ugly. Never mind. The restaurants are good, room service is efficient, the staff is great, and the location will serve you well. Rooms go for around $200. The adjacent ATM is a blessing. U.S. reservations ✆ **800/HILTONS** (445-8667). Local ✆ 04/933-0500. www.hilton.com.

InterContinental Westlake Hanoi
1A Nghi Tam Village, Tay Ho District, Hanoi.

This is a five-star resort that appears to float on a lake. It has 327 rooms and 36 apartments. Note that Westlake is becoming a destination unto itself, but it is not in downtown Hanoi. Rooms have either city or lake views. There is a surcharge of

$50 for the high season around Christmas. Otherwise, rooms begin around $220 and go up. But wait, in an article in the *New York Times,* the reporter found a room in April 2009 for $128.

Just to demonstrate how reasonable everything is, the hotel fee for airport transfer in a sedan is $18; in a van, $25. (A taxi is about $15.)

The hotel stretches over the water so there is a lounge and bar with large wicker beds right up against the lake itself—very romantic. At night there are torches burning, music playing, and at some times of the year, mosquitoes biting. Oh well. U.S. reservations ✆ **800/496-7621.** Local ✆ 04/270-8888. www.ichotelsgroup.com.

Sofitel Metropole Hanoi
15 Ngo Guyen St., Hanoi.

This is the most historic hotel in town—the grande dame in a super location; the hotel that is a movie star in its own right. The Sofitel Metropole prides itself on being a shopping headquarters and provides all guests with a local map and shopping resource list. Unfortunately, most of the great shops in the lobby are now gone, but there's a wing of designer stores off to one side. This is the hotel you swing by to visit even if you aren't staying here. Eat a few meals. Sigh a few sighs. Sign up for cooking lessons (p. 199).

Promotional rates sometimes list two prices, one for the modern wing of the hotel and one for the older portion. Expect to pay about $200 for the newer part and $250 or more for the historic part. We got our rooms online for about $180 a night and on arrival were asked if we wanted to pay another $30 a night to trade up to the old part of the hotel. You betcha!

Don't miss a meal at **Spices,** whether you stay here or not. You can take a special tour from this hotel in a vintage (1935) car that will really make your trip. Please note that there is another Sofitel hotel nearby, the **Sofitel Plaza.** This is a modern high-rise halfway between West Lake and downtown.

U.S. reservations © **800/SOFITEL** (763-4835). Local © 04/826-6919. www.accorhotels.asia.com.

WATCH OUT

There is a business in war souvenirs; I could not stomach the idea of shopping for them. Rumor has it that most are fakes anyway. The specialty is sixties-era watches and lighters.

SHOPPING HANOI

Hanoi has quickly grasped the concepts of the glam slam and the good deal. It has stores that would do Paris, New York, and Tokyo proud. The locally made merchandise is far more sophisticated than in Hong Kong and China; designer and brand business is just getting going. Obviously, you don't go to Vietnam to buy designer merchandise anyway.

I shopped nonstop for 3 full days and returned to Hong Kong kicking myself for not buying more. The raw authenticity of the setting is pure charm; the prices are heaven (few items cost more than $25; most cost $5) and you can truly shop 'til you drop. You'll also get a good giggle, perverse as it may be, in buying a size XXXXL; in having a tailor-made dress created for $12. Actually the asking price for the dress I wanted copied was $11 but when I asked to have pockets put in, it went up to $12.

MOTO SHOPPING

As you probably know, this is a motorcycle culture (*moto* in French). Do not be surprised if you are working with your tailor or some other artisan and you are invited to hop on back of their moto to go to the fabric market or some other venue with them. Wear a helmet? What helmet? This will be the ride of your life, and yes, you are likely to survive. Somehow.

SNACK & SHOP

The food in Hanoi is fabulous; you will have no trouble enjoying yourself, eating well, and staying on your diet as everything is tasty but not fattening. I don't do street food, which many claim is a shame. For the most part, I like to test hotel dining rooms as part of visiting a new hotel and I hang out a lot during any given day at the **Metropole Hotel** (good food, clean bathrooms, great location).

Fanny, at 48 Le Thai To, is actually a cafe but it is best known for its ice cream—give me ginger or give me death.

Pho 24 is a well-known place for expat ladies who shop.

SHOPPING DAYS & HOURS

Stores are open 7 days a week. Some close for lunch. Hours are normally 9am to 6 or 7pm. Stores close during Tet, the new year's celebration, sometime in January or early February. (Tet is lunar, so the date changes every year.) On weekends some stores stay open until 9 or 10pm.

THE ART SCENE

Contemporary art from local artists is not only the rage of Vietnam but also of Hong Kong and other parts of Asia. There are galleries everywhere—entire streets of galleries and neighborhoods of dealers.

You may want to begin to educate your eye to the artists from Vietnam, and the most often displayed styles, while still in Honkers and then hit the streets wide-eyed. Subject matter is split about fifty-fifty between local subjects and abstracts. Remember that shipping becomes an issue with a large picture under your arm. Hanoi has more galleries than HCMC.

I spent about 5 days negotiating over a painting—it was in a big heavy frame, which I obviously didn't want. The only allowance I was given pricewise for the canvas without the frame was $50. Note that it took five different visits and much haggling to get that canvas from $480 to $250. I had it framed at Michaels in my hometown during one of their 50%-off framing specials—now it's in my dining room. When we struck the deal, I paid in cash and the canvas was taken out of the frame, rolled in parchment and put into a tube. I carried it by hand halfway around the world.

I call this the No Name Gallery although it says **Ha Noi Gallery** out front; you will know it as the dive on the corner, directly across the street from the Metropole Hotel. I have bought some wonderful oils here: small-size canvases, maybe 8×8 inches, of flowers in vases for $25 each. These were easy to pack, made wonderful gifts and were not expensive to have framed at Michaels in the U.S.

On many side streets in the heart of the downtown guild district, you will find studios where copy artists are busy at work with a van Gogh or Monet. I spied a not-completed Cezanne that I fell in love with, as it was. The gallery rudely refused to sell it to me in that form.

There are some hotshot galleries with big-time works in various mediums; I like **Bui Gallery** (which also has a gallery in Paris) because they have enormous paintings that make a statement as well as a splash. Go to www.thebuigallery.com.

WEB TIPS 🖰 This particular website is extensive with a blog, press info, events calendar, and plenty of information on the local art scene.

The most famous contemporary art gallery is **Art Viet Nam Gallery** (7 Nguyen Khac Nhu St.; ⓒ 04/3927-2349), where my fellow Texan, Suzanne Lecht, is credited with starting and growing the Vietnam contemporary art scene internationally. She also has a gallery in Austin. **Mai Gallery** and **Apricot Gallery** are two other very well-known and respected galleries.

For yet another vision of the art scene, please note that there is a hot new trend in both original and reproduction worker's posters from the communist era. These works are absolutely gorgeous. The posters are not as large as the Soviet or Chinese ones so they can be easily tubed and carried home and cost about $15 each. Originals cost about $200.

There are assorted styles within this genre. I personally am not interested in Uncle Ho or in giant works with red and black as dominant colors—I like workers in fields, elephants and donkeys, happy workers with big smiles and outstretched arms, and pastel shades. I bought several posters from **Old Propaganda Art,** 122 Hang Bac (© **04/926-2493**).

There is a similar shop nearby, **Propoganda Art,** 17 Nha Chung St.

MARKETS

The **1912 Market** is named for a date in December, so you say "nineteen twelve." It sells everything. And I mean everything, but not the everything you are looking for. It's in a dark alley and, frankly, you can give it a miss. On a charm scale of 1 to 10, I'd give it a minus 10.

Buoi Market is slightly outside of town but very close to West Lake, so it's right in your world of travel. This is a very authentic market, serving the villages built along the north delta where boats once brought merchants and their wares to the communities. There are crafts, fruits, and veggies and more. Avoid the exotic birds because it's heartbreaking and because these days we avoid all birds in Asia for health reasons. And yes, those with black teeth have been hanging out with Bloody Mary and chewing betel nuts. There are also plants and seedlings for sale; these are illegal to bring into the U.S.

Dong Xuan is a series of street markets and market buildings not too far from the cathedral—a tad rough, but very low cost and easy to get to. This is the market you want, just avoid the live-bird portion. One floor is devoted to fabric vendors. Various portions of the outdoor streets are devoted to subject matter of merchandise—china or paper…or anything. This market can get very crowded. I have heard complaints from some people, but I love it.

Cho Hom isn't really a market; it's a street filled with shops in a row, on both sides of the street—all of which sell fabrics. Now here's my favorite part—the fabrics are marked in Vietnamese, which may not be your language of choice. Just sound it out! *Lahn* sounds like "laine" in French, which is wool. See, it's easy. This market is much less junky compared to Dong Xuan and is about 20 minutes farther away from town.

Flower Market is a visual treat but since you really don't need to buy flowers or plants, you might not want to stop. It's right near Long Bien RR Station on the edge of town. If you want to be part of the action, get there at 7am. This market dwindles down during the day and closes by noon.

Pho Hang Dau is a shoe market for those with Vietnamese-size feet.

Long Bien Market is not particularly interesting, although it beats the 1912 Market by a long shot. This is a food and veg market underneath the railroad bridges at Long Bien Station; you will pass it automatically as you drive to West Lake. The really neat thing about this market is that it employs only women as porters.

Night Market is, uh, at night. This is complicated, so please pay attention. As your Shopping Goddess, I will tell you flat out, this is not a good market. But, there's more to it. This is a must do because of the market's location by the lake, the brick-and-mortar stores that stay open into the night, and the little lights strung in the night sky. This isn't about buying much; it's about being out in the streets and part of the adventure. Balloons optional.

STREET VENDORS

Street vendors abound during daylight hours, so I don't mean market vendors here—I mean roving entrepreneurs. Most sell the same old stuff: postcards and guidebooks, along with a few Graham Greene titles (*The Quiet American* is the most popular). The "books," which appear to be photocopies of page proofs or computer printouts, are pretty hard on the eyes and have numerous typos.

INTERNATIONAL BRANDS

Brands are discovering Vietnam and vice versa. Hanoi currently has a short string of brand-name stores ranging from **Pierre Cardin** (which looks nothing like anything you might guess was French) to **L'Occitane,** which is identical to its stores all over the world. The Sofitel Metropole has a very spiffy branch of **Louis Vuitton, Hermès** and several other big–time, who-ha names in a small arcade of luxe stores. There are no bargains. Duh.

WESTERN MERCHANDISE

Most of the hotels have gift shops that sell American and European magazines. The **Press Club,** 59A Ly Thai To, behind the Metropole, sells cookbooks in English and in French. The Metropole has a grocery store that sells French foodstuffs.

HANOI'S BEST SHOPPING STREET

You'll find the best stores, but not necessarily the best prices, on **Nha Tho,** a short street in the heart of the shopping district, on the side of Nha Chung, a more mainstream shopping street. Nha Chung means Church Street; the street runs alongside St. Joseph's Cathedral. The good stores include **Mosaique, Kien Boutique,** and **LaCasa.**

COOKING CLASS

It's the vogue now for many hotels to show off their chefs by allowing them to teach a cooking class. The most famous in town is held Tuesday to Saturday through the Hotel Metropole. The half-day program costs $85 per person; the full day costs $110. On the full day, you go to a Noodle Village. I tried to find a Noodle Village on my own but was unsuccessful. E-mail concierge@sofitelhanooi.vnn.vn or call to reserve © 04/826-6919, ext. 8110.

LOCAL HEROES

Merchandise is very much how you hit it when you visit, so a great source may be great when I visit and not so hot when you visit. The Local Heroes listed below are stores I've shopped in during many visits and they remain consistently good.

The downtown guild streets are very much divided into sections, such as Silk Street, Lacquer Corner, and Sewing Notions Avenue. Go to the district and then keep your eyes open.

Chi Vang Embroidery
63 Hang Gai

This large store is close to the Hilton and the Metropole, but slightly out of the mainstream downtown shopping district. It's worth the walk for the architecture of the building and the merchandise—more chic embroidery than you can imagine, at prices that will make your palms sweat. I saw an entire bed set for $150. Table linens begin at $100. Don't forget to go upstairs to see the house and the merchandise.

Now then, one tacky report: We had a salesgirl who decided to change the price on an item at the cash register. The price was marked in U.S. dollars but she added on a few dollars because the dollar was falling. We walked out. ✆ 844/3828-6576. chivang@fpt.vn.

CoCoon
30 Nha Chung.

I went downright nuts my first time in this store—everything whispered my name, from the shawls to the bathrobes. I bought handbags, tote bags, drawstring silk pouches, and then more bathrobes. I bought so much that I got a 15% discount. I tried to charge it, but the sales clerk was not adept at using Visa and kept saying my card had expired. A few years later, the store was still good, but not as good. You never know until you try. ✆ 844/928-6922.

Khai Silk
121 Nguyen Thai Hoc St.

This is the best-known name in local silks in the country. A few other branches are dotted around town, with another store in HCMC. This is somewhat of a TT (tourist trap) but is nonetheless a good source for everything silk from bathrobes to umbrellas. For me, the clothes on offer are too traditional and not funky enough. Many people love the store. ✆ 04/747-0583.

Marie Linh Home Decor
38 Hang Trong.

Although Mme Linh has two stores that sell fashion, you want to have a look at her home-style and most particularly her lacquer work. I will not say she has the best lacquer in town. I will say hers is totally different from everyone else's and is quite amazing, possibly collectible. © 04/3938-0436. www.marie-linh-design.com.

Minh Ngoc
26 Hang Bong.

Extraordinary smocked and embroidered old-fashioned baby clothes.

Mosaique Decoration
12 Hoa Ma St.

Furniture, tabletop, some fashion—the gamut of locally made chic. Mosaique has other stores around town and a bar. It's a lifestyle thing. © 04/971-3797.

54 Traditions
30 Hang Bun.

This is the most-famous and trusted gallery for handcrafts, tribal arts, and cultural antiques. I am still dreaming of the 2m (7-ft.) long articulated wooden dragon puppet that would be fabulous hanging from my high, high ceiling. The gallery is in a house; you take off your shoes to visit the various rooms, which are organized by subject matter. The owner, Mark Rapoport, is an American, who will arrange shipping for you. His expertise in the works he sells is inspiring. © 04/715-0194. www.54Traditions.com.vn.

Nguyen Frères
3 Phan Chu Trinh St.

Study your copy of the movie *Indochine* and get ready to shop: The style here is pure colonial chic. This is not in the regular downtown shopping area but is within walking distance of the Metropole. It is a house turned into a store that sells home decor—of the glam *Indochine* variety. Remember that lamps are 220-volt and must be converted for the U.S.; furniture has to be shipped. Small items are great for table accessorizing and gift giving. This is one of the most chic stores in the city.

Quang's Ceramic
63 Hang Trong.

This is not a cutie-pie shop and may not really even be a consumer shop—it sort of feels like a hotel supply showroom. Not all of the ceramics are attractive (to my taste), but some of the wares are both stunning and inexpensive. A teapot with six cups was $12 for the set. I bought many things that I swear were twins of items I saw at Armani Casa in Milan. The shop takes credit cards and even shows in Germany. © 04/928-6349. www.quangceramic.com.

Song
27 Pho Nha Tho.

Be still my heart; stop breaking. What was once one of the best stores in the world is now sort of ho-hum. While the merch is chic and elegant and can be amazing, you won't rate this as a life-changing experience. The brainchild of an Australian designer, Song sells home-style, women's fashion, and accessories. Prices are high for the locale, and you can find similar merchandise for less. On the other hand, these guys know style. © 04/928-8733. www.asiasongdesign.com.

Three Trees
Sheraton Hanoi Hotel & Towers, 11 Xuan Dieu St., West Lake.

This is a small jewelry shop outside the Sheraton Hanoi, across the entry from the main lobby. There's gold and diamonds and many very creative pieces, real stuff for around

$200. © 04/719-2438. There is a second shop at 15 Nha Tho St. © 04/928-8725.

Traveler's Tip

FYI, Nha Tho Street (p. 199), which has a Three Trees location, is the best shopping street in town.

Trang & Anh
3 Ly Kuoc Su.

God forgive me for being the type who shares sacred information, but this is the name and address of my wonderful tailor. We've had success in men's tailored shirts, bed quilts, copies of simple linen dresses, and an evening gown or two. Please do not make her work all night on your order. Don't miss her quilted baby jackets, which are ready-made. © **04/826-7122.**

EXCURSION TO BAT TRANG

Once I found out that there was an entire village of ceramics shops, I hired a taxi for the half-day excursion (about $40). The drive took almost an hour. There is a city bus and someday I am going to take it—looks like my kind of fun.

The town is larger than you think, and shopping it all takes a good eye and a strong back. In no time at all, everything starts to look alike. I have heard of people who hated it here, mostly because there is a lot of junk and they don't care if the vases cost $3. I've now been here four times and brought a tour group. I've had the time of my life, although I bought little and was exhausted afterward.

Most members of the tour group felt take-it-or-leave it about the town and none was impressed with the tour by ox cart that I thought would be an amazing novelty. Actually no one cared about the ox after the photo op; they wanted to go shopping and were delighted to buy pottery destined for Provence.

I guess I have a different kind of eye, or maybe it's that I already own a house in Provence, but my interest is in monochromes and I especially like the green that isn't really celadon but looks like it. I did a huge haul at **Phuong Hoa Ceramic Co.** (© 04/874-0883; phuonghoa@fpt.vn).

If you want the ox-cart tour, go to **Minh Hai Ceramic Co.,** Giang Cao, Gia Lam District of Bat Trang (© **04/874-1995;** www.minhhaiceramic.com), which is considered a suburb of Hanoi. (Hey, I'm just the messenger.) To tell the truth, communications with the oxen were a tad difficult; it seems there's no charge for the tour if you buy from the shop. We didn't want to buy from the shop—too touristy—and in the end gave the driver $10.

EXCURSION TO VAN PHUC

I am mentioning this because it may be offered to you and you may shrug and say, "Why not?" Van Phuc is a so-called silk village right outside of town—maybe a 20-minute drive. I found it very, very touristy, and prices are the same as in town. You can tour the factories, and you'll find a little bit of rural charm. But I'd go with the ox carts in Bat Trang (see above).

DEPARTING HANOI

Remember that you are most likely flying to another Asian or European city, so you'll be governed by the kilo weight system, not the piece system. Show an onward-bound ticket for the USA for leniency. If you just came with weekend gear and left everything else in Hong Kong, you can buy inexpensive luggage from one of the shops and stalls on the far side of the lake. You are allowed two valises of 22 kilos (49 lb.) each.

Departure tax is paid after you check your luggage. Note that because Chinese airports now charge their departure tax in a ticket, you may not be used to the concept of "departure tax" or the need to stand in a different line to pay it.

If you have a "through ticket" to the U.S., you will be allowed the weight allowance per your class of service on the long haul. If you are going back to Hong Kong, since the whole idea of this trip was a weekend away, then you have the intra-Asian weight allowance you came with. Now here's the hard part: If you are going on to another Asia destination on a multileg ticket and are at your long-haul weight, you will pay a tremendous amount of overweight surcharge, possibly $200 worth just to get to Bangkok. Honest.

Welcome to Ho Chi Minh City

While the city is called Ho Chi Minh City (HCMC) in newspapers and magazine articles, most people still call it Saigon when they refer to the southern city and former capital of Vietnam.

I am often asked which of the two cities—Hanoi or HCMC—has the better shopping. I invariably say Hanoi, but I think it's just because I have been to Hanoi more often and know it better. Not only is there nothing wrong with the shopping in HCMC, but you also find pretty much the same merchandise as up north and you have the delight of strolling a lovely lantern-lit night market.

You'll find more rebuilt colonial architecture in HCMC than in Hanoi; a bit of a funky, down-home feeling pervades the city and the old airport. But, oh my, do I see a hammer-and-sickle flag flying from yonder flag post?

GETTING THERE

You can actually fly into HCMC nonstop from some European capitals or from the U.S. United and Delta (Northwest) have service, although the Delta flight is from Tokyo and the United flight is from Chicago, making it quite historic. You can also get here from most Asian hub cities such as Hong Kong and Bangkok. In fact, you are little more than an hour or two in flight from everywhere in Asia. (Mind the 1-hr. time change.) Note that in travel, the name of the city will always be HCMC, never Saigon.

Ho Chi Minh City (Saigon)

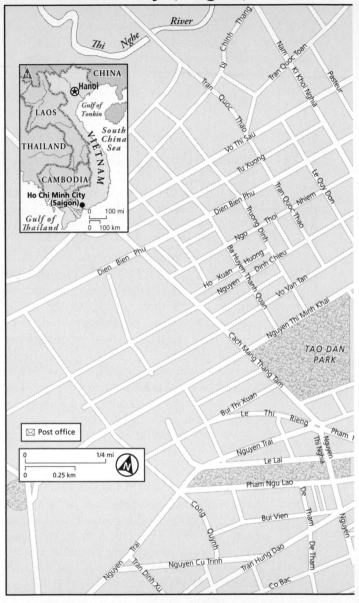

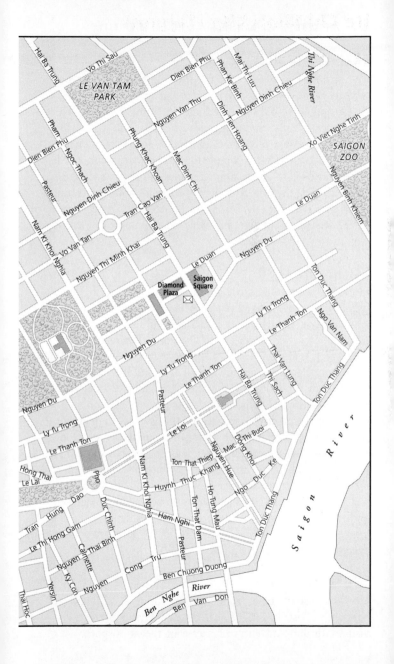

ARRIVING IN HCMC

The airport has two terminals; the international one has recently been renovated and is somewhat spiffy, while domestic remains sorta old fashioned and stuck in, uh, 1975. The old airport was/is charming and adorable, but it is being replaced by a big, modern, 21st-century job, similar to the one in Hanoi. A date for completion has not been announced.

The airport is about 8km (5 miles) from downtown. I loved arriving there because it was so small and simple and thrust you right into the middle of the fantasy. We were met by a hotel representative and whisked right on our way. It was all very Graham Greene.

LAY OF THE LAND

HCMC is a large city (pop. around 7 million) and is divided into districts, sort of like French *arrondissements*. The district system may make sense to a local, but you'll find it a tad disjointed. District 3 is adjacent to District 1; District 10 abuts Districts 3, 1, and 5.

District 1 is the main downtown area and the most likely place to stay and shop. The market, and most of the shopping, is in District 1, which may be written as "D1" on maps.

Just go up and down each street—this is easier than Hanoi, that's for sure. The main shopping thoroughfares are Dong Khoi, HaiBa Trug, Le Thank Ton, and Le Loi. For those in a hurry, Dong Khoi has just about everything you might want, from silks to lacquer. District 5 is a bit out of the way, but it has no tourists and two big markets, one called Chinatown and the other, Cholon, an indoor job for residents. This is a wholesale market where bulks of 10 or 12 units are sold at everyday low prices. Much fun.

SHOPPING HOURS

Stores are usually open from 10am to 10pm, 7/7. The Night Market, in District 1 right near the Ben Thanh Market, is a visually thrilling adventure because of the atmosphere—it's almost like a movie set. The shopping becomes secondary to the outdoor dining, the families on motorbikes, and the softly lit lanterns.

SLEEPING IN HCMC

Caravelle
19 Lom Son, District 1.

Before the Park Hyatt opened, this was the best hotel in town and the most sought after. And for good reason: The location is great (it's across the street from the Park Hyatt), and the hotel not only offers everything you want and need (good eats, nice bar scene, pool, gym), but the rates are also a little lower than average, from $175 to $250. © 848/8243-4999. www.caravellehotel.com.

Intercontinental Asiana Saigon
Hai Ba Rung, Kinho Centre.

This brand new high-rise, newly opened glam spot is a two-tower hotel with residences and regular 4-star hotel joined by dining and modern conveniences and a fabulous concierge. The pastry chef does French pastry as good as in France. It's two blocks from the heart of town; grab new opening rates. © 08/3520-9999. www.ihg.com.

Park Hyatt Saigon
2 Lam Son Sq., District 1.

HCMC has other hotels, but forget about them: This hotel is simply a miracle. If you can't get a room here, change your dates of travel or save your dong until you can spring for the best. This is a modern European-style luxury hotel set into the middle of Asian history.

Within walking distance to everything, the hotel is drop-dead chic, gorgeous, wonderful, heavenly, and is a welcome respite from the buzz of motorcycles outside. Every detail of the hotel is sublime from the room decor to the jazzy little free map of the city they give you to the low-cost dry cleaning. (Send out all your clothes.) The food is great, too; I suggest you eat here at least once a day.

There is a pool, spa, and all the amenities and services you would expect from a five-star property. The hotel is also situated right smack in the middle of everything. U.S. reservations © 800/492-8804. Local © 824-1234. www.saigon.park.hyatt. com.

SNACK & SHOP

I use lunch or between shopping meals as a time to explore the various hotels, some of which are quite famous (don't miss the Rex). One of the most famous luncheon chains in Hanoi also has a restaurant here, **Pho 24,** 5 Nguyen Thiep, District 1, in the thick of the shopping area. Don't miss their baseball cap that says "magnify pho cent."

SHOPPING HCMC

Aside from the magic of HCMC's Night Market, the city is simply not as cute as Hanoi in terms of the shopping atmosphere. The goods are very much the same, but I prefer the ambience of Hanoi.

Several of the best stores in Hanoi also have branches in HCMC. I don't think **Song** here is nearly as good as in Hanoi, but I could have hit it on a bad day—and Song in Hanoi has changed a lot lately so it's not as exciting as it once was either. **Nguyen Frères,** one of the best furniture and home-style shops in Hanoi, also has a branch. **Mosaique** has their flagship here; there are branches of **Khai Silk** and **Ipanema** as well.

I say you'll have a whole lot of fun at the indoor market. The main market building, **Ben Thanh Market,** is filled with stalls selling clothes, souvenirs, silk tops for $5, wigs, makeup, and sunglasses (Ray-Bans, $3). Illegal DVDs tend to be hidden but can be found. There are rows of shoe and handbag dealers. The foodstuffs are to the rear and left—avoid the fish department perhaps.

The scene is great fun and very interactive—more fun than the similar market in Hanoi. When Sarah and I sat down at a stall, tried on wigs, and took turns holding the mirror for the other, a crowd of locals drew around us and cheered the wigs they preferred. Yes, gentlemen do prefer blondes, even in Vietnam.

As you walk the alleys and stalls, shop girls pop up to talk to you. "You my best friend, lady? I like-a you. You good luck. You see my shop?"

Nearby, a few streets are lined with stores. For me, I'll take the string of shops on Le Loi that sells silk and velvet clothing; I'd swear it came from Bergdorf. Try **Orchids,** 84–86 Le Loi St., with three other branches in District 1 as well.

There are art galleries, many of which you will see again or recognize from Hanoi—start at **Apricot Gallery,** which is pricey but puts an international reputation behind their sales. Most major artists are sold in the handful of galleries here, but the real contemporary art scene is in Hanoi, see p. 195.

The most important new address in town is a gallery cum boutique called **Mai on Dong Khai** in the lobby of the Continental Hotel at Opera Square. This showcase to one woman's talent is a case of Bergdorf's meets Anthropologie with a religious creativity that will wow you. The designer began with embroidery on army surplus and went from there.

Chapter 8

Shanghai

Welcome to Shanghai

Shang Ten, everyone, Shang Ten! That's my new motto. If it's 2010, then it's time for World Expo and it's time you got to Shanghai—no excuses.

Shanghai was once the Paris of the West, the Whore of Asia. You should see the old girl now. She is, without a doubt, one of the most exciting cities in the world. And yeah, Barbie—kind of an old girl herself but not an old China hand—has arrived with her own shop.

Westerners are welcome to visit, explore, and check out the surrounding area. Hell, visitors are now even allowed to buy in. The New Shanghai seduces you with the delicious state of euphoria generated by luxury hotels, fine restaurants, clean streets, and fabulous shopping. All those antiques and DVDs can't possibly be fake, can they?

There's dinner for two at about $50 a head at a restaurant that would cost four times that in London or New York; there's the world's largest Louis Vuitton store; there's a brand-new circular train station (South Station) that required the invention of the world's first circular crane for construction to be completed. It looks like a sports stadium ready for the

World Series. This is the train station that will lead you to Hangzhou (p. 264) which I promise, you will love.

If you're expecting a honky-tonk scene or the sing-song girls pictured on cigarette cards and calendars, forget it, pal. Twenty-five new malls opened last year alone. Twelve Carrefour hypermarkets (these are French, *bien sur*) are open as we go to press, with who knows how many by the time you read this. Over 150 hypermarkets from various brands dot the landscape—Wal-Mart has opened less than a mile from Lotus Centre. Hmmm, too bad about my favorite branch of Lotus Centre, but that's another story completely (p. 252). The Pen is in place, yup, Peninsula Hotel just opened and the wonders never cease.

About World Expo

You might not know that Shanghai has its own world fair, called World Expo, right here in PuXi to the tune of 70 million expected visitors. Fair dates are May 1 to October 1, 2010; the theme of the show is somewhat scientific and very green. It will be held on both sides of the Huang Pu River, easy to get to and near great shopping venues. It will be an international binge of pavilions and sites. Hot line: ✆ 8621/962-010. www.expo2010.cn/expoenglish.

Getting There

ARRIVING BY AIR

See chapter 2 for information about carriers and Asian travel details; the information here is more city specific.

Shanghai has two international airports; most international long-haul flights serve the newer one, Pudong. The other airport, Hong Qiao, is more for domestic and nearby destinations. In the next few years, the two airports are expected to welcome some 80 million people a year—each.

You can fly nonstop to Shanghai on transpacific routes from the U.S., transcontinental routes from Europe, transpolar routing from the U.K., and from down under via Dubai or Australia. I frequently go to Shanghai from Hong Kong; there is a **Dragonair** (www.dragonair.com) flight just about every hour. You can also get there through Taipei, on **EVA Air** (www.evaair.com). **American Airlines** has nonstops from Chicago and L.A.; **United** flies from Chicago; **Continental** flies from New York/Newark.

If you arrive in Shanghai from an international destination (including Hong Kong), you will be asked to fill out a landing card and should, of course, already have a visa. You may also have to fill out a health card. The lines move quickly; you will be through immigration in no time, waiting at carousels for your luggage. Luggage carts are available.

About that visa: Don't panic. Under some circumstances, you don't need a visa—if you are in the country fewer than 48 hours with a group (possibly on a cruise) or you hold a passport from 1 of the 17 countries that have recently relaxed their relationship with China and waived the visa requirement. Normally, of course, Americans and Brits do need visas. For more on how to obtain a visa, see p. 18.

The **Pudong International Airport** is one of Shanghai's architectural highlights, with lots of glass and light, reflecting the latest trend in airports that resemble museums. This airport is so well hidden in the middle of nowhere that you may be shocked at how far out it is. Don't worry about the distance, or about the fact that you may have to stand in line for 30 to 50 minutes if you want a legal taxi. You sure don't want an illegal one, so ignore those bozos who ask to ferry you about town.

After clearing formalities, you go to the hotel desk for your transfer—or outside for a taxi. Driving time from the Pudong International Airport to the InterContinental Hotel in Pudong is about 45 minutes, so figure at least an hour to a hotel on the other side of the river—on the Bund or in Shanghai proper.

There is a fast train—one of those fancy maglev jobs—from the Pudong airport right to Pudong. The bad news: This train doesn't go directly to downtown Pudong. It stops at Long Yang Road; you can change there to a train to downtown Pudong or deeper into Shanghai. Besides, you may not arrive with much luggage, but I promise you will leave with more than you can handle on a train.

LOW-COST CARRIERS

Most of the Asian low-cost carriers are based in Bangkok, but local **Shanghai Airlines** (© 021/6255–0550 in Shanghai, © 800/820-1018 elsewhere in China; www.shanghai-air.com) may or may not meet your needs for travel in China. Of course, if you want to go to Bangkok, you're all set with many choices. Try **AirAsia** (© **8659/2516-7777**; www.airasia.com).

ARRIVAL BY CRUISE SHIP

Shanghai's importance to China has always been its port; today many cruise ships call here at a number of berths on the Huangpu River, not that far from where you want to be. A new cruise terminal has been built in what's called the North Bund District. This is the largest terminal in China and it can welcome up to three cruise ships at once. Expect to see ships in the bay (to paraphrase Stephen Sondheim) especially during World Expo 2010. Hey, here's my improved motto: Hang Ten on the Hang Pu!

TRAIN TRAVEL

You may want to travel within China by train—I regularly use the overnight service between Shanghai and Beijing. Whether you are coming or going, your biggest problem will be luggage. I shop, therefore, I schlep.

If you arrive in Shanghai by train, don't plan to meet up with friends for a ride. With four exits, the terminal can be very confusing. (I fear Peter and Louisa are still waiting for me.) However, if you have a cell phone and can relay your car number, you can be met directly on the tracks. We were recently met by the uniformed porters from the Portman Ritz-Carlton and actually burst into tears when we saw them. We were so happy for the help and to escape the stress of the crush to unload baggage.

If you are departing Shanghai by train, don't rush to the station because you will not be allowed out of the lounge area until 30 minutes before the train leaves. The lounge area is quite nice (for China), but you are a long way from done with the journey. You may have to go up an escalator, trek down a hall, climb down sets of stairs, and walk a mile along the plat-form before you find your car. You may find this a rather tense adventure—until you are onboard and marveling at how chic the train is (complete with video screens).

Warning: Last time we did this train, it was disgusting! We got a lemon. Know that it's not all perfect. See p. 275.

Porters are not plentiful and are normally banned from taking you directly to the platform or from actually loading the luggage onto the train for you. This can be overcome with an extra ticket for your porter—I usually buy all four of the beds in a compartment, even if there aren't four of us travel-ing. Those who can easily manage their luggage were not born to shop.

WEB TIPS ⌐ I found this fabu site (www.seat61.com) that offers reports from the so-called man in seat 61. It's in Eng-lish, gives you tons of train info, and will even tell you how to get from Beijing to Shanghai on the train.

Fast Train, Going So Fast

The bullet train to connect Beijing and Shanghai is still a work in progress. This also means no fast train service is available to Hangzhou; see p. 264. I remain hopeful because the Chi-nese can do anything. When this train is operational, travel between these two cities will be 4 hours.

MONEY ON ARRIVAL

If you have not arranged a hotel pickup, which will be charged to your room, you will need yuan for paying your taxi fare. If you don't have any on you, expect a nice long line at the exchange booth. The ATM is at the departure gate.

The Lay of the Land

If you're familiar with Hong Kong, you'll quickly understand my Hong Kong parallels. Pudong is the equivalent of Kowloon—the boomtown on the far side of the river. Today it has an impressive array of towers and tenants, all with breathtaking views of the waterfront promenade known as the Bund. But Pudong is far more than a contained space on the "other side of the river"—it is an enormous metro area and includes much, much more than what we have been led to believe is the sum total of the city. The "new territories" of Pudong are also very convenient to the airport and downtown.

If you've never been to Hong Kong, don't fret. You can still find your way around simply by realizing that the Huang Pu River runs through Shanghai and separates the two parts of town. I use the giant Pearl Tower, which is in Pudong, on the far side of the river, as my visual landmark to know where the river is located and therefore find my way around town.

PuXi lies on the west bank of the Huangpu River. The neighborhoods bear the traces of the original Chinese city (though the walls are long gone) and the foreign concessions, or territories, of the 19th century (the French concession is still the nicest). Despite its size, there actually is a system, especially for the streets in "downtown": North-south streets are named after Chinese provinces, and east-west streets after Chinese cities. Of course, you need to learn your provinces in order to use this information—or keep a map on you at all times.

Shanghai Orientation

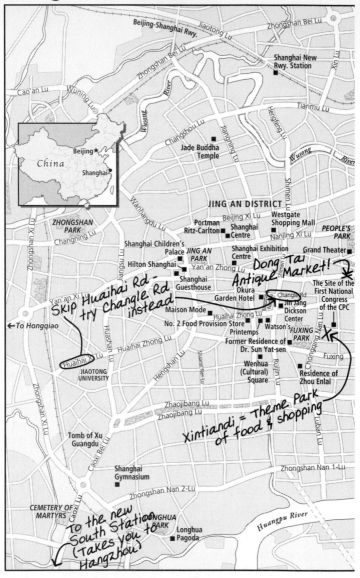

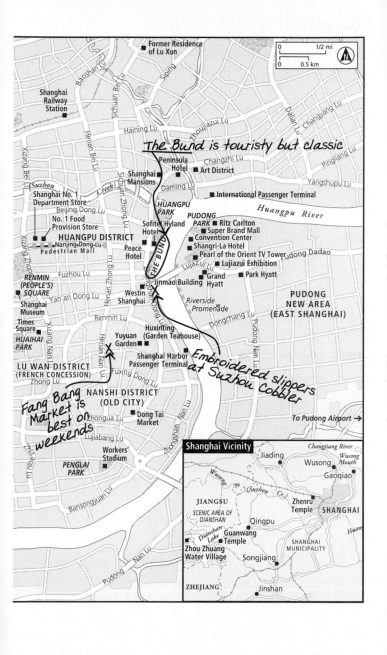

Getting Around

This is an enormous city that is getting bigger as I type. Oops, another high-rise just went up.

Traffic is bad and will only get worse. I recently suffered a shopping adventure outside of town that took over an hour to reach—yet the return trip to my hotel only took 20 minutes. Traffic increases in certain directions at certain times of day—ask.

Even the leap from Pudong into "town" can take time if you get stuck in traffic, so plan ahead.

TAXIS

Taxis are inexpensive and, especially at hotels, plentiful. There are new, clean cars and fleets that can be identified by their livery colors, such as metallic soft green or bordeaux lacquer. The good taxi companies give you a receipt (keep it) and promise that if you were cheated, you will get your money back, plus some. Drivers don't expect to be tipped. You can hail a taxi on the street or find one at any hotel. White gloves are optional but are indicative of a higher level of service.

I stumbled upon a taxi driver with a van I loved, had some Chinese friends make a deal with him, and used him as my private car and driver for $10 an hour.

PRIVATE CARS

Most luxury hotels do a good business in private cars; this pays if you have lots of stops to make or need to be dressed up for appointments. Fees are based on the type of car and length of time; there are also flat fees for airport transfers and for day trips. Half a day in a Lexus costs about $125; a car to Suzhou for the day (and back) is about $300. A private taxi company can also provide a car and driver, but it is unlikely that the driver will speak English.

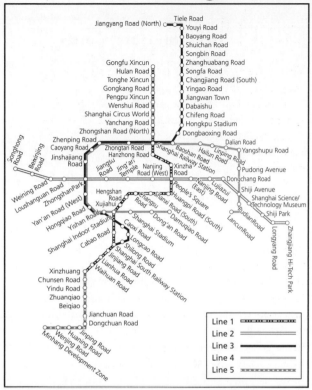

Shanghai Metro

Line 1 ▬▬▬▬▬
Line 2 ═════
Line 3 ▬▬▬▬▬
Line 4 ▬▬▬▬▬
Line 5 ●●●●●

METRO

Shanghai has a great Metro system, and it's growing constantly (see map, above). It now has five lines with an additional four branches—it's busy, it's pushy, it's not as clean as Beijing's Metro, and it's not a summer sport. If you ride during nonrush hours, you should be fine. A different color designates each line. Note that all station names are written in Pinyin and that the Renmin Guangchang station is also called People's Square.

Line 2 serves Pudong and connects the two international airports; in so doing, it connects the two sides of the city. Metro Line 3 is an east-west sort of transverse, all on the PuXi side of the river and crossing the Suchow Creek.

Important: Hotel Cards

No matter where you go or how you get around town, make sure you have one of the hotel cards on you that says "My hotel is...." Hotels give them out by the zillion. Most hotels also have short charts of addresses in English and in Chinese and often also in Pinyin so you can point to where you want to go and show it to the driver. Take it from me: No Chinese person will understand your Pinyin pronunciation of anything more extravagant than hello: nihau ("knee-how").

ABOUT ADDRESSES & GUIDEBOOKS

A guidebook to China is a good starting point, but no guidebook can keep up with the changes in China, especially in Shanghai. Buildings and stores are being torn down in Shanghai so fast that they can disappear overnight.

This problem doesn't exist just with guides; many (maybe most) concierges don't know what's going on either. No one in Shanghai can keep up with the changes. Hearsay—even concierge hearsay—is cheap and cannot be trusted. Sometimes you just have to get out there and see for yourself.

Sleeping in Shanghai

Shanghai has attracted enough business travelers over the last decade to ensure that there are plenty of suitable hotels with Western-style amenities. Just about every big, four-star chain already has at least one hotel here, and it is not unusual for a chain to have a hotel on each side of the river. The fight now isn't over beds; it's over luxury and amenities.

Because Shanghai is so spread out, where you stay can be important to how you feel about the city; on the other hand, where you stay doesn't matter that much because little in Shanghai is within walking distance and taxis are cheap.

The Chain Gang Opens with Deals

Most new hotels offer opening specials and new hotels and chains continue to expand in Shanghai, despite the fact that hotels in Beijing that were built specifically for the Olympics have not been full since the Games.

- When the **Shangri-La**—the first really razzmatazz luxury hotel in Pudong—opened, rates began at $138.
- **Ritz-Carlton** had a summer special for Visa cardholders of $130 per night on the weekend and $150 per night on weekdays. **Ritz-Carlton Pudong** opens in April 2010. **Four Seasons** is working on a second hotel in Shanghai as well.
- **Westin, Sheraton,** and **St. Regis** chains are all part of the **Starwood** group. As a member of AAA (American Automobile Association), I get a coupon for a discount at Starwood hotels if I book 14 days in advance. The Westin had a winter rate of about $200, while the St. Regis—in a far corner of Pudong—was about $180. The **W Hotel** is opening in Pudong as we go to press.

Most of these hotel chains have executive floors with many perks that often make paying more an actual bargain.

Do note that hotels always have promotional rates, depending on their occupancy or whims. Ask.

HOTELS/CENTRAL (PUXI)
Peninsula Hotel Shanghai
32 the Bund; 32 Zhongshan Dang Yi Rd.

Located right off the Bund where the British Embassy once stood, the Peninsula brings all of its charms and wonders to one of the best locations in town—the northern part of the Bund, just south of the creek. The hotel was not open when we traveled through, but as longtime and big-time fans of the Pen Group, we stand by this as a top choice. www.peninsula.com.

Portman Ritz-Carlton

Shanghai Centre, 1376 Nanjing Xi Lu (Metro: Jing An Temple).

This hotel is not the new "it" hotel of the moment—it's one of the first luxury hotels to open in Shanghai and has withstood the test of time. I have been staying here for years and it continues as one of the best hotels in Shanghai. The executive floors offer lounge privileges that really make a difference in the comfort of your stay and more than balance out the price of the upgrade with the perks you gain. There is also an excellent business center and what many expats say is the best hairdresser in town.

The hotel is large, and I think the concierge staff downstairs is overworked, which is one reason it pays to upgrade to a room that has use of a lounge and a private concierge service—which is fabulous.

Regular rooms cost under $200 a night but can go to $400; it's usually about $50 more per night for the club rooms, which pay for themselves in extras. U.S. reservations ✆ 800/241-3333. Local ✆ 021/6279-8888. Fax 021/6279-8887. www.ritzcarlton.com/hotels/shanghai.

Sofitel Hyland Hotel

505 Nanjing Rd. E. (Metro: Renmin Guangchang or He Nan Rd.).

This is one of my secret finds, although since it has just been renovated, the secret could be out. The hotel is small and in one of the most fabulous locations in town—smack-dab in the middle of the shopping district right on Nanjing Road. The hotel is French, has a French GM, and has fabulous croissants (and more, of course). You'll save money by staying here and be treated with tender loving French hands.

Prices are less than at other luxury hotels ($105 on a winter special); I paid $200 for my room on the club floor, which offers many, many perks, making it worth the splurge. Prices are higher in market weeks, during fairs and events.

You can also get a package with the **Sofitel Westlake** in Hangzhou which is very much worth doing, see p. 267. U.S. reservations © **800/SOFITEL** (763-4835). Local © 021/6351-5888. www.accorhotels.com/asia.

HOTELS/PUDONG

Pudong, as mentioned, is gigantic—the two hotels that I have the most experience with, herewith reviewed, are in different parts of Pudong, and there are other parts of Pudong with yet other hotels, some of them very fancy. If you shop by brand and find your favorite is in Pudong, please look at a map to understand where it is. Pudong is not very pedestrian friendly unless you are at the **Shangri-La,** across from a mall.

Before I go rambling on about the new and the now, note that the first luxury hotel in Pudong was the Shangri-La and that it's got a great location and is a super hotel. I've stayed there many times; a lot of businessmen use it too.

InterContinental Hotel Shanghai
777 Zhangyang Rd., Pudong (Metro: Dong Fang).

This hotel looks average from the outside, so step inside for the atrium, the chic Chinese style, and a hidden destination you might not otherwise discover. The hotel is not on the waterfront in Pudong, but it's not inconvenient and the Metro is nearby. And taxis are cheap.

Rooms are large, decor is Chinese modern, and the lounge floor and facilities are excellent. The hotel has a wonderful spa, and good eats are available on the ground floor. It's also far more cozy than most Shanghai hotels. It pays to upgrade to a club lounge room for all the extras.

BEST BUY   Spa packages with four treatments often go for about $130 for 2½ hours of bliss—try to book ahead to help cure jet lag.

Rates on a standard room are about $175 per night; a king-size-bed business suite is $250. U.S. reservations ✆ 800/496-7621. Local ✆ 8621/5835-6666. www.ihg.com.

Park Hyatt Shanghai
Shanghai World Financial Center, 100 Century Ave., Pudong (Metro: Century Ave.).

There are other Hyatt hotels in Shanghai, but there is no other Park Hyatt—nor is there anything in the world like this hotel. This is the one by which you measure all others; this is the one you visit even if you can't stay here. But, if you don't sleep here, you don't get to take the picture from your bed of the crown of the tower, like King Kong, smiling outside in clouds.

The hotel is not in the cluster of luxury hotels around the Pearl Tower, it is set just over a block or two so that you think you can touch the Pearl Tower (and others too) from your window. You can reach out and touch the stars from this hotel—the rest of the stars are guests.

Currently, this is the highest building in town. The hotel is swanky and peacefully decorated in a French-Zen-chinoiserie attitude. The spa is amazing; the corridors are so wide they are divided by bookshelves stacked with, uh, real books. There was no retail when we arrived; maybe soon.

The upper level restaurant is the place to be seen; don't miss the enamel tea caddies in the lobby—they're French, so no, you won't find them in a nearby market. Fashionistas should save up for this experience. Local ✆ 21/6888-1234. www.parkhyattshanghai.com.

Dining in Shanghai

Should you happen to be a street-food person, there are a few streets for wandering and eating your way to heaven...or somewhere. Check out **Wujiang Lu,** near the Shi Men Road Metro station. This is a strolling street—the first part is devoted to Western-style fast-food, and the second part is for local diners who prefer the real thing. Chef Jean-Georges says his street food of choice comes from **Xiang Yang Road,** between Julu and Changle roads.

Shanghai has a growing reputation as the swinging spot in the Pacific Rim, and a lot of this is related to European-style dining. Shanghai could be in London, New York, or Paris.

RESTAURANT CONCEPTS
Three on the Bund

No. 3 the Bund, 3 Zhong Shan Dong Yi Rd., at Guang-dong Rd. (Metro: Renmin Guangchang).

About the address: The building is on the Bund, but the door is on Guangdong Road. About the concept: Until recently, the Bund was best seen in the opening scenes of *Empire of the Sun.* About 10 years ago, an Australian chef by way of Hong Kong opened M on the Bund, the first of the Western-style fusion-chic restaurants—and with a spectacular view. Now the concept has gone further, with the first Western-owned landmark building on the Bund, across the street from M on the Bund in a building that was once "the club" to local foreigners. It's been totally redone—the decor is stunning—with a handful of designer restaurants and the only Evian health and beauty spa this side of France. This is also home to a few stores, including two Armani shops and 3, a designer store on two levels that carries many Euro big names. www.threeonthebund.com.

Make a reservation for all of the Bund's restaurants:

The Cupola: Dinner *à deux*? This is marriage-proposal central. The private dining room in the building's cupola has a view to die for. You ring for the waiter; otherwise, it's private. It is amazingly gorgeous and dreamy. © 021/6321-1101.

Jean-Georges: I visited for lunch, which was a good insight into the fashion scene, but dinner is probably better—for the view and the dress-up version of the fashion scene. The food at either meal is sublime; the bar is a re-creation of the famed Long Bar of Shanghai's storied past—where each man had a position at the bar based on his status in the business world. *Shopper's tip:* There is a prix-fixe lunch, three courses, about $40 that is a must do. Weekend brunch is also a steal. © 021/6321-7733.

Laris: Perhaps this was the most exciting of my meals at Three on the Bund because I already knew the Jean-Georges concept so well from Market in Paris, one of my favorite restaurants. The chef here came from Paris, so there is some crossover in the fusion. (Laris also has a cafe in the new Barbie store. See p. 234.) Don't miss the homemade chocolates after dinner. © 021/6321-9922.

New Heights: This is a bar, cafe, and casual restaurant that includes a terrace—the easy spot to see the view of the Bund and the river and grab a bite without making any big deal out of the event. © 021/6321-0909.

Whampoa Club: This is the Chinese restaurant of the group; I am over the moon for the private rooms for tea service. My lunch here was a tad too Chinese for me, but the place was full, and the locals love it. The decor is gorgeous, the view sublime, and the food creative Shanghainese, by a chef who made his name in Singapore. With six you do *not* get egg roll. © 021/6321-3737.

Xintiandi
Huaihai Rd. E. (Metro: Huang Pi Nan Rd.).

This is a destination, not a restaurant—it's sort of a theme park of great architecture, some stores, and many bars and restaurants. This is surely a must for seeing what's hot. I'd suggest just wandering and picking a restaurant that appeals to you. Or you may prefer to barhop. If you're looking for addresses to check out, there's **Nooch,** 123 Xinye Lu (© 021/6386-1281), and **TMSK,** 11 Beili Lu (© 021/6326-2227), which is best as a bar or a lesson in design. The prices in all the restaurants are more in keeping with New York than China.

MUSEUM DINING CONCEPTS

First things first (I screwed up on this, so there's a chance you will, too): The Shanghai Art Museum and the Shanghai Museum are two different places.

Kathleen5, a restaurant in the Shanghai Art Museum, is the talk of the town. The chef is American-raised Chinese, and this is her fifth restaurant since returning to Shanghai. For off-the-Bund dining, this is the place for taste, view, and new style, complete with a large terrace. Even when the museum is closed, lunch is served; just take the elevator upstairs. *Be warned:* I happened to come here one day and almost left due to language problems, despite a luncheon reservation. A Western menu is available. Shanghai Art Museum, 325 Nanjing Rd. W., Fifth Floor (© **021/6327-2221;** Metro: Renmin Guangchang or Shi Men Rd.).

Nearby is the **Shanghai Museum Café,** located in the Shanghai Museum. This modern cafe is on the ground floor and serves Western-style snacks. It's chic, clean, and convenient. Good bathrooms, too. Figure $15 per head without drinks. Shanghai Museum, 201 Renmin Da Dao (© **021/6372-3500;** Metro: Renmin Guangchang).

Shopping Shanghai

Stores in Shanghai are an incredible jumble of styles. Communist-era shops, however, are disappearing. Shanghai has a far greater rep for trendiness than Beijing—there's lots of fashion, from Euro name brands to Chinese no-names. This is the place to shop for clothing, especially for teens, 'tweens, and others in need of the latest thing.

The flea markets (there are several for antiques) are pure heaven; the museum stores are also good—especially the one at the Shanghai Museum. Most hotels have shops; prices in hotel gift shops are always higher than elsewhere, but at least you don't have to deal with crazy salespeople or bargaining techniques…often hotels have bought with a discerning eye so that the price difference is worth it in editing. There are malls with all the big names; there's shopping and browsing streets; there's old China and new China.

BRAND AWARENESS

Duties on foreign-made merchandise are incredibly high, so brand-name goods sold in China have never offered any value. Although all brands are now available in Shanghai, even Hong Kong is cheaper for such items. In fact, many say that Hong Kong has survived the latest financial downturn because the wealthy Chinese go there to shop.

We all know that China is expected to be the world's largest consumer market. With Shanghai considered a more fashion-motivated city than Beijing, most brands have tried to break into the Shanghai market. The brands already established in both cities often say they have better customers in Beijing and that Shanghai shoppers are too picky. How ya gonna keep 'em down on the farm now that they've seen Peking?

BUND AWARENESS

The Bund is still *the* place to be, to see, and even to dance (ask your concierge about the dance lessons). The big-name stores (Saks) and hotels (the Pen) continue to move into historical buildings and sites, further enriching the scene. If you do nothing else, stroll the Bund and shop at **Shiatzy Chen** (p. 231), and you will understand the new China in a blink.

MONEY MATTERS

See the "Money Matters" section in chapter 2 for a complete discussion of money in China. ATMs are readily available. You should bargain in all markets.

SHIPPING TIPS

DHL: This company has a comprehensive shipping network throughout China and Hong Kong. For Express Centre locations, call © 021/6536-2900 or search www.cn.dhl.com.

UPS Shanghai: To find shipping locations or to arrange for pickup, call © 021/6391-5555.

BEST STORES IN SHANGHAI

Each of these stores is described in "Shanghai Resources A to Z," later in this chapter. But if you're in a hurry, consider these your must sees. They all take plastic.

Hu & Hu

8, Lane 1886, Caobao Lu (no nearby Metro).

Out in the boonies a bit (have your taxi wait), but worth it if you are looking for mostly restored antiques. This large warehouse has incredible home-style. A limited selection of original ancestor scrolls is available, too. An extra shed or two houses stock that you can buy and restore yourself or have restored to your color and finishing choices. The staff will arrange shipping and even send you e-mail photos of pieces that may come in after you've left town. The owner is wonderful and speaks English.

Paterns

19 Fuzhou Rd., Shanghai.

This teeny-weeny boutique is near the Bund and near Suzhou Cobblers. In fact the designer started Suzhou Cobblers. Here she creates her own prints and fabric and then jumbles them together in a Betsey Johnson Goes to China manner in fashions and tote bags and accessories that is creative, endearing, shocking, and delicious. There are also goldfish lanterns that are to yearn for. © 21/6329-9656.

Shiatzy Chen

The Bund, Shanghai.

This is simply one of the most incredible stores you will ever see in your life. Shiatzy Chen is from Taiwan, and her husband is a wealthy garmento. Her work is more sublime than Armani and encompasses men's and women's clothing—both work and dress-up clothes—home-style, and women's accessories.

Suzhou Cobblers

17 Fuzhou Rd. (Metro: Renmin Guangchang).

The world's tiniest store, right off the Bund, sells embroidered slippers in Chinese styles that have been Westernized to the point of high chic. Don't miss it! *Note:* This store is just around the corner from Shiatzy Chen, described above. You can shop online; they will take custom orders. www.suzhou-cobblers.com.

Urban Tribe

133 Fuxing Rd., W.; also Portman Ritz-Carlton Hotel; Lane 248 Tai Kang Rd.; hours of operation vary with each location.

I happen to be a sucker for "tribal" as a fashion statement. In this case, the clothes and accessories are actually classical styles with drape and droop and natural fabrics and a whole lot of style. Excellent for the flawed figure. This is a lifestyle brand. Fuxing Rd. flagship © 021/6433-5366. www.urbantribe.cn.

PUXI SHOPPING NEIGHBORHOODS
ART DISTRICT

Chinese contemporary art has become a huge business; Shanghai has a part of town devoted to galleries and exhibition space although if you start at **Art Scene China,** you are well placed. This district is on the far side of Suchow Creek (p. 239) which isn't very far, but you probably won't walk, although you might from the new Peninsula, maybe. What you want is **Moganshan Road.** Some go directly to **50 Moganshan Road Art Center** to begin explorations of the area; this address is written on most hotel taxi cards. Art Scene China is in no. 50. Note gallery hours are usually daily 11am to 8pm.

A Hong Kong Tailor, at Home in Shanghai

The best tailors in Hong Kong have traditionally been from Shanghai families who fled in 1949. Now they are beginning to come back to serve the new China. **W. W. Chan & Sons,** 129A Mao Ming Rd. (© **021/5404-1469;** www. wwchan.com; Metro: Shi Men Rd.) is one such tailor—one of the big two in Hong Kong (p. 128).

This free-standing store across the street from the Okura Garden Hotel off Huaihai Road is swank and Western and all you need. It offers men's suits, shirts, ties, and such. Prices are about 20% less than in Hong Kong. However, this is also the last of the handmade suits. You may pay $3,000 for it. For an appointment e-mail sales@wwchan.com. This is for serious gentlemen only; this is not the home of the $400 suit. Note: Women's clothing is not made at this branch of W. W. Chan—go to Hong Kong for Irene Fashions.

THE BUND

Located on a bend in the Huangpu River, the Bund is enhanced by the river's natural curve in the heart of what we'd call downtown. It is called *Waitan* in Chinese. There are buildings on one side of the waterfront, then comes the part for cars (some call this a street), and then, right along the quayside, there's a large boardwalk so that one can promenade along the river. Yes, there are guys with cameras who will take your picture for a small fee; it's just like Atlantic City. This is not a great shopping street, but it is an important landmark. *Note:* **Armani** is here as is **Shiatzy Chen** (see above). The side streets jutting away from the river right off the Bund are the ones to watch, starting with Fuchow Street.

HONG QIAO

This area includes the Hong Qiao International Airport, many furniture and antiques warehouses, a mall or two, and huge gated communities where wealthy expats live in either modern high-rises or town houses organized as village developments. Even though traffic can be fierce, if you have any interest in furniture, you won't want to miss this district. This is an area in transition, going from funky to fab on a daily basis. It requires a lot of coming-and-going shopping, which must be done with car and driver; you'll need a list written in Chinese and the ability to be organized, flexible, and a little bold.

Get a taxi to stay with you and wait as you shop.

HUAIHAI ROAD

If you care about your sanity, avoid Huaihai Road (formerly Ave. Joffre to the French, and also written as "Weihai Rd.") on Saturday. This is the main drag of the fashionable French concession and the high street for local fashionistas ages 20 to 30. Most of the stores are either big-name global brands or Chinese inspirations—copies of European trends selling at low Chinese prices, with equally low quality. In no time at all, you can have a Huaihai headache.

But wait—did I tell you that **H&M** has opened? Their first Chinese store opened last year at 645–659 Middle Huaihai Rd. (As we went to press there were four H&M stores in town.) But the clothes are cut to what's called "Asian fit." That means small. And now we have **Barbie Store,** also in Middle Huaihai Road—a big store for a small lady. I am not amused. This store is five stories tall and has a David Laris cafe. Frankly, I just don't get it.

Note: Do a drive-by in a taxi first to find the areas you want to explore on foot. Not only is the street very long, but it also has east and west portions. The western portion has the shops you will be most interested in; the eastern portion is just now getting it together.

JING AN

The Portman Ritz-Carlton, the Four Seasons, and many, many other hotels—and a few shopping malls—are in this part of town. It includes West Nanjing Road and the Shanghai

Jangle My Changle

While staying at the Okura Garden Hotel, I decided to take advantage of the fact that the famed **Huaihai Road** was a block away. This bustling street of consumerism has the reputation of being the "it" road for shopping in Shanghai. What I found was the same-old Western and global stores you find at home—and way too many people.

There were crowds, bad attitudes, and much shoving and pushing—and that was just in Starbucks. I was quickly losing my sanity. Luckily, on the way back to the hotel, I discovered **Changle Road,** a street that anyone could fall in love with. This smaller, less-busy street not only runs east-west, but it also sells East and West stylewise. It parallels Huaihai Road, but it is much more than a parallel universe.

The atmosphere and merchandise in half the shops were funky and trendy. Think Greenwich Village in New York or Melrose Avenue in L.A. The rest of the stores have high-quality, traditional Chinese merchandise—both fashion and accessories. This street is perfect for both the young and the hip or the older and more sophisticated.

More importantly, Changle Road has it all, without lines, crowds, or pushy people. The street is almost as long as Huaihai Road, and the best shopping parts are near the Okura Garden Hotel. There's no bargaining, but prices are more than fair. There are fancy malls nearby. —*Jenny McCormick*

Exhibition Centre, which is across the street from the Portman Ritz-Carlton. This is not much of a funky shopping district, although it has a big mall, **Westgate;** several other malls are building up around here, such as **Plaza 66.**

This part of town is also called Nanjing Road West because the far-reaching Nanjing Road comes up here, but it is not the same animal as the Nanjing Road you will learn to love in the center of town near the Sofitel Hyland Hotel.

Insider's tip: The outlet store for **Lilli's** is in this area; there is also another branch of Lilli's upstairs in the tower housing the Ritz-Carlton, see p. 247.

MAO MING

I'd rather call this a subneighborhood of both Changle Road and Huaihai Road. It is, in fact, a cross street that not only connects these two shopping streets, but is the center of the shopping universe and is home to several of the fanciest Western stores and malls in town.

There's a row of tailor shops directly across from the **Okura Garden Hotel** in the central block. If you want to know how to tackle this area, have your taxi drop you here.

I often use the Okura Garden Hotel as home base for this neighborhood (including Changle Road and Huaihai Road). The hotel has several restaurants, including a Japanese one (duh), which has a bento box lunch that is a real treat. The lobby also has very good shops. Don't miss the souvenir part of the Mitsokoshi Department Store (there are several stores in the lobby)—this is the home to many fine $10 to $15 gift items.

MOVIE LANE

Yeah, sure, you can still bump into vendors of illegal DVDs in all sorts of shopping situations. The true sport is to go to this 1-block lane (right near the Four Seasons Hotel) and shop the half dozen or so stores that sell DVDs and CDs. The official name of this street is **Da Gu Lane** and it is upmarket and somewhat small-town Midwestern USA residential and exactly where you wouldn't mind living. The stores are bright and clean; the clerks all speak English. Hours are usually 10am to midnight.

The stores do have different merchandise, so please see more than one. Most movies are in English, but there are international sections for perhaps a dozen different languages. Among the delights of shopping in this area is the ability to find many BBC series (all with Judi Dench) and get some classic French films (alas, in French). Try **Movie House,** 391 Da Gu Rd. (© 21/6327-5022); open 9am to midnight. I also like **Le Ka De Club,** 378 Da Gu Rd. (© 6340-0451); open 10am to 1am. You can get a taxi on the nearby main road.

THE BUND PROMENADE
Zhongshan Dong Yi Lu
Peace Hotel
Sichuan Lu
Jangxi Lu
Henan Zhong Lu
Shanxi Nan Lu
Fujian Zhong Lu
Guang Bei Lu
Like Shanghai's own Harrod's
Xizang Zhong Lu
Pacific Hotel
Huanghe Lu
Huangpu Bei Lu
Xi Lu
Chengdu Bei Lu
"Fenshine Market"
Nanjing
Shimen Lu
Shimen Yi Lu
Maoming Lu
Shaanxi Bei Lu
Portman Ritz Carlton
Jing An Temple
Jing An Si

Feng Xiang Market **14**
Nanjing Road Pedestrian Mall **6**
No. 1 Food Provision Store **4**
Plaza 66 mall **10**
Peninsula Hotel **13**
Shanghai Arts &
    Crafts Center **8**
Shanghai Centre
    (Portman Ritz-Carlton) **11**
Shanghai City of Books **3**
Shanghai Exhibition Centre **12**
Shanghai Number One
    Department Store **5**
Shiatzy-Chen **1**
Sofitel Hyland Hotel **7**
Three on the Bund **2**
Westgate Shopping Mall **9**

Ⓜ **Metro station**

Area of detail

JING AN DISTRICT
HUANGPU DISTRICT
PUDONG NEW AREA (EAST SHANGHAI)
LU WAN DISTRICT
NANSHI DISTRICT (OLD TOWN)
Shanghai

NANJING ROAD PEDESTRIAN STREET

Perhaps the most famous street in Shanghai after the Bund, Nanjing Road is also the city's main shopping drag, despite its enormous length (over 10km/6¼ miles). Much of the main shopping district is a pedestrian mall. Don't miss this at night—stores are open until 10pm. If you plan to have a stroll to see a good bit of this famous street, begin at the Bund and the Peace Hotel (be sure to see the renovation at Peace Hotel). After a few banks and hotels and after you cross Shanxi Road, you'll be in the heart of the pedestrian mall and shopping greats. This is the eastern part of Nanjing Road. It is not really within walking distance of the western portion of Nanjing Road which is where you find the Portman Ritz-Carlton.

In the eastern district, you'll find everything from silk shops to TTs (tourist traps), to pearl shops, to stores that specialize in gadgets or sports equipment. There's Western style, Eastern style, and no style whatsoever. But plenty of McDonald's and big bright lights. *Note:* In between the neon and the teenagers are some old-fashioned Chinese stores, just like the ones you won't find back home.

NANJING ROAD EAST

I understand that all these locations and directions for Nanjing Road are very confusing and I am sorry about that. Life is confusing, cope. I will only tell you about one address on Nanjing Road East and it is specifically because of this building that I even include this part of town as an important shopping neighborhood. Remember the name **Fenshine** and see p. 251 for more.

NANJING ROAD WEST

See "Jing An," above for the area also known as Nanjing Road West.

OLD CITY

This is the name most often given to the oldest part of town, which is also known as **Nanshi.** This was the Chinese city in the days of the foreign concessions. It was walled many years ago. The wall is quickly being torn down and replaced with the new China, but some quaint winding roads, alleys, and tin shanties remain to fill you with glee.

The Old City is home to the **Dong Tai Antiques Market,** which feels a lot more authentic than just about any other part of town. Also here are the **Yuyuan Gardens,** a Disney-meets-Chinatown parcel of land with buildings and gardens, a teahouse, a temple, a market, and antiques stores. It's the city's number-one tourist attraction—and for good reason, although I am sick at just how touristy this area has become.

SOUTH BUND

This is one of my made-up names, so don't panic; it will not remind you of South Bend, Indiana. There is a large redevelopment area called South Bund, which has been made ready for World Expo 2010. In the traffic and the construction and the new buildings, there are two fabric markets that are very much worth your time. Okay, one of them may be touristy (**Spinning Market**) but the **Shi Lui Pi Market** is a big-time favorite of ours. See p. 249 for the differences between the two and directions to each.

SUCHOW CREEK

Back in the old days, the international concessions ended at the Suchow River at Henan Nan Lu, just north of the Bund. That area is now being turned into a hot new enclave for artists, and warehouses are filled with ateliers.

Note: Do not get the area known as Suchow Creek mixed up with the city named Suchow, aka Suzhou (p. 261), even though the creek once was a river that connected the two.

A fairly large market (lotsa fakes and much junk) is in this area; it's called **QiPu Market** because, yup, it's on QiPu Road. Take Henan Nan Lu north from the Bund, cross the creek, and turn left on QiPu Road. *Xie xie.*

TAIKANG ROAD

This is perhaps the most-charming part of the shopping scene in Shanghai. A few stores are actually located on Taikang Road itself, but you will be sorely disappointed if you don't go into the little lanes: The shops, many of them in restored buildings, are chockablock cute. There are cafes, too.

The lanes, like all proper Asian lanes, have numbers, not names. You'll want to pay attention to several of them. Lane 248 is indeed an alley—mostly pedestrian traffic, although a car can catch you off guard. I like Lane 210 the best; most taxi cards are marked with 210 Taikang in Chinese.

Ask the taxi driver to drop you at the main road where it intersects with this series of lanes; if you want an exact starting point, head to **Suzaar,** Lane 210, Taikang Rd., building 5, room 108 (© **8621/6473-4388**), or **ShirtFlag,** No. 7, Lane 210, Taikang Rd., room 8 (© **8621/6466-7009**).

Note: Stores typically open around 11am and stay open until 8 or 9pm. You can easily hail taxis on this main street when you are ready to depart.

XINTIANDI

Xintiandi is in the French concession and resembles a film set or an American festival marketplace, although it was built with Hong Kong money. It is said to be a restoration of old houses, converted to stores and restaurants. The feel is nothing like Colonial Williamsburg or even Disney but is wall-to-wall charm with tons of hot design looks in the use of tiles, inventive seating, and unusual light fixtures. In short, this is a village of cutting-edge chic.

This complex—a true must do—is at the eastern end of Huaihai Road, a part of town where redevelopment began only recently. Office buildings have arrived; luxury housing is expected soon. The bars are downright inspirational, from a design point of view. In a not-so-obvious part of the complex, you'll find the design atelier of **Xavier** (p. 247), one of the leading style mavens of the city. Just taxi on over here at least once, and surely for a meal—it's especially nice at night, and the stores are open 'til about 10pm.

Also note that several new hotels are springing up here, the Conrad is on hold but look at the **Landis Skyway Hotel.**

PUDONG SHOPPING NEIGHBORHOODS

Pudong isn't really a neighborhood, it's a big district with many neighborhoods. It is sometimes written as "Putong."

DOWNTOWN PUDONG

Maybe I am the only one who calls this "downtown," but as an American shopper, when you see the lay of the land, you will get the gist. The business district of Pudong is called **Lu Jia Zui;** the Stock Exchange is here, as are many main offices of the big banks, the Jin Mao Tower, the Shangri-La Hotel, and, of course, the Pearl TV Tower. In short, tourists call it Pudong and some business guys call it Lu Jia Zui.

Whether you stay in this part of town or not, you must, must, must come over and get a view of the Bund at night.

The main shopping portion of this area is the Brand Name Mall, which is pretty much your standard Chinese mall. It has a Sephora in it (many Chinese brands here) as well as a food court and a small branch of **Lotus Centre,** a supermarket owned in partnership with Tesco (U.K.). This supermarket has changed a lot in recent years and I don't like it as much as I once did, but it's still fun. It's in the basement of the mall.

HUAMU

Whoooaaa, I mention this because it's my job to tell you. Once you know, you can ignore it. This interesting part of Pudong is interesting because of the fabulous Science and Technology Museum. Across the yard from the museum is a Metro station inside of which there is a "market." It is about the worst market I have ever been to. It is sometimes referred to as Pudong Fakes Market. I'd give it a miss.

YANGSI & NANMATOU

This is the Pudong side of the river between Central PuXi and the South Bund area and part of the site for World Expo 2010. Nanmatou is the portion just south of the Nanpu Bridge. This bridge is easy to spot because of its construction and is a landmark to where you are, especially because it is in the heart of the expo sites.

Shanghai Resources A to Z

Note: If you don't find listings here that are mentioned in other guidebooks, there's a good reason. Maybe the stores no longer exist, or maybe I didn't think them worth your time, or maybe something else happened. I recommend all of the following.

ANTIQUES MARKETS

If you go to Shanghai for one shopping experience, it has to be for buying antiques, both small decorative pieces and furniture. The antiques markets are heaven, and the prices are so low you will want to weep. There are also good markets in Beijing, so don't blow your wad. Remember, most of this stuff is fake; trust no one. But if you see any more of those pewter and ceramic bowls, get me a few, please.

Dong Tai Market

Dong Tai Lu (no nearby Metro).

This is one of my favorite addresses in Shanghai, where I want to buy out all of the stalls. An outdoorsy type of thing, the market is not particularly large and takes place on just two perpendicular streets. The vendors sell from wagons or little trailers; there are a few shops. Not too many dealers speak English, but I didn't find that to be a problem.

Whatever you do, the first time you fall in love with an item, price it but don't buy. You tend to see a lot of similar things, and prices can vary dramatically—even without bargaining. I almost bought a set of three blue-and-white ceramic men for $100. I figured I could get them for $50 and liked the idea a whole lot. I didn't do it because they were hard to pack. Days later I found them, priced at $50 for the set of three, at a fancy hotel gift shop. The market price should have been $30!

Fang Bang Market/Shanghai Old Street

Henan Nan Lu and Fuxing Zhong Lu/Fang Bang Zhong Lu (no nearby Metro).

I have seen this market written as **"FuYu Market,"** and I bet you know what I have to say to that. But then, who cares? This is an amazing market if you go on a weekend.

Shanghai Old Street is a very commercial section that looks almost like a festival marketplace from a bad American mall, with carts in the street and vendors selling baskets and kites. The closer you get to Henan Nan Lu (and the farther from Yuyuan), the more it turns into something that feels like an authentic neighborhood. Finally you get to a dumpy little building that will surely be condemned soon. This is the home of the Fang Bang Market. On weekends there are antiques in the street and more dealers sitting on the curbs bearing tote bags crammed with hot or fake (or both) Ming vases that they will try to entice you to buy.

The market takes place every day. *But* it's not very good on weekdays, when only about 30% of the vendors show up. On weekends, especially Sunday, it is crammed and quite the scene.

To get here, I suggest a taxi to the Henan Nan Lu side (after 11am on weekdays, 9am on weekends). Or walk from the **Haobao Building** (see below). Look for rather touristy torii gates and a pedestrian shopping street. Before your eye can figure out which part is real and which is stagecraft, you see the dealers and spy the heaps of delicious junk, on the curbs and falling out of stalls and tiny shops. They're to your left if your back is to the torii gate and Henan Nan Lu.

Haobao Building
Yuyuan Gardens (no nearby Metro).

Many people don't even know that there is an antiques mart within the "village" of the gardens, or another one a few blocks away. This market has changed in recent years and now leans toward the Tibetan. The prices on antique silk garments and other items here are so low that I became giddy on my first trip; I touched and tried on everything from padded silk jackets in dusty mauve to small embroidered pockets (popular because Chinese clothes do not come with pockets). Bargain like mad. Many dealers speak English.

ARTS & CRAFTS
Friendship Store
68 East Jinling Lu (Metro: Middle Henan Nan Lu).

I write this with a heavy heart as the Friendship Stores are not as good as they used to be, and the mother of all Friendship

Stores in Shanghai is a bit out of the way from the normal tourist thrust. This is the state-owned department store of everything Chinese. It is large, and the area is interesting to me, sort of middle–class, downtownish, and real Chinese. The hours are 9:30am to 9:30pm. I like to do this at night, seeing the shoppers doing their afterwork bustling around, and eat around here in any old crowded place with lotsa neon.

If you haven't been to Shanghai in a while, note that the old Friendship Store has been torn down to make space for the new Peninsula Hotel.

Shanghai Arts & Crafts Center
190–208 Nanjing Rd. E. (Metro: Henan Rd.).

Four floors of fun—every type of crafts product you can imagine is sold here, including silk by the bolt and all sorts of silk products. I bought printed silk scarves and cut-velvet silk scarves. The pajamas were rather expensive; no one at home would ever believe you paid that much ($85–$100) for them.

Suzhou Cobblers
17 Fuzhou Rd. (Metro: Renmin Guangchang).

This is the cutest little store in Shanghai. It sells amazing embroidered shoes of a quality far above souvenir slippers, and the designs employ modern motifs. My favorite is the green satin with bok choy dancing across the toes. Prices are about $50 to $75 per pair. Horribly chic; an undeniable must have. The store offers a few tote bags and handbags also and see p. 231 for information about the clothing and fabric location, Paterns.

BOOKS
If you stroll the midsection of Fuzhou Lu, on what was once called Culture Street, you will find an entire street of Chinese booksellers. I like a small chain called **Shanghai City of Books;** there's one on Nanjing Road near the entrance to the Hyland Sofitel and another on the above-mentioned Fuzhou

Lu (no. 465). You can find legal CDs and DVDs here at low prices. Fuzhou Lu is a good stroll because it starts at the Bund, has some fabulous shops for the first 2 blocks, and then turns into books and art and culture.

Chaterhouse

Shanghai Centre (next to the Portman Ritz-Carlton); Shanghai Times Square Mall; Super Brand Mall (Pudong).

This is a British-style bookstore where most titles are in English but you will find some other languages, such as French or Italian. Good for bestsellers, guidebooks, maps, and the famed taxi book (p. 34).

CERAMICS

Haichen Ceramics

17 Fuzhou Rd. (Metro: East Nanjing Rd.).

This tiny store is next-door to Suzhou Cobblers, a few meters off the Bund, so you have no excuse to miss it. I realize that packing and schlepping breakables is annoying, but several items here are not only stunning but also well worth the trouble. Check out the mugs with Chinese tassels attached. © 8621/6323-0856. haichenceramics@hotmail.com.

Spin

758 Julu Lu, building 3 (Metro: Changshu Lu).

Japanese restaurateurs began to have their simple and classic styles made locally, and *voilà*, now a shop. If you don't feel comfortable sending home a set of dishes, look at the platters or the teapots. For about $100, you can get an eat-your-heart-out Martha Stewart teapot with teacups. © 8621/6279-2545.

CHINESE STYLE (SERIOUS STUFF)

Shanghai Tang

Jin Jang Hotel, 59 Mao Ming Rd. (Metro: Shi Men Rd.); Xintiandi, 15 North Block, 181 Tai Cang Rd. (no nearby Metro).

The selection here is not as good as in Hong Kong. The style is fabulous, but the prices are high. Check out the cashmere Mao sweaters. There are a few stores dotted around town. *Shopper's tip:* Go with your eyes on fine-tune and then go to the fabric markets and have this style copied for $30 to $50. Ooops, did I say that? www.shanghaitang.com.

Shiatzy Chen
9 the Bund, 9 Zhongshan Dong Yi Rd. (Metro: Henan Rd.).

The first time I visited this store I was so profoundly moved that I booked air tickets to Taiwan to see the mother store (p. 231). As it turns out, the flagship is nowhere near as glam as this temple to men's, women's, home, and accessory styles. No stroll on the Bund is complete without a stop here. Classic Chinese styles are whipped together with couture and high fashion to create timeless beauty. Figure on prices to be $1,000 and up (although I did buy a blazer for $450 on sale in Taipei). There is also a small branch on Mao Ming Nan Lu near Changle. It is open 10am to 10pm. © 8621/6321-9155. www.shiatzychen.com.

Zhang's Textiles
Shanghai Centre, Nanjing Xi Lu (Metro: Jiang An Temple).

This place offers antique textiles for collectors. The most famous dealer in China, Zhang's also does business in Beijing.

DEPARTMENT STORES
Isetan
1038 Nanjing Xi Lu W. (Metro: Jing An Temple).

This branch of Isetan is about 1 block from the Portman Ritz-Carlton in a modern, Western-style mall that was recently remodeled and filled with big-name stores. Isetan is a Japanese department store known for younger brands, kickier fashions, and lower prices than some of the other Japanese department stores. Not only does it carry an international lineup of brands, but also many name (such as Michel Klein) specialty lines, and there are many super brands you just haven't ever seen before. Large sizes need not apply.

Yuyuan Department Store
Yuyuan Gardens (no nearby Metro).

I discovered this department store by accident while shopping at the downstairs flea market. It not only has a good fabric department, but the staff also bargained with me while the salesgirls fought each other for my business. I paid $12 per meter for silk *dévoré* (cut velvet).

DESIGNERS/LOCAL TALENT

European and international designer stores are popping up everywhere, especially in hotel lobbies and big, fat malls. Prices are at least 20% more than in Hong Kong and may be even higher compared to your local mall in Hometown, USA. And did you really come to China to see Louis Vuitton?

But wait! There are a few hidden resources. You might not know about **Xavier** (www.xavier.cn). As an important design fixture in Shanghai for 20 years, Anthony, Xavier's British designer, was well positioned to become one of the best-known and most-influential designers in town. Then all the new money showed up, hungry for feathers, Art Deco, and high style, and... *vavavavroom*! Anthony designs ready-to-wear, accessories, bridal, some furs, and, of course, bespoke. Boutique: 181 Taicang Rd., unit 2, no. 15 (© **8621/6328-7111**). Studio: 119 Madang Rd., unit 603 (© **8621/6385-1155**).

Now I have a most curious tale of the brand **Lilli's,** which I first discovered in a variety of upmarket hotel gift shops and went wild over: accessories and fun stuff with a Chinese twist, but very sophisticated. I was very excited to find the Lilli's outlet store (not far from Portman Ritz-Carlton) and terribly upset with the merchandise inside it. When I thought all was lost, I found amazing little mesh zip bags trimmed off with Chinese pattern silks in the gift shop at the Okura Garden Hotel. These cost $10 and made wonderful gifts because they seem so unique and chic. There was nothing to want in the outlet and everything to covet in the gift shop.

The outlet/showroom: Maosheng Mansion (this appears to be an apartment building), 1051 Xin Zha Rd., 1-D (© 21/6215-5031). There's another, smaller, showroom inside the Shanghai Centre (Portman Ritz-Carlton), no. 602.

I also like **Annabel Lee,** who does a very different kind of look—less edgy, softer, and very chic—in both home-style and accessories. I bought a white shirt from her that was totally simple but the buttons were tiny green jade discs. Her designs are sold in various hotel gift shops or in her own flagship store, Zhongshun Dong Yi Lu, Lane 8, no. 1 (© 8621/6445-8218; www.annabel-lee.com), slightly after no. 3 on the Bund, but before the Peace Hotel. She also has a small shop in **Xintandi.**

WEB TIPS 🖑 The website comes up in English but you can switch to Chinese or Japanese as desired. You get to see enough of the merchandise to understand what she makes before you get to China, which is helpful. This is not touristy stuff.

Finally we get to my heroine, **Denise Huang,** who began **Suzhou Cobblers** (p. 232) and now has a new shop for style, **Paterns** (p. 231). E-mail her at suzhou_cobblers@yahoo.com.

DRUGSTORES
Watson's, the Chemist
Huaihai Rd. W. (no nearby Metro); also Super Brand Mall, Pudong, and other locations.

Americans would call this a full-service drugstore. I spend a few minutes each day loading up on candy bars and soft drinks, Watson's brand of bottled water, some health and beauty products, medicines (often without Rx), and gadgets. Avoid U.S.- and European-brand makeup and fragrances, which are stunningly expensive. I've bought many marvelous

$3 gifts here for my friends; the gifts look like they're worth at least $5, maybe more.

DVDS

Do not finish reading this book. Walk out of your hotel, flag a taxi, and head to **Da Gu Road.** (It's near the Four Season's Hotel and not far from the Portman Ritz-Carlton.) Turn to p. 236 while you are on your way there.

FABRICS
Shanghai Shi Lui Pi Cloth Market
168 Dong Men Rd. (no nearby Metro).

This market isn't showy; it doesn't have a lot of space or a lot of tourists. It is quietly sublime and our new number-one choice for fabrics and for tailoring. There are four floors and you will have to do your own explorations and poking around. Do not expect too much English spoken by tailors.

The tailor I use is in room 244 (2nd floor) where I pick fabric and have them make me a rather standard Mao jacket. I had them copy one I loved and then had one made-to-order. They cost the same price ($30) but the made-to-order fit a lot better. (Duh.)

One of the vendors here just sells linen and only makes Mao jackets from sherbet-toned linens a la Shanghai Tang. Of course you can pick whatever colors you want, but you may need a dozen since narrowing it down is nearly impossible. These jackets also cost $30 when finished. They are reversible, so you pick two colors—get it?

On yet another floor, I found a purple cashmere cocoon jacket for a girlfriend in New York who actually asked me to find something like this for her. It cost $50.

We had 24-hour service from our tailor and paid $5 extra for Pudong delivery to our hotel on a Sunday.

Traveler's Tip

Now, some geographic references: Lujiabang is a major thoroughfare that comes off the Nanpu Bridge; Zhonghua Road runs along side it, to the north. You get to the Shanghai Shi Lui Pi Cloth Market by way of Zhonghua Road. It and the Shanghai South Bund Soft Spinning Material Market (below) are close enough to walk between, or have a car wait for you.

Shanghai South Bund Soft Spinning Material Market

399 Lujiabang Lu (Metro: Nanpu Bridge).

This is not an easy confession. I loved this mall of materials and tailors and shopping ops when it opened, but I was so horrified with it on the last visit that I returned two more times to make certain of myself. I know things change, and you may have luck here—there sure are a lot of tourists around, so somebody has found this place. There are floors and floors of vendors, and you can bargain a little bit. My favorites are the totes, handbags, and gift items on the ground floor.

Silk King

819 Nanjing Xi Lu (Metro: Henan Rd.), and other locations.

The stores in this chain vary with the location. They are easy to shop; usually at least one salesperson speaks English. Prices are higher than in the fabric market, but the store is almost Western in style and is right in the thick of tourist land. You'll pay $10 to $15 per yard for silk, so there are no immediate bargains. It also has tailors. The Nanjing Xi Lu location is open 9:30am to 10pm. Other branches (there are 10 locations in Shanghai) may have different hours. ✆ **21/6215-0706.**

Zhang Yan Juan

Wife Ding Cloth Store, 438 Fang Bang Zhong Lu (no nearby Metro).

This store is part of a development called Old Shanghai Street, which I adore. The store features only fabric and items made of the fabric in the homespun blue cloth of the Henan region of China. For blue-and-white freaks, this is really a find.

FAKES

Oy vey, as we say in French. Talking about fakes in China is like discussing real estate in Manhattan—still a hot topic but there's not much good stuff out there. With the demise of the HuaiHai Road flea market several years ago, several markets for fakes have popped up in oddball locations. One of them was so bad that we were goofy with laughter. The other was easy and fun to shop. Not that we would ever buy anything, of course.

THE GOOD MARKET

Feng Xiang Market
580 Nanjing Rd. W. (Metro: West Nanjing Rd.).

This market is sometimes written as "Fenshine Market" in Pinyin or on taxi cards. Let me count the ways this market makes your life easy: The bathrooms are clean; the market is right on Nanjing Road in the heart of "downtown"; the market sells just about everything; and the fakes part of the business is just scary enough to be fun. Almost all vendors have fake doors that lead to inner chambers; some doors lead to other doors, which lead to…well you get the idea. In the end, everything leads to Louis Vuitton.

As in all markets like this, you find a dealer you like for some reason, glom on hard, and bargain like crazy. We got your basic designer tote to $50 and handbag to about $100. The Mulberry-style bag for $100 turned out to be better made and more stunning than anything we later found in Italy shy of about $2,000. Honest.

Buyer Beware

To add to the fakes confusion at Feng Xiang: Sarah and I bought identical watches from the same guy. Mine has never worked. Sarah's keeps on ticking. I paid about $150 for my watch and do not find this funny.

THE BAD MARKET
Yatai Yinyang/Pudong Fakes Market
(Metro: Science & Technology Museum).

Oy vey! Despite whatever you read or hear from others, trust us on this one—come out here for the Science & Technology Museum. Do not come for the market. This is a $15 taxi ride from the heart of Pudong (although you can come on the Metro) and is junky enough to bring you to tears of frustration. Should you have fond memories of the old market on Huaihai Road and ask someone what happened to it and be directed here—forget it! It is open daily from 10am to 6pm.

FOODSTUFFS
Lotus Centre
Super Brand Mall, Pudong (Metro: Lu Jia Zui).

This was created in partnership with the U.K.'s Tesco and is not nearly the fun it used to be (at least, at this location). There is a floor of groceries and if you want to browse or shop, go for it. I used to bring tour groups here, so the changes have made me weep with despair. Now it's just a supermarket in Pudong.

No. 1 Food Provision Store
720 Nanjing Rd. E. (Metro: Renmin Guangchang).

This just might be my favorite store in Shanghai. It is on the pedestrian mall part of Nanjing Road and is open in the evening, so you can come here for a nighttime stroll. The store is large, in the colonial European architectural style, but only two stories high. The ground floor sells fresh produce, dried fruit, liquor, and gift baskets. It's like Harrods Food Hall in Shanghai. All signs are in Chinese (no Pinyin, even). Upstairs there's a supermarket.

No. 2 Food Provision Store
887 Huaihai Rd. W. (Metro: Shan Xi Nan Rd.).

This store is smaller than No. 1, not nearly as much fun, and somewhat ruined by the enormous KFC sign out front. It's worth a visit if you are strolling this part of Huaihai Road and haven't been spoiled by No. 1.

FURNITURE

There are so many furniture warehouses in Shanghai that you will go nuts with greed and desire (at least, I did). In terms of bargaining on final price and making shipping arrangements, it's easiest to give all your business to one dealer.

You'll pass many furniture warehouses as you drive into town from the Hong Qiao Airport—Hong Qiao is the main district for antiques furniture warehouses, but not the only one.

Note that many an expat has taken furniture back to a different climate in the United States, only to have it crack during the first winter. Consider buying a humidifier once in the U.S.

If you plan to ship your purchases, consider several factors: Prices on shipping are not that high, and you will be impressed. However, prices on clearing goods through a Customs broker and trucking from the port of entry may be obscene. I paid $125 to ship a piece and an additional $425 to have it delivered, a mere 161km (100 miles) from the port.

And speaking of money: While I found prices in Shanghai laughably inexpensive, dealers say that outside of town there are warehouses that are even cheaper, such as **Nineteen Town,** 19 Jin Xin Lu, Jiu Ting. Needless to say, the farther off the beaten path you wander, the more you need a translator.

G-E Tang Antiques
8 Hu Qing Ping Hwy. (no nearby Metro).

This establishment is extremely tourist oriented; it has a website (www.getang.com), advertises in the city's freebie tourist map, and has a reputation among visitors and expats. There's even a most-impressive English-language brochure.

The shop is very chic and sleek; the young men who work here could have stepped out of an Armani showroom. Many speak English. The goods are gorgeous (too gorgeous—and too expensive—for my taste).

I asked the staff to show me the junk and was led to a warehouse of unrestored furniture in the rear. This was much more fun. I was quoted various prices for the same piece—as is, cleaned up, or restored. Shipping usually doubles the cost, and—having seen the quality of the pieces before they were restored—I simply didn't think they were worth it.

The place is very seductive—and a good starting point as you learn what you want and what you want to spend. ✆ 6268-5968.

WEB TIPS 🖱 This is an excellent website that even answers questions like "Are the antiques fake?" and has an online boutique. www.getang.com.

Henry Antique Warehouse
359 Hongzhong Lu (Metro: Xujiahui).

This is an enormous warehouse with excellent salespeople. There are more than 2,000 pieces of furniture on hand. They have been restored and, yes, you will want them all. Due to the incoming, ongoing Metro construction, the warehouse moved since we were here last. It is open daily 9am to 6pm. It accepts all major credit cards; international shipping is available. ✆ 8621/6401-0831. henryantique@eastday.com.

Hu & Hu Antiques
8 Lane 1886, Caobao Lu (no nearby Metro).

First off, one Hu is a Chinese woman named Marybelle Hu, who attended Smith College and has since come back to China. I hope she gets into politics and becomes president, or whatever China has—empress? She worked for Sotheby's and obviously knows everything and can explain it to you in flawless English. Her organizational skills are amazing; the store functions like a professional New York showroom. I haven't ever seen anything like this in China. She's warm, she's wonderful, she makes you feel at home, and—most importantly—she's honest. I bought an ancestor painting from her—so I know it's real—for about $800. It's a real beaut.

The warehouse is modern, not crammed or dirty and dusty. There's an open-air shed with not-yet-restored furniture; you can negotiate a price. © 8621/3431-1212.

MALLS
Jing Jang Dickson Centre
400 Changle Rd. at Mao Ming Rd. (Metro: Shi Men Rd.).

The fanciest and most upscale Western mall in Shanghai is owned by the same businessman who owns Harvey Nichols in London. The mall is so chic it doesn't open until 11am (but it stays open until 9pm). Most of the really big-name shops, including Ralph Lauren, Lalique, and so on, are in this mall, which is the kingpin of the Huaihai Road shopping district. The building is done up like redbrick goes Art Deco. Remember, there are no bargains on designer goods in China because the import taxes are outrageously high. The stores are mostly empty and the help is very cool, probably terrified you will require them to speak English.

Mao Ming Centre
Mao Ming Rd. at Changle Rd. (Metro: Shi Men Rd.).

This luxury mall is right near the Dickson Centre and across the street from the Okura Garden Hotel. It boasts the usual Western suspects.

Plaza 66
1266 Nanjing Xi Lu (Metro: Jing An Temple).

Yawn, another fancy mall with big, big, big, Euro names. Here's the largest Louis Vuitton store in the world, along with brands like Chanel, Dior, and ESCADA. You get the picture.

Shanghai Centre
Nanjing Xi Lu (Metro: Jing An Temple).

This is not a traditional mall but a multiuse center with a hotel, an apartment block, and various stores. It has Gucci, Ferragamo, a Starbucks, and so on.

Times Square
93–99 Huaihai Rd. E. (Metro: Renmin Guangchang).

This is the first mainland China branch of the mall that changed a portion of Hong Kong's shopping style. It's a youth-oriented mall with name brands and attitude—but wait, it has a branch of my favorite supermarket, City Super.

Westgate Shopping Mall
1038 Nanjing Xi Lu (Metro: Jing An Temple).

I like this mall because it's 1 block from the Portman Ritz-Carlton, across the street from the JC Mandarin, and near the Four Seasons hotel. It's very Western, and it has a branch of Isetan, the Japanese department store—and a branch of everything else, too.

MARTS

I'm calling a difference between a mart and an antiques market and a fakes market, all of these categories have their own listings in this book.

Children's Clothing Mart
10 Puan Lu.

If you have young children in your life or you are in a gotta-give-a-gift situation, you will go nuts with the selection of beautiful baby clothes and accessories. The best, to my eye, are in traditional styles. This market is sometimes called Puan market or by its Chinese Name, Ni Hong Children's Plaza. It is open 10am to 6pm.

Cybermart
1 Huaihai Middle Rd. at Yizang Rd. (Metro: Huangpi Nan Lu).

You should be very computer/digitally savvy to shop here; there are programs and parts and cables and wires and phones and systems and serious boy toys. This address is written on your hotel's taxi card, so don't bother with the Metro—and then you are on Huaihai Road right where you want to be.

The market moved in 2007 so there are some people who use the address noted above and others who say 282 is the right number. Have your hotel concierge check before you leave and make sure the taxi card has the right address.

Note that "real" items will be more expensive than in the U.S.; there is a business in "used and real" but they will be more than in the U.S. and of course, no returns or repairs if you can't get back here. Buy a memory card for your camera and save off Wal-Mart low everyday prices.

Fenshine Mart

E. Nanjing Rd.

See p. 251 for a report on this market for copyright infringements of all sorts.

PEARLS

If you are going on to Beijing, I suggest you wait for the Pearl Market there. Go to the original building. But you can do just fine in Shanghai, believe me.

Pearls and jewelry can be bought ready-made or to be strung according to your instructions.

Look at **Pearl City,** 558 Nanjing Rd. E., a minimall of dealers right on the pedestrian part of Nanjing Road. Expats like **Pearl's Circle,** in First Asia Plaza and some go out to Hong Qiao (many expats live in this area) for the **New World Pearl Mart** on Hongmei Road, which is open 10am to 10pm.

SPAS

Evian Spa

Three on the Bund, 3 Zhongshan Dong Yi Lu (Metro: Remin Sq.).

This is perhaps the most glorious spa you have ever seen in your life, or in Shanghai. The multilevel spa is almost like a grotto: You step over stones and running water, go up and down stairs, and nestle into heated beds for heavenly treatments. Since this is not part of a hotel, anyone can book. The spa is for women guests, but Barbers Three does designer shaves and treatments for men. It is open daily 10:30am to 10:30pm. © 8621/6321-6622.

Tang Dynasty Health Care Centre

339 Shang Cheng Rd., upstairs (Metro: Pudong).

This is around the corner from the InterConti Shanghai, which is how I found it. It's a clinical kind of place where you go for reflexology. I've been here several times and referred many people. I wouldn't taxi all the way over here, but if you're in the 'hood, don't miss it. Treatments are $10 to $25. ✆ 8621/5882-0653.

TAILORS

Before the communist takeover, Shanghai was famous for its community of tailors. Most of them left in the late 1940s and reestablished themselves in Hong Kong. Now the trend is reversing. The block of Mao Ming Road right off Huaihai Road is now filled with tailors. If they all seem the same to you, try **Sam's** from Hong Kong.

W. W. Chan & Sons Tailor Ltd.
129A-2 Mao Ming Rd. (Metro: Shi Men Rd.).

These are not quickie, cutie-pie, cheapie, ho-ho suits in the manner of some of the other tailors in the area; this is Savile Row style and quality at a Chinese price, which is still about $3,000. This is much, much less than London with the same quality, but may not be in your budget. *Note:* Prices are approximately 20% less than in Hong Kong. See p. 128. To make an appointment prior to arrival, e-mail sales@wwchan. com or call ✆ 8621/6248-2768.

Aaron Strikes Out at the Shoe Stores

I saw some amazing shoes in China. I'm big on Puma and Adidas's Kick brand. In China I saw lots of cool designs that aren't available in the States. One pair of blue Adidas will forever be the pair that got away; it was pure love. Alas, I have size 13 (American) feet, and the largest pair of shoes I saw in China was size 10. And these were considered something of a novelty.

I was so depressed about having to leave stores without shoes that I actually started taking pictures of the shoes I couldn't have. Talk about desperation. —*Aaron Gershman*

TEA

There are a few tea markets for locals, but they are far out and you will need a local guide or interpreter. The best-known market, **Tian San ChaCha,** is in Hong Qiao. (*Cha* is "tea" in Chinese.) All grocery stores and Chinese herbal shops sell tea.

For a more upmarket experience, begin your quest at Three on the Bund, which has a tea sommelier and 80 different kinds of tea.

Also try your hand at the teeny-weeny stall of **Yun Tian Tea Shop,** 347 Fang Bang Zhong Rd., located between the flea market and Yuyuan Gardens. The teas here are in flower-bud format, and the staff will be happy to demonstrate for you or do a tasting. The buds open in hot water, providing a performance that is great at dinner parties. You'll pay $8 to $10 per box of tea; jasmine is always a popular one. © 8621/6330-2906.

Chapter 9

Beyond Shanghai

Day Trips & Overnight Excursions

There's no question that Shanghai is the Pearl of the Orient. Nor should there be any question that it is not indicative of the real China, new or old. Not to fret. Shanghai's location, and the new fast trains in the you've-really-gotta-see-it South Station make getting anywhere nearby not only a breeze, but also an essential part of your trip.

For years I've been toying with the idea of a weekend away in Hangzhou, but I never got there 'til recently. My report is later in this chapter. What's fascinating is that there are a handful of strong possibilities within your reach and you don't have to go for the obvious choice of Suzhou because it's gotten the most press. Spend a few moments with a map of Eastern China and the Shanghai area—you'll see Nanjing, Hangzhou, and Ningbo are all fanned out along newly built highways.

SUZHOU

I am thinking of changing my name to Suzhou Gershman; I'd still be Suzy, right? And then I could share the glory of the new Suzhou, because, baby, has this place perked up.

I once dreamed of Suzhou as one of those destinations on my list of places I had to see before I died; it was part of my Shanghai fantasies. The Venice of China, a city of canals, home of the old silk factories, pearl-bargain heaven. What's not to like?

Well, then I got there. *Oy vey*, as my Grandma Jessie used to say. What a bore. I was crushed. For years I have used these pages to advise people to skip Suzhou and to try something more rewarding, like Zhouzhang (p. 264).

Now, everything's up-to-date in Suzhou. Business is booming because real estate in Shanghai is so dear that many companies are relocating here. Meet the new Silicon Valley. So what if it's not the Venice of China; you come here for the I. M. Pei–designed Suzhou Museum, not for the shopping. (Local boy makes good.) The gardens are excellent; there are things to see…and, of course, things to buy.

The silk factories are a joke. The unattractive main shopping street is amusing only in that a) you're a long way from Shanghai architecturally, and b) it looks like news footage of Hanoi in 1969. Sure, the pearls are cheap; they're cheap everywhere. You'll have more fun buying pearls in Beijing—I promise. People come here to see the pagodas, the stone bridges, the architecture, and the city that is 2,500 years old. It does not speak to my soul and is my least favorite of the cities in this section—but hey, that's just me.

GETTING THERE

Most people take tours to Suzhou, enjoy its delights as part of their China package, or take a hotel car and driver. You can get there and back by train—it's about an hour-long ride; there are trains every hour. My hotel concierge quoted a flat fee of $300 for a Mercedes with driver for the day trip. You can get a taxi off the street to drive you around for $30 to $50. Express buses from the Hong Qiao Airport operate between 10am and 4pm. The bus ride is about an hour and a half.

SHOPPING SUZHOU

Not the main thrill. I hate the so-called silk factories because they are TTs (tourist traps) to me. But wait, you may find a selection of silk duvets here—a far better selection than in Shanghai or other big cities—and this could be reason enough to shop. The duvets are not inexpensive ($200 and up), the sizes are by Chinese standards (figure a Chinese king is a U.S. queen), and they are bulky to carry home. Though the factory will air pack the quilt so it's smaller and easier to pack. Silk factories also sell the usual suspects in clothes, robes, scarves, and the like.

STAYING IN SUZHOU

Many international hotels have branches in Suzhou, most of them being modern, business-oriented hotels. The priciest and fanciest is **Shangri-La,** but the **Holiday Inn** (the Holiday Inn Jasmine) is very, very nice. The number of brand-new hotels increases steadily; there's also a **Sheraton Hotel & Towers** and a **Renaissance.**

If you spend a night, you can explore the area and get a much better feel for the real China than just big-city Shanghai. You can also take an overnight boat trip to Hangzhou from Suzhou, and since Hangzhou is one of my favorite cities in China, I think this is a fabulous idea for the adventure minded.

Hotel One

379 Chang Jiang Rd., New District, Suzhou.

Hotel One is a division of the Landis Hotel Group, a group I have only recently met, but have already come to trust. This is a contemporary hotel with minimal design and maximum amenities, including Wi-Fi, a variety of dining choices, and any other features the business traveler could want. Rooms cost about $100. © **86-512/6878-1111.** www.hotelone.com.cn.

THE MAGIC CITY OF ZHOUZHANG

I am reluctant to tell you about this because it is so fabulous that you will rush there immediately and then it will be over-run with tourists and ruined. But because you've just read my rip on Suzhou, and you're thinking I'm as bad as any theater or restaurant critic, and you're mumbling that it's easy to find what's wrong without finding what's right—well, I have found the real Shangri-La. Zhouzhang is everything that I wanted Suzhou to be.

Zhouzhang is an ancient city, southeast of Suzhou and about 2 hours from Shanghai, in the "Water Country." The city consists of two parts, modern town and old city, which is across a series of bridges from modern town and is closed to vehicular traffic. You can walk or take a pedicab to the old city and then stroll the landmarks at your leisure. Because it's so scenic, it might be the most romantic place on Earth at night, but taking advantage of it would entail an overnight in a hotel that does not compete with Four Seasons or Shangri-La.

You can get here by private car, by taxi, or by express bus from Shanghai Stadium. The bus fare includes the ride and the entrance fee to the village. About four buses make the run per day (the last bus departs Shanghai at 2pm); check with your concierge.

HANGZHOU

I might have jokingly said "shang ten" when I wrote about Shanghai, but we can truly hang ten in Hangzhou—this is my new favorite city in China and where I actually think I could move, retire, and live happily ever after. This is the best of the new China and is only 2 hours away on the fast train. It's new, it's modern, and it's real.

Hangzhou is a Chinese resort city and has been for eons, but it is also known for tea and silk...and some nuts, yes, it's true. Wait 'til I take you to the Nut House...make that Nut Market. And just so you know, shorthand among old China hands for this city is HZ.

THE LAY OF THE LAND

The center piece of Hangzhou is West Lake, which is in the center of town. If there is an old or crummy part of town, I haven't seen it. There is a shopping street of older buildings, but it's done in a cutie-pie theme.

From the train station to the edge of the lake, all I saw was new streets, new highways, new buildings, and the new China. When you drive around the lake, you get a feel for some of the resort architecture, the pagodas, and the magic of the lake itself. In the hills above the lake, the villas of the rich, famous, and governmentally powerful sparkle as if in the Chinese version of the Italian Riviera.

GETTING THERE

You are undoubtedly coming from Shanghai, hopefully as an overnight guest or weekend visitor—you can do this as a day trip but you will miss a lot.

By train: In coming from Shanghai, the easiest thing to do is to hop the new fast train at the South Station. This train station is circular, but everything is marked in English and fairly simple to use. Now then, study the schedule or do so with your hotel concierge as some trains take the full 2 hours and some take an hour and a half. The train is new and Western and a total breeze.

By bus: Coming from Shanghai, you leave from the Shanghai Long Distance Bus Station and arrive at the Hangzhou East Station. I have not done this nor do I particularly suggest this. However, there are airport bus shuttles that could work for you, either from Pudong or Hong Qiao airports. Hangzhou has four bus terminals; the East Station serves Shanghai arrivals.

By plane: You probably don't want to fly from Shanghai to Hangzhou because they are so close and the train service is so great, but note you can fly to/from Hong Kong via Dragonair, ANA, JAL, and Asiana. You can also fly to numerous Japanese cities as well as other Asian cities. The most popular route is to Hong Kong International Airport; Dragonair has several flights each day. Note that if you are arriving from Hong Kong, you will need a visa to enter China. Hangzhou Xiaoshan International Airport (airport code HGH) is about 30km (19 miles) outside the city, so allow about an hour to get into town. Note that the Sofitel resort, mentioned in passing but not fully covered in this chapter, is closer to the airport than to town. A taxi from the airport to downtown is about $20.

By car: We took the train down to Hangzhou but returned to Shanghai by car so we could stop at the various factory outlet cities and pop into **CHN** (*©* **573/8701-0001;** www.chinaleather.com), in Haning (also known as China Leather City), an entire mall of leather goods at wholesale prices.

ARRIVAL IN HANGZHOU

If you are on a day trip, before you leave Shanghai ask your hotel concierge to write out a few directions for you in Chinese. You probably want the taxi to drop you at the Starbucks on West Lake (I'm not kidding) or on Hefang Street, the main drag. To really see the town, you'll need taxi transportation and a taxi card. If you just want to walk around the lake and eyeball what's going on, you can rent a bike, a boat, or, yup, walk.

The smartest thing is to spend at least 1 night and to arrange pickup at the train station. You'll exit the station following the crowds (no signs in English on our last visit) and then come to the barriers where friends and family wait. Your hotel rep will be standing there with a sign with your name… in English!

SLEEPING IN HANGZHOU

The best hotels are located around West Lake, some of these are isolated from town. For that reason, I feel strongly that the Sofitel Westlake is the right choice. Please read and pay attention because there are two Sofitel properties in town— the other is a lovely, beautiful resort (Sofitel Xanadu Resort), but it's out of the way. You want Westlake!

Do Not Miss Impressions Westlake

One of my main reasons for spending the night here was rumors of a great **Night Market** that I felt compelled to shop before I died. As it turns out, the market is not the most important reason to spend a night. Through a friend in Hangzhou, I learned about Impressions Westlake, a theatrical presentation very similar to the opening ceremony of the 2008 Beijing Olympics (same director and team). This is something you will remember the rest of your life and is the real reason you should spend a night in Hangzhou as the performance can only be done in the dark. You also need time in Hangzhou, so I say stay 2 nights or longer.

Sofitel Westlake
333 Westlake Ave., Hangzhou.

While Hangzhou has many modern hotels, this is the hotel of choice because it's intimate, small, right on the lake, and perfect in its combination of French-, Chinese-, and English-speaking know-how and *ni hou*. I swear, but when we got out of our car, the doorman said "Bonjour and ni hou."

The hotel is modern but not so contemporary that it is uncomfortable. There are restaurants overlooking the lake; one restaurant specializes in the local cuisine, which is related to the lake itself (fish and algae!). Yet when we wanted an afternoon break, we had coffee and French pastries in the lobby lounge. There is also a club floor with a gorgeous view and a splendid buffet.

Note: You can get a package of room nights with Sofitel for Shanghai and Hangzhou that includes transfer to the various train stations and back.

Rates in Hangzhou are about $125 per night on the weekend but there are seasonal deals and promotions. Local © 571/8707-5858. www.sofitel.com.

ABOUT ZHANG YIMOU & YOU

Millions of Americans saw the opening ceremony of the 2008 Beijing Olympics and were stunned with the creative ingenuity and the dramatic effects of the performances.

While I watched it at home in San Diego, not only was I transported, but the creative/technical part of my brain also wondered where the production came from within the director himself—how did he get to the ideas for the drummers, the man walking on the projection world, the drama?

At that time, I did not know who Zhang Yimou was or what works he had created in China already. Suddenly I was bundled in a coat and blanket outdoors in the dark at West Lake, watching a performance of people who floated on water, neon fish that danced, and a couple that flew to the moon and back. All of my senses were stunned.

Zhang Yimou is the most famous Chinese filmmaker, cinematographer, producer, and director working in China today. He has made many movies of international reputation (the one I know is *Raise the Red Lantern,* a must see, although it is depressing) and he is the go-to guy for Chinese government official events, be it the Olympics or the birthday of the Communist Party in China.

It turns out that there are several of these performances at various landmarks in the most famous Chinese tourist cities. Tickets for the best seats are about $50 each; this is one of the most important theatrical experiences you will ever enjoy. For tickets call © **571/8796-2222** or visit www.hzyxxh.com.

Don't trust me on this because there's no shopping involved? Well, do an online search. There is footage on YouTube posted by people just as impressed as I.

CULTURE IN HANGZHOU

While I consider shopping to be sociology and do not usually report on the cultural landmarks of a destination, I do want you to know that this city has a boatload of stuff going on. You can tour and do tastings at nearby tea plantations (try Dragon Well Tea Village); there are half a dozen excellent museums. My favorite is the Scissors Museum. All kidding aside, without bias, this town has much to offer and you could be happy here for 4 or 5 days of shopping and sightseeing.

GETTING AROUND

We made this trip on the train with Peter Chan, Born to Shop regional editor for Asia. He sent his driver (along with GPS) via the highway while we all took the train. Because we had a driver and a native speaker, we were set to explore. You will either need a taxi and a taxi card, a car and driver, or an interest in exploring just the parts of town that you can walk to (although bike rentals are readily available). There is a metro (Hangzhou Metro) but this won't do you much good. I am forced to confess there is a metro stop right in front of the Sofitel Westlake hotel.

SHOPPING IN HANGZHOU

Because Hangzhou is part of the new China, there are plenty of malls and plenty of Adidas stores. This is obviously not what we came for. The main shopping streets are Hefang Street, Hubin Street, and Qinghefang Historical Block (part of Hefang St.).

There are modern malls in the **Hangzhou Tower, Hangzhou Jiebai, GDA Plaza,** and the **In Times** mall, which has two branches, one of which is near West Lake. All the luxe brands have stores here, such as **Hermès, Gucci,** and **Armani.** Give me a break. If you're going to the branch of a famous name, I'd rather see you go to **Starbucks** where at least you can buy a coffee mug from the city mug series, one that says "Hangzhou" on it.

If you are familiar with Xintandi in Shanghai then you will immediately grasp the concept of **Xihu Tiandi,** a similar cultural, historical, touristic, shopping venue located on West Lake.

The infamous **Night Market** is held near Wulin Square, begins around 6pm, and frankly, is merely so-so. It's okay, but nothing to plan a trip around and is not essential for your shopping pleasure. It helps to have had some bargaining experience in other Chinese markets and to know the street prices; few items cost less than in the major cities—even with bargaining.

There are numerous other markets in town; if we didn't get there, I have not written about it. Several of the markets that sounded so promising were truly dismal, so I don't want to lead anyone on with misinformation. I have not been to the **Ceramics Market,** since I can't ship home all that I buy, nor have I been to the **Drum Tower Antiques Market.** There is also a **Saturday Antiques Market** next to Number Two Department Store, Wenhui Road. Write if you get work. Since I wear at least a size 11 shoe, maybe a 42 or 43 in European size, I saw no reason whatsoever to even glance at the **Shoe Market** at Wusin Lu Square. Sorry, call me a selfish bitch.

In directing shopping suggestions, I will make the assumption that you are going to be in other Chinese cities, so that I will not take time out to direct you to the French *hypermarché* (supermarket) **Carrefour** (which is almost across the street from the Sofitel Westlake), or to the Hong Kong hero **Watson's,** the chemist—the source of many hours of shopping joy for me.

LOCAL HEROES

Emvon
87 Lianhua St., Hangzhou.

This spa is best known for its mineral salt foot therapy, about $12 for an 80-minute session. It offers other treatments, but they make me nervous…intracranial therapy, anyone? Not me! © 0571/8523-7777.

Hangzhou China Silk Town
West Jiankang Rd., Hangzhou.

Hmmm, well, this isn't terrible, but it's very clean and touristy and ho-hum. Certainly no bargains here and that's after bargaining! We did find various silk scarves that we hadn't seen in other markets in Beijing and/or Shanghai and we still regret the ones not bought. Hermès-style scarves for $15 are worthy of attention when hand-rolled hems are in order and you don't mind a fake or two. Brushed coffee brown denim Mao jackets for $35 (the going rate) are a must have at one time or another in your life. This is by no means a fabric market. It's a kind of outdoor mall. No Starbucks.

Hangzhou Tea & Nut Market
Nanban Lane, Hangzhou.

Because this area is famous for its tea (we were here, unfortunately, a few weeks before the harvest), I was very interested in the tea market, which was fun. What really knocked me out, however, were the nut sellers. I am still singing about Bloody Mary chewing betel nuts (now ain't that too damn bad) and marveling over the extraordinary tastes introduced by Peter Chan, Born to Shop Asia editor. I don't like walnuts in real life—these were a different size and taste from what I know. I do like Texas pecans; Chinese pecans have a totally different flavor—they melt like butter pecan ice cream and fade from the tongue to a memory. This was worth doing with a native speaker to guide you through assorted tastings.

Outlet Shopping in China

Aside from China Leather City, which I mention above, there are also some factory outlets; even a branch of **Foxtown** in Xinbang, about 45 minutes from Shanghai. It has 90 brands.

There are also the **Shanghai Outlets,** near the Hong Qiao Airport on the A9—as if you are driving (ha). This one is in the town of Qingpu in Zhoa Xing and has 240 stores, including Armani.

Die-hard shoppers from Hong Kong sometimes like to visit these outlets; I didn't come to China to do this, sorry. Clothes in the U.S. may be made in China, but the markers (pattern dimensions) are for American bodies. Asian fit is proportioned smaller than petite—beware.

Hefeng Street

Ding An Rd. and Hefeng St., Hangzhou.

It is touristy. We're all tourists in this together and if you aren't using a car and driver and just want to walk and snoop around, you can stroll this long street and even time it into the evening so that you end up at the Night Market. Stores here are open daily from 10am to 9pm.

Night Market

Renhe Rd. and Huixing Rd., Hangzhou.

Not only was I disappointed in this market, but I was frustrated with the number of opinions as to when it is open. Most people said 7pm to midnight. We went at 6pm and things were just getting going and one hour was all we needed. We were on the way to *Impressions Westlake* (p. 267) but I couldn't bear the thought of missing the Night Market. Ha. Live and learn.

Chapter 10

Beijing

Welcome to Beijing

If you are expecting old-world China when you arrive in Beijing, you can forget that right now. Surely the 2008 Olympic Games taught us all about the new China—the art, the theater, the architecture, and the ability to accomplish just about anything. The small amount of old China that still stands is hard to find and is either being "improved" (ruined) or eliminated. Your visit to Beijing will include world-class hotels, fabulous shopping, take-your-breath-away sights, and yes, even Starbucks and McDonald's, plus all the Peking duck you can eat. I wish you double happiness and many ducks to go. Get to a *hutong* (traditional nabe) before it's too late.

Getting There

See chapter 2 for information on air carriers that serve all parts of China, including Beijing.

More and more U.S. flag carriers are serving Beijing with direct and even nonstop flights. **Northwest** (now merged with Delta) was a leader in this, and **American Airlines** now has a Chicago to Beijing flight. **Continental** has nonstops from

---

Electronically Yours: Beijing

Please note that these sites are specific to Beijing:

- **www.timeout.com/beijing.** Time Out Beijing is a freebie magazine, but you can check its website for lotsa info, too.
- **www.thebeijingguide.com.** This is an English-language resource of culture to dining and, yes, shopping.
- **www.beijingpage.com.** This site is similar to the previous site but also has links to additional resources, such as Beijing photos, traveler blogs, and advice on touring the city.

New York to Beijing, Shanghai, and Hong Kong. For Chinese carriers, **Air China** has flights from New York to Beijing. Traditionally, flights from the U.S. depart from the West Coast and Vancouver. Now Chicago, Detroit, and even New York City are hot.

If you want to hub in Asia, take a good look at a map before you choose the carrier, as Beijing may be farther north than you imagine—easier to get to from Seoul or Narita than Taipei or Hong Kong.

ARRIVAL BY AIR

The new Terminal Three at Beijing Capital Airport has been created to impress. Taxi service from the airport to central Beijing runs about $15. All major hotels have transfer packages that cost about $40 to $50. There is a long line for taxis, but it is orderly.

OTHER POSSIBILITIES
TRAIN

Beijing has five train stations, so if you arrive or depart by train, know which is where.

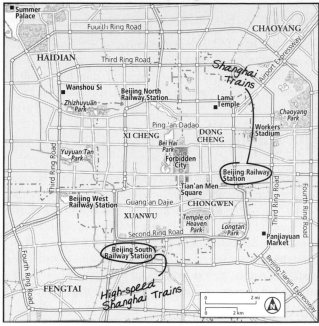

Travelers from Shanghai arrive at the Central Station (CK). The train station is blocked off to taxis and hotel cars, so you have to walk quite a distance. If you have a lot of luggage, it pays to arrange a hotel transfer (ask to be met at the tracks).

If you want train tickets departing from Beijing, call and fax your hotel concierge as soon as you choose your dates. Tickets are sold only a certain number of days before travel and go quickly. The overnight train is Western; ask for a "soft seat." We usually book all four bunks in a sleeping cabin for privacy and space for the luggage (about $250 total).

Traveler's Tip: Speed Demon

Our last overnight train trip was a disaster! The train took 2 hours longer than other trains (talk about a slow boat to China) and was filthy. Disgusting. Furthermore, the bookings were made by the concierge at the fanciest hotel in town. To ensure a modern train, book the fastest train.

CRUISE SHIP

Beijing is landlocked; however, it is not terribly far from the sea, and many cruise ships use Beijing as a "turnaround city" and transfer passengers by bus to Tianjin. Tianjin has rebuilt its consumer portion of the port and has a new cruise terminal.

The Lay of the Land

Beijing has purposefully been built in a series of circles, starting with the Forbidden City as the core, surrounded by ring roads: "First Ring Road," and so on. There is a clear north-south axis as well as a modern east-west main drag, making it easy to divide central Beijing into four quadrants for directional purposes. Even if your hotel is located on an outer ring road, you will be able to get around relatively easily. On the other hand, since the Olympics, there are more roads and more ways for taxi drivers to cheat you. You will be taken the long way, count on it.

Getting Around

TAXIS

Taxis are plentiful and cheap, which is good because you will not find too many honest drivers. Before you leave your hotel, ask for its preprinted taxi checklist of destinations written out in English and Chinese. Taxis are fairly easy to hail in busy shopping districts, but not in out-of-the-way districts or at some tourist sights. If you take a taxi to the Summer Palace, have your driver wait for you. Don't tip a cheater.

PEDICABS

I am a little embarrassed to say this—it must be quite socially incorrect—but I love the pedicabs in Beijing and I will be sorry when they disappear, as invariably they must.

The drivers range in age, which I always take into account, depending on the difficulty of the journey. A few speak some words of English, but don't count on it. Always determine price before you get in. A tip is not expected, but I tip if extra effort has been made.

Shopper Beware

I traditionally take a pedicab from the Big Duck back to my hotel, usually Peninsula Palace. Last trip, the driver got lost, or frustrated, or was drunk, or all of these and dropped us plunk down in the middle of nowhere—and I know my way around Beijing. It's a miracle we are still alive. Do not pedicab at night.

THE METRO

The Metro (also called "the subway") is marked in Pinyin. You can easily connect to "downtown" (Tiananmen) on your own. This subway is far nicer than the one in Shanghai. The subway opens around 5:30am and runs until 10:30 or 11:30pm, depending on the line. The fare is about 25¢. The symbol for the subway is a little square inside an incomplete circle, sort of like the letter G.

Sleeping in Beijing

Because Beijing is a city of neighborhoods and traffic is so terrible, where you stay very much defines your trip. Luxury is also important if you are used to Western-style hotels and want the electronics to function. Several hotels have two (or more) branches, so be careful and smart when you choose.

Park Hyatt Beijing

2 Jianguomenwai St., inside Yintai Center, Central Business District (Metro: Jianguomen).

This is a hotel in a high rise and you may not have extraordinary expectations as you arrive—in fact, your taxi driver may

Beijing

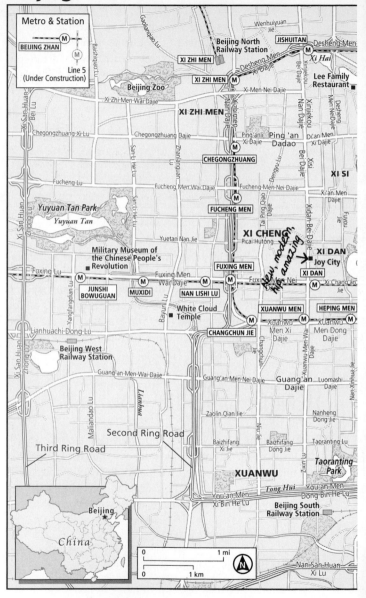

Metro & Station

BEIJING ZHAN Ⓜ
Ⓜ
Line 5
(Under Construction)

Gaoliangqiao Lu
Baishiqiao Lu

Wenhuiyuan Jie

Beijing North Railway Station

JISHUITAN

Desheng Men

XI ZHI MEN

Desheng Men Nei Dajie

Xi Hai

Beijing Zoo

XI ZHI MEN

Xi-Men-Nei-Dajie

Xinjiekou Bei Dajie
Xinjiekou Nan Dajie

Men NeiDajie

Desheng Men NeiDajie

Xi-Zhi-Men-Wai-Dajie

Zhanlanguan

Lee Family Restaurant

XI ZHI MEN

Chegongzhuang Xi-Lu

Chegongzhuang Dajie

Ping'anli Xi Dajie

Ping 'an Dadao

Di'an Men Xi Dajie

Xisi Bei Dajie

Xi-San-Huan Bei Lu

Sanli He Lu

Fucheng Lu

CHEGONGZHUANG

Xidan-Bei-Dajie

XI SI

Xi'an-Men Dajie

Dengyu Lu

Xi-an-Men-Nei-Dajie

Fucheng Men-Wai-Dajie

Fucheng Men-Nei-Dajie

Fuyou Jie

Yuyuan Tan Park

Yuyuan Tan

Xi-San-Huan Zhong-Lu

Sanli He Lu

Zhanlanguan Lu

Yuetan Nan Jie

FUCHENG MEN

XI CHENG

Picai Hutong

*New, modern,
truly amazing!* →

XI DAN
Joy City

XI DAN

Military Museum of the Chinese People's Revolution

Fuxing Lu

Fuxing Men Wai Dajie

FUXING MEN

Fuxing Men Nei

Xi-Chang'an Jie

JUNSHI BOWUGUAN

MUXIDI

NAN LISHI LU

HEPING MEN

Yangfangdian Lu

Bayun Lu

White Cloud Temple

XUANWU MEN

Xuanwu Men Dong Dajie

Lianhuachi-Dong-Lu

CHANGCHUN JIE

Xuanwu Men Xi Dajie

Nan-Xinhua Jie

Beijing West Railway Station

Guang'an-Men-Wai-Dajie

Changchun Jie

Guang'an-Men-Nei-Dajie

Guang'an Dajie

Luomashi Dajie

Maliandao Lu

Lianhua

Second Ring Road

Zaolin Qian Jie

Baizhifang Xi Jie

Niu Jie

Baizhifang Dong Jie

Nanheng Dong Jie

Taoranting Lu

Taoranting Park

Third Ring Road

Xi-San-Huan Zhong-Lu

XUANWU

Tong Hui

You'an-Men Xi-Bin-He-Lu

You'an-Men Dong-Bin-He-Lu

Beijing South Railway Station

Nan-San-Huan Xi Lu

Beijing ★

China

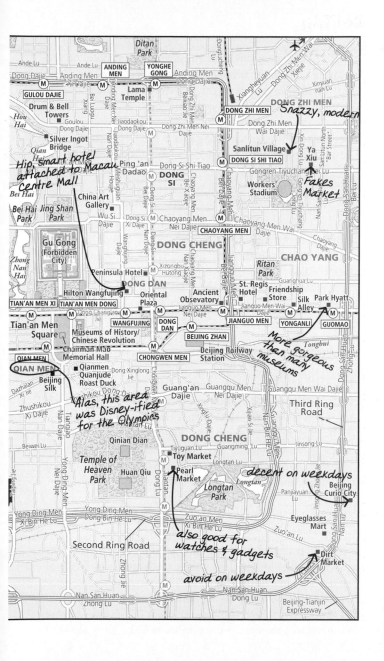

have trouble finding the front entrance. Once you are on the lobby floor, up above Beijing, you'll know you're not in Kansas anymore. The view is spectacular as is the Ed Tuttle design. Guest rooms are swank, the spa is yummy and the restaurants are perched way up high in the tower for views of the middle kingdom as well as lip-smacking fusion food. The space is airy, chic and rich without being precious. © 10/8567-1234.

Peninsula Hotel Beijing
8 Goldfish Lane, Wangfujing (Metro: Wangfujing).

How do I love the Pen? Let me count the ways. Rooms are decorated in Armani-Zen-chinoiserie chic. Standard deluxe rooms are traditional, with great bathroom amenities. An executive floor offers extra privileges and a private lounge. The presidential suite made the cover of *Architectural Digest*.

One of the best things about this hotel is the location, which is among the most convenient in Beijing: 1 block from the famed Wangfujing, the pedestrian shopping street; right near Food Street (not that we eat too much street food in China); and you can walk to Tiananmen Square and the Forbidden City (a long walk, but doable). The Peninsula has excellent restaurants, a multilevel mall of big names (including Chanel), and even an ATM machine.

The E'Spa is to swoon for; Peninsula Academy offers classes in local customs and inscrutable ways...and even some shopping. Prices are uptown but vary with seasons and promotions. Local © 8610/6512-8899. www.peninsula.com.

Hilton Beijing Wangfujing
8 Wangfujing St. (Metro: Wangfujing).

Not to be confused with the Hilton Beijing, this hotel is the new kid on the block and is on the exactly right, best block of Beijing. It is imperative that you understand the difference between the two hotels as this hotel is new and a national treasure, so swank and sophisticated that I don't know where to start. It was the first in town to serve Coke Zero; the staff

Beijing Metro

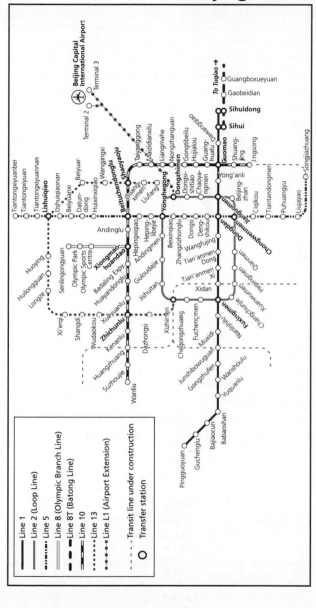

sends a goldfish in a bowl to your room to help you sleep; the restaurants belong in both *Saveur* and *Architectural Digest*— and there is a water bar.

The location is right on the main shopping drag and there's an attached mall called Macau Centre. You will not believe your luck or smarts if you book this hotel. Try for Hilton promotions for price breaks. Local ✆ **10/5812-8888,** or U.S. reservations ✆ 800/HILTONS (445-8667). www. wangfujing.hilton.com.

Intercontinental Beijing Beichen
8 Beichen West Rd. (Metro: Olympic Green).

This may not be the world's best shopping location, but the location is halfway to Tiananmen and halfway to the Great Wall and, most importantly, the hotel is on the main Olympics site and overlooks the Water Cube. You may never have a more memorable view in your travel career. Note that the hotel has a huge convention and catering business, so rates vary with what's happening in town. Many fashion shows and big-time events are held in the Water Cube and catered by the hotel. Also note that the subway stop isn't that far away but you do not want to walk. You can get a taxi from the subway to the hotel or vice versa; you can also taxi to the nearby shopping malls and real-people districts, $5 does it. Once in a lifetime experience. Local ✆ **10/8437-1188,** or U.S. reservations ✆ 888/424-6835. www.ihg.com.

Dining in Beijing

Qianmen Quanjude Roast Duck
32 Qianmen St. (Metro: Tian'an Men Dong).

This famous eatery is on the far side of Tiananmen Square and remains the only "old" building on a totally new and "improved" Beijing street that looks like Main Street Disneyland. Never mind the 'hood, you came for the duck. We always have the hotel reserve but like to go early due to the crowds; perfect on arrival day if you have jet lag. Most diners are Chinese, but this is a major tourist destination and several members of the waitstaff speak English and helped us order. Why a duck? Surely you know by now.

Red Capital Club
66 Dongsi Jiutiao, Dongcheng (no nearby Metro).

This restaurant is in a private home, which is restored to old Shanghai–communist brotherhood style; there is also an adjoining guesthouse. The menu is a parody of old communist tricks; the style is very Shanghai Tang commie kitsch. Three of us ate here for $100, but we were careful on alcoholic drinks and wine and skipped dessert. Expect your taxi to get lost, but it's worth it. © **8610/6402-7150.**

Shopping Beijing

There's no question that Beijing's shopping scene is funkier than Shanghai's. There's a marvelous congregation of fancy stores and big-name boutiques, but prices on designer goods are 20% higher than elsewhere. Do you really want to buy Hermès here? Chanel? I'd go more funky.

Beijing to me means pearls, souvenirs, antiques, and fakes (I don't buy them, I just like to look). This is also DVD heaven for legal discs at good prices. Forget the illegal ones available on the street—none of mine were as advertised, most didn't even work, and some were porn in sheep's clothing.

MONEY MATTERS
ATMs are easy to find. Most banks have them as do most hotels—even the Pen.

SHOPPING HOURS

Stores are open daily, usually from 9:30am until 8pm, but many malls stay open until 10pm, as do stores on the pedestrian street, Wangfujing. Note that office workers have both Saturday and Sunday off. As a result, they often spend their leisure time shopping. You might want to plan your ventures accordingly. Beware weekend crowds.

SHIPPING

It costs between $300 and $500 to send a 20-pound package to the United States by FedEx. I suggest you do some research before you leave the United States, then be prepared to take care of the phone calls yourself once in China. There are a handful of FedEx offices in Beijing, but I'd call © **8610/6466-5566** before jumping in a taxi. Your hotel business office can probably help with shipping or the concierge will lend a hand. Ship "returned American goods," to avoid duty; hand carry any treasures.

For more serious freight, there's a shipping desk that specializes in containers at **Beijing Curio City** (p. 297).

HOTEL GIFT SHOPS

Several hotels are attached to small or even medium-size malls; the **Peninsula Palace Hotel** has a lock on the luxury big names. The **China World Hotel's** mall (China World Shopping Centre) is more like a mall, and it's attached by some tunnels to the **Kerry Centre,** another mall (with its own hotel). The Kempinski Hotel is also attached to a mall (**Lufthansa Centre**) as is the Wangfujing Hilton (**Macau Centre**) and the Hyatt (**Oriental Plaza mall**).

All the big Western-style hotels have some sort of gift shop. Prices in hotel gift shops are always higher than on the street. Usually hotel gift-shop merchandise is classier than what you find on the street and, therefore, worth the extra price. Many hotels have antiques shops in their lobbies.

MUSEUM SHOPPING

Beijing is one giant museum and has plenty of shopping inside museums, although nothing as sensational as the museum gift shops in Shanghai. On the other hand, there's nothing like a little shopping at Mao's Mausoleum Museum (for kitsch).

TOUR & GUIDED SHOPPING

All motorcoach tours will make shopping stops whether you want them or not. Yes, of course, the guides get kickbacks. Even if you take a taxi or a private driver, expect kickbacks to be involved, especially when drivers or guides accompany you.

Most hotels offer their own private tours, so you need not travel by motorcoach; hotel excursions are often in a Mercedes-Benz with an English-speaking driver and may even include a picnic lunch. Prices can be as high as $150 for a single traveler or $90 each for two people together in a private car. Keep in mind that you can invariably do these "tours" on your own with a taxi and save a lot of money.

Beijing Neighborhoods

WANGFUJING

This is the main drag in Beijing. It is a pedestrian-only street that spans 1.5 million sq. m (16 million sq. ft.), of selling space—larger than any megamall in the United States. I think that might possibly be the good news and the bad news all crammed into one big wonton.

A food and street market takes up one portion of the main street—it is adorable and terrifying at the same time. It's cute to look at and easy to shop but very, very touristy—very American-Disney-does-Chinatown, and very much in keeping with the new redo. I, personally, am desperate for a little authenticity somewhere. It ain't here.

There's the Western-style Oriental Plaza mall, which is at the end of the street and includes the Grand Hyatt hotel. In the middle of the street—lined up on the walking blocks— are the big Chinese department stores; fast-food places, like McDonald's; some local pharmacies (Chinese medicine–type stores); and bookstores. There are also some discount stores, a silk shop, a few arts-and-crafts stores, banks, Popeye's Fried Chicken, and so on.

There is a lot of action in the evening during good weather. One of the reasons is that this is truly a one-stop location—you can buy tea (**Tianfu Tea Shop**), get a **Big Mac** (order by look- ing and pointing at the pictograms), have dessert at **Häagen- Dazs,** have your photos developed or digitalized, and go to gourmet food stores or the supermarket under the **Oriental Plaza mall.** You can even replenish your supply of meds, have your watch cleaned, get postcards and books, and shop the local version of the 99-cent store. Should you run low on funds, not to worry—there are scads of ATMs and banks.

LIULICHANG

I call this "Lily Street" because I can't pronounce the name in Chinese. A fun part of the shopping scene has been cleaned up and faked up, and is not nearly as inviting or rewarding as it once was. I am sick over this insult. How can you trust a squeaky clean antiques shop?

If you decide to visit anyway, note there are two parts to this street, and they do not readily connect visually. On one end, it's more like a series of indoor markets selling fun junk; the other is lined with high-end stores that mostly sell the real thing, and I don't mean Coca-Cola. There are also some bookstores and art-supply stores here.

Don't get here too early. I stopped by at 9:30 one morning and stores were just barely opening. The area is very conve- nient to Tiananmen Square.

Wangfujing

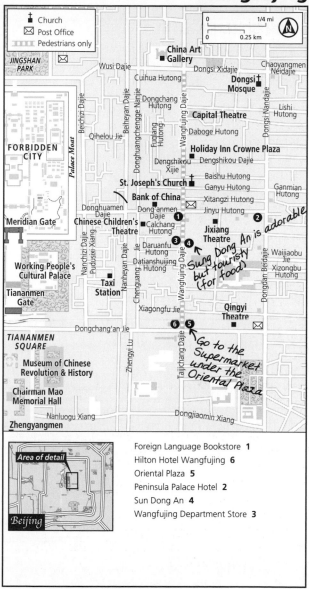

Map legend:
- ✝ Church
- ✉ Post Office
- ▥▥▥ Pedestrians only

0 — 1/4 mi
0 — 0.25 km

JINGSHAN PARK

Wusi Dajie

China Art Gallery

Dongsi Xidajie

Chaoyangmen Neidajie

Cuihua Hutong

Dongsi Mosque ✝

Dongchang Hutong

Lishi Hutong

Wangfujing Dajie

Capital Theatre

Qihelou Jie

Daboge Hutong

FORBIDDEN CITY

Beichizi Dajie

Beiheyan Dajie

Donghuangchengge Nanjie

Fuqiang Hutong

Palace Moat

Dengshikou Xijie

Holiday Inn Crowne Plaza

Dengshikou Dajie

Baishu Hutong

St. Joseph's Church ✝

Ganyu Hutong

Ganmian Hutong

Bank of China

Xitangzi Hutong

Dong'anmen Dajie

Jinyu Hutong

Donghuamen Dajie

Chinese Children's Theatre

Calchang Hutong

Jixiang Theatre ❷

Sung Dong An is adorable but touristy (for food)

Meridian Gate

Nanchizi Dajie

Pudusixi Xiang

Daruanfu Hutong ❸ ❹

Waijiaobu Jie

Dongdan Beidajie

Working People's Cultural Palace

Datianshuijing Hutong

Xizongbu Hutong

Nanheyan Dajie

Chenguang Jie

Taxi Station

Tiananmen Gate

Xiagongfu Jie

Qingyi Theatre

Dongchang'an Jie ❻ ❺

Go to the Supermarket under the Oriental Plaza

TIANANMEN SQUARE

Zhengyi Lu

Taijichang Dajie

Museum of Chinese Revolution & History

Chairman Mao Memorial Hall

Nanluogu Xiang

Dongjiaomin Xiang

Zhengyangmen

Area of detail

Beijing

Foreign Language Bookstore **1**

Hilton Hotel Wangfujing **6**

Oriental Plaza **5**

Peninsula Palace Hotel **2**

Sun Dong An **4**

Wangfujing Department Store **3**

QIANMEN/TIANANMEN

If these sound suspiciously alike to you, it's because they are basically the same; the Qianmen shopping district is a spoke off Tiananmen Square. This area was cleaned up and reinvented for the Olympics; I don't really even know what to say. Many of the original stores were hundreds of years old; it was one of the oldest shopping districts in town. Now it's somewhat bizarre and Disneyesque.

As for Tiananmen Square itself, many vendors wander around the vast plaza, selling things like snacks, postcards, or kites. Inside the nearby museums (and mausoleum), you'll find souvenirs for sale.

FORBIDDEN CITY

The royal residence part of the old Imperial City, the Forbidden City is a now living museum, with several opportunities to shop. They begin immediately as you enter the front gate and pay your entrance fee. The best thing I saw to buy here—and never saw anywhere else in Beijing or in China—was a silk scarf with a map of the Forbidden City printed on it for about $25.

SANLITUN

Most of the old shopping portion of this area was razed, but there is a very new, snazzy retail center as well as an indoor-style market (which is almost like a supermarket) filled with fake designer merchandise. The contrast between the two is pretty funny.

The fakes market is named **Ya Xiu,** which often appears on a hotel taxi checklist. (In English, you'd pronounce it "Ya Show," which is how it is often written in guide books.) Note that the fakes may be hidden per the new antifraud measures.

The new-fangled modern mall is called **Sanlitun Village;** there are a handful of designer stores here as well as youth-oriented stores, such as Adidas and Apple.

The little lanes that make up the bar district have a few cute boutiques, but the big news is the new mall and adjacent design hotel—Opposite House.

CAOCHANGDI

Beijing has been known for its local contemporary art scene for a number of years; galleries and warehouses for artists are multiplying. This is now the avant-garde area du jour. (I prefer **Space 798**; p. 292.) The area is northeast of Dashanzi, around the Huantie railroad ties (farther out than Space 798). Locals like this area because they feel it is more authentic than Space 798 and more cutting edge. As we went to press, there were about six galleries here.

TEMPLE OF HEAVEN

Okay, so it's a cultural site to you. To me, it's a shopping neighborhood—and talk about heaven! This is where you'll find the **Pearl Market** (Hong Qiao) and its next-door neighbor, the **Toy Market** and their newest family member, the addition to the Pearl Market, which is bold and new and well, not funky. Hong Qiao appears on every hotel taxi checklist, the new portion of the market is not delineated. This could be an all-day adventure if you do all three buildings, although after a while everything will look alike. The original Pearl Market has clothes, "antiques," small electronics, makeup and beauty supplies, hair accessories, luggage, shoes, and many floors of bead vendors and jewelry stores. Note that to get to the upper level jewelry stores, you must use another staircase—the main escalators do not lead there. There are two more floors of nice shops up there.

NANLUOGU XIANG

This is a gussied-up version of a hutong, the Chinese village-city-housing unit of ancient times. It is an official tourist area, so there isn't too much that is authentic in an old-fashioned sense, but this is the new China, remember? *Xiang* is the word for alley and this particular alley is meant to mix shopping and culture. Stores are open daily from 10am to 10pm with some variations, such as **Woo Scarf & Shawl** (17–4 Nanluogu Xiang), which is open 9am to 11pm. This area is particularly fun at night when you get the mix of locals. There are many cafes.

OLYMPIC GREEN

This is not really a shopping neighborhood—at least, until they make bargain hunting an Olympic event. Most of the Olympic sites are directly north of city center; there are hotels there (p. 282) as well as a very nice mall.

PANJIAYUAN

This district of Beijing plays host to the weekend **Panjiayuan Antique and Curio Market** (read: flea market), which has become synonymous with the name of the destination. Expats often call it the "Dirt Market" because it used to have a dirt yard. (Alas, past tense—this is another place that has been seriously spiffed up.) Nearby (around the corner) is the **Beijing Eye Mart** (Ming Jin Yuan) and then **Beijing Curio City** and other furniture warehouses. Arrive in a taxi; return in a truck.

Note: This location is not far from **China World** and the **Park Hyatt Hotel**—you need a taxi, but this is not really out in the far boonies. The Dirt Market is now open during the week, but there are only a handful of vendors doing business then. **Beijing Curio City** is a better bet during the week.

GREAT WALL (BADALING)

The most commercial parts of the wall (Badaling being *the* most commercial and closest to Beijing) have tons of shopping, in terms of souvenirs stalls, and even free-standing antiques shops. Get this: There's even a Starbucks!

SUMMER PALACE

There isn't a lot of shopping at the Summer Palace (at least, not a lot of good shopping)—but there are certainly more retail opportunities than I had expected. The most important thing you will buy—and it pays to get it from the vendors out front—is a map in English and Chinese. You might also want to splurge for a private guide—there are several (also out front) who will be hawking their services.

Beijing Resources A to Z

*A **note about addresses:*** Although addresses are often listed below, most of the destinations in this section are on the standard preprinted hotel taxi checklists, already written out for you in English and Chinese, which is far more useful than my listings. I've been to every venue on every major hotel checklist; if said venue is not mentioned in this section, there is a reason.

ANTIQUES

Also see "Flea Markets" and "Markets," later in this chapter.

You may not know it, but you came to Beijing to buy antiques or so-called antiques. This is tchotchke heaven. You will find everything from fake to real, valuable to worthless, and much that looks great and therefore means something to you, regardless of its true value.

Although there are some nice furniture stores here (p. 299), remember to buy furniture in Shanghai if you can because the air there is less dry and furniture is less likely to crack or suffer winter damage.

If you are in town over the weekend and like flea markets, get to the **Panjiayuan Antique & Curio Market.** Do remember that a lot of the "antiques" were made last week. The Panjiayuan Market claims that it is now open daily. Born to Shop editorial director Sarah Lahey and I specifically went to check it out on a weekday and had two problems: 1) the taxi driver insisted there was no market during the week and therefore took us to nearby **Beijing Curio City** (we had fun); 2) when we got to Panjiayuan Market on a weekday (we walked), there were only a few vendors open.

ART
Commune by the Great Wall
Shuigan exit, Badaling (no nearby Metro).

This is an architecture exhibit and should not be confused with the listing below. There is a resort as well; you can rent the architectural property. As noted by the name and address, this is not in downtown Beijing but out very close to the Great Wall of China. There is also a spa at the resort.

Space 798
Dashanzi Art District (no nearby Metro).

If you are in Beijing for only a few days, you will be tempted to write off this destination because it's far away and traffic is bad, because you aren't interested in buying art, or because you want the old China, not the new. Silly *yu*! This is one of the most fabulous places in the world and worth a visit by anyone who likes to see what's hot and trendy.

The basic space is a former factory, now converted into the SoHo of Beijing. Along with the factory itself is an entire neighborhood with cafes, artists' workshops, galleries, photographic studios, and a few fashion boutiques. It has very much been discovered, so there's nothing raw or dangerous about it. This is truly fun...and interesting.

Take a taxi; have the driver wait. Allow an hour each way in drive time from the Peninsula Palace Hotel (due to traffic, not distance). *Note:* The name in English is sometimes written as "Factory 798," so don't be fooled. © 8610/6437-6248. www.798space.com.

WEB TIPS 🖐 The excellent website is in English and offers a complete guide to the 'hood, among other things.

ARTS & CRAFTS
A few stores on Wangfujing sell arts and crafts to tourists; mostly, I hated them—way, way too touristy. All markets

have some crafts; you will probably find what you want at the **Hong Qiao Market** (Pearl Market)—note that merchandise in both of the markets is very similar.

I'm not crazy about the arts and crafts selection at **Ya Xiu** market, but you'll be there anyway for some serious shopping, so take a look.

Beijing Curio City (p. 297) is an excellent source for arts and crafts, as is the **Panjiayuan Antique and Curio Market** (p. 297), possibly the best flea market in the world.

There is a small selection of arts and crafts at the duty-free store in the Beijing airport; almost all hotel gift shops also sell arts and crafts at elevated prices.

BOOKS
Foreign Language Bookstore
219 Wangfujing (Metro: Wangfujing).

This wonderful store is toward the Peninsula/Hilton end of Wangfujing (right across from McDonald's). The Foreign Language Bookstore also sells videos and computer programs. On the street level are a large selection of fabulous postcards (the artsy kind), many slides of tourist and artist sites and sights, books in foreign languages, textbooks, medical books, newspapers, and kids' books. My favorites are the language books for children—I think they make good gifts.

CASHMERE & PASHMINA
King Deer Cashmere
135 Chaoyangmen.

This chain of tourist stores, which sells all kinds of souvenirs and stuff, has eight shops in Beijing and stores all over China. There is one in the mall near the InterConti Beichen; the group flagship (above) is for tour groups. © 010/8403-6979. www.kingdeer.com.cn.

Silk Alley
Jianguomenwai Dajie (Metro: Dong Dan).

This is not an alley but an enclosed mall filled with stalls that sell everything. Many stores and stalls in Silk Alley sell pashmina and cashmere, some seasonally, others year-round. Just be careful you know what you're getting with anything you buy in Silk Alley. This place is jammed on weekends, but on our last research trip, it was better than Ya Show (Ya Xui Market) for similar merchandise. Note that this area is near what's called the Embassy District; it isn't hard to get to, is surrounded by fast-food chains, and has a DVD center in the arcade on the street level.

DEPARTMENT STORES
Lane Crawford
Seasons Place, 2 Jinchengfang St., Xicheng, (no nearby Metro).

Anchoring the new Seasons Place luxe shopping mall, Hong Kong retail giant Lane Crawford has arrived in Beijing. More than half of the more than 600 brands available in this sprawling trilevel department store are exclusive to the Beijing market and, like its Hong Kong sister, this prestigious Western-style store offers one-stop shopping for top international designer labels. The hours are 11am to 8:30pm Monday to Sunday. ✆ 8610/6622-0808.

Wangfujing Department Store
255 Wangfujing (Metro: Wangfujing).

Happy days are here again: a true 1950s-style department store that's been renovated as such. I love it, if only because it makes me laugh. I also use it as my local one-stop shopping source when I'm staying at the Peninsula. I've bought luggage and all sorts of things here. Glam it is not, but it works. The fountains out front are a hoot.

Ya Xui Market

58 Gong Ti Beilu, Sanlitan (no nearby Metro).

This is also known as Ya Show, which is how it is pronounced. I have classified this as a department store, but you might call it an indoor market. It's clean and bright, and everything (even the cafe) is marked in English. Each floor offers a different kind of product, so you can truly buy everything here—from fake designer goods to luggage, to arts and crafts, to fabulous flower-stenciled enamel Chinese thermos bottles for $3 each.

The basement sells handbags and shoes of questionable origins; the ground floor has mostly clothes, and up the escalators there's just more and more merchandise. Yes, of course, you can bargain. You might want to call this a cleaned-up version of Silk Alley. *Note:* There are several ATMs at the entrance.

Insider's tip: This mall has the best DVD store in Beijing. You can approach from either side of the building and end up in a back corridor, closed into a semidark room. You keep your clothes on. All products tested worked in the U.S.

DESIGNER BOUTIQUES

Many international designers now have stores in Beijing. The most exclusive names are located in a three-level shopping arcade in the **Peninsula Hotel Beijing,** but there are also some in the Hyatt. Expect prices to be 20% higher than in Hong Kong, the United States, and Europe. The reason no one cares is A) you can often get a Birkin without waiting and B) when you're rich and Chinese, money is meaningless.

DOWN

Why eat Peking duck? Simple—so there are plenty of duck feathers to go into down coats and down products, which are laughably inexpensive all over China. Although they are bulky, the comforters, pillows, and coats cost a small fraction of what you'd pay in the U.S. Every department store, including the Friendship Store, has a selection. I actually found down pillows and comforters in a grocery store. Twin-size comforters cost about $30 each; coats and pillows are less. Note that the down is usually packed tightly for travel—you will never get it this small again.

FABRICS

See p. 303 for more on silks by the yard. Note that we searched and searched for a fabric market like the many we know in Shanghai and wasted our time and taxi fare. We followed many leads from various sources—all were disappointing or even heartbreaking. Buy in Shanghai. Oh yes, we did hear about a market and were told it was not particularly safe.

FAKES

I cannot condone fake merchandise, but I will tell you that it's pretty easy to find in Beijing. The best places for a wide selection of fake anything are the **Ya Xiu Market** in Sanlitan and **Silk Alley.** There are some at **Hong Qiao** (the Pearl Market); watches are on the ground floor, and leather goods are upstairs before you get to the antiques and crafts. Pearl Market is not really the place for well-made fakes.

Jenny's Turn: Are You Faking It?

Fake handbags in Beijing are as abundant as bicycles. Around every bend there's another false Fendi; behind every door, a knockoff Dior. You become obsessed with finding the best bag at the best price because different markets seem to have different merchandise and different quality. Where did I see that Dior bag? Can we get back there? It was almost as good as the one at Dior in the Pen, wasn't it?

We did have a good time at **Ya Xui,** but we were getting tired by all the haggling, and all the fakes began to look alike. We eventually found a stall that sold triple-A (the best grade of fake) merchandise, and we got purse-size notebooks with calculators inside for about $15. They do make great gifts. The sentiment is real even if the merchandise is not. —*Jenny McCormick*

FLEA MARKETS

Beijing Curio City

21 Dongsanhuan Nanlu (no nearby Metro).

Be warned: The "lobby floor" is a tad tacky and overwhelming. Also, the place is very touristy—prices are high, and many vendors speak English. But once you get into the recesses of the ground floor, or up on the other levels, it isn't bad at all. That said; it's a good one-stop shopping place if it's the best you can do or if you hate the real China. There is a shipping desk in the lobby—naturally, it was closed each time I visited. This market has much the same merchandise as the Dirt Market but sold in a more upmarket, indoor venue. Most items here (as elsewhere) have been created for the tourist market. It is open daily 9:30am to 6:30pm. ✆ **10/6774-7711.**

Panjiayuan Antique and Curio Market/ Dirt Market

Huaweiqiaxi Nan Dajie (no nearby Metro).

Many guidebooks report that this is a "Sunday only" affair, but it takes place on both Saturday and Sunday. From 8:30 to 9:55am, it's a pleasure. Then, at approximately 10am, the market is suddenly mobbed.

This market has been cleaned up enormously, but the layout remains the same; the vendors on the left (as you face into the market) with their wares on the ground are still the least expensive and most likely to have fun merchandise.

Bargaining is expected. Some of the stuff is fake (really!). Few dealers want American dollars, and they don't take credit cards, so have yuan on you. Prices range from good to better to you've-got-to-be-kidding lows. I bought two porte-mirrors (a matched set) for $30. How could I leave them behind? I made three necklaces from one strand of $10 beads.

You will have the time of your life. Bargain hard and carry a tote bag or backpack for small items. Dress down; bring small bills; consider having a porter to carry your buys.

This market is 14km (8¾ miles) from the city center; take a taxi south. It cost me about ¥60 ($10) to get there.

FOODSTUFFS

Carrefour Chuang Yi Jia

International Exhibition Center, 6 Bei San Huan Dong Lu (no nearby Metro).

One of the branches of the French *hypermarché*, this enormous modern supermarket is a destination for those in the neighborhood. There's another Carrefour in the Haidian district.

Ole Supermarket

China World Hotel, basement (Metro: Jianguomen); Oriental Plaza mall, B level (Metro: Wangfujing).

This upmarket chain seems to have replaced CRC and is the Western-style market of choice in fancy-schmancy malls. You can buy snacks for your hotel room and picnics to take to the Great Wall, or for the plane home, or for the kids. *Gift tip:* Take home packages of international brands with Chinese labels.

Wangfujing Food Plaza

Wangfujing (Metro: Wangfujing).

Harrods Food Hall meets the new China; many of the gorgeous examples of produce are engineered and have no taste. Other than that, it's great fun to look. I bought many items just for their wrappings; I have no idea what's inside, nor do I care. Think gift shopping.

Yaohan Supermarket

Sci-Tech Plaza, 22 Jianguomenwai Dajie (Metro: Fuxing Men).

This place is not worth the schlep unless you're already in the area—then you will find it great fun. This is a famous Japanese market, quite established in China.

Aaron's Turn: Gadgets & Watches

You'll encounter quite a few bizarre and unique electronic devices in both Beijing and Shanghai. The greatest selection is in markets, and in Beijing the best choice is at **Hong Qiao** (the Pearl Market). Mostly you'll see watches—the best pay homage to Chairman Mao, the local equivalent of Elvis. At Hong Qiao, the watches are sold from cases and possibly have a longer battery life. They cost $2 to $5.
—Aaron Gershman

FURNITURE

Gao Bei Dian (Furniture Street)

Jingtong Expwy., opposite the Chinese Sandalwood Museum, Gaobeidian exit (no nearby Metro).

A whole street of shops, warehouses, and dealers—complete with a torii gate to welcome you. Some stores sell small decorative items. Okay, so they're reproductions—that doesn't mean the merch isn't fun to look at, to touch, and to buy.

FURS

Winter in Beijing wouldn't be nearly as much fun if it weren't for the fur business. Furs are inexpensive by U.S. and European standards, and probably not well-made.

But wait. The furs I saw in the fur boutique of the Friendship Store were so chic I could have wept. The prices were competitive with New York prices, and I wanted them all.

HOME-STYLE

My idea of Chinese home-style is, uh, Chinese. All you minimalists out there, however, should know that the Japanese chain **Muji** has arrived in Beijing with a few branch stores as well as a **Muji Living** (www.mujiliving.com). We actually had a ball there and bought far more than home-style. There were zillions of little travel bags and zip containers and all sorts of thingamabobs. And while you're looking for hot and/or interesting merchandise, check out **Potato & Co.,** which is not a restaurant but a design store in China World mall.

MALLS

Malls are relatively new to Beijing; most arrived in the late 1990s. They are, as everywhere else in the world, a big hangout for teens and 'tweens on weekends. The current thinking is that traffic is so bad in Beijing that people don't want to travel out of their district or away from their hotels, so most of the new malls are attached to big-name hotels. The Macau Centre, at the Hilton Beijing Wangfujing, was not open when we last stayed at that hotel, but promises to add another dimension to the Wangfujing shopping district.

China World Shopping Centre
China World Hotel (Metro: Jianguomen).

Half the brand-name stores in Beijing are in this mall (the other half are in the Peninsula Beijing). There's also a supermarket, a bank, and courier offices, as well as shops on the hotel lobby level (which is not actually part of the mall, but while you're there—it shouldn't be a loss). It's also easy to get here on the Metro. There's a terrific food mart, including **Starbucks** and **Cold Stone.** It's all clean and easy to shop.

Shopper's Tip

Use the Metro station to cut across to the other side of the road to explore the **Park Hyatt Hotel,** which is more gorgeous than many museums.

Joy City
Financial Street, 131 Xidan (Metro: Xidan).

If my teeth were not glued into my gums, they would have fallen out when I saw this mall. It's new, it's modern, it's hip, it's amazing. It may seem too much like home to you if you consider it as a shopping experience, but as a cultural event, this is a must do. There's a cinema, young people, fashion, big brands, and food.

Financial Street is an entire district unto itself, about 4 or 5 years old. There are several luxury hotels lined up here, as well as businesses and, of course, this mall. Things can be dead at night.

Oriental Plaza
No. 1 East Chang An Ave., Wangfujing (Metro: Wangfujing).

One of the fancier malls in town, Oriental Plaza is attached to the Grand Hyatt Hotel. Sony has an Exploratorium museum here; I liked the supermarket (Ole). For some reason, the mall is designed sort of like a snail, which is to say that the designer shops facing outward on the streets do not open into the mall itself. These designer shops are as fancy as they come, but there are no bargains. I popped in to **Tse Cashmere,** thinking that because it's a Chinese-based firm, there might be a price break. Ha. Sweaters are $500. The mall is divided by themed areas. www.orientalplaza.com.

WEB TIPS ✎   The website is in English and is so organized that you can get a directory with a photo of each storefront as well as a map.

Peninsula Beijing
8 Goldfish Lane, Wangfujing (Metro: Wangfujing).

This isn't really a mall, but it functions sort of like one. It's like the Galleria in Houston: small and select, with only designer stores on three levels of marble floors. Little about it is Chinese, except that the prices are sky-high. If you have no interest in expensive designer items, go anyway for a quick look because the locals who shop in these stores are so gorgeous that they're worthy of a good long stare.

MARKETS
Hong Qiao (the Pearl Market)
Across from the Temple of Heaven (no nearby Metro).

The so-called market itself is in a modern demi-high-rise with about four floors of merchandise and an additional two floors of fancy jewelry showrooms. The antiques portion has been totally redone so it's very small and cleaned up—stick to the jewelry instead. There is a new building next door that sells very similar merchandise, without a jewelry mart.

There is nothing Chinese or even attractive about the market as you walk into a room filled with small electronics. Past that is a room with counters of dealers who sell watches. Many of the watch dealers have fakes, but you must ask for them. Some of these dealers also sell musical Mao lighters, which you cannot take on the airplane.

Upstairs feels sort of like a cheap department store, but there's luggage if you need some. There's also—at the other end—sweaters, some clothes, and handbags; again, copies are out but also hidden. The good stuff is put away. Then you get to the pearl floor, which must have at least 100 dealers selling all sorts of pearls and semiprecious stones. The "pearls" that I liked (for style and price) were not from oysters, but were made of crushed shells.

At one end of the pearl portion on this top floor, a stairway goes up to two more floors. Ask for the fourth floor or for **Sharon's Stone** (www.sharonpearl.com), a good place for everyday needs. **Fanghua** (www.fanghua.com) is the fancy showroom that takes up half the floor as well as a portion of the new building. Hong Giao market hot line ✆ **10/6713-3354.** www.hongqiao-pearl-market.com.

Ming Jin Yuan (Eye Glasses Mart)
Chao Yang District East, 3rd Ring Rd., Huawei Beili 43 (no nearby Metro).

Located around the corner from the famed Dirt Market, this market is filled with 100 or more shops selling designer and no-name optical frames. Most will make up your Rx in an hour although complicated prescriptions may take several days. I had a pair of trifocals made in a day, frames and lenses, for $99—with snap on sunglasses.

My Christian Dior nonscrip sunglasses said "Dior" in proper logo script when I bought them and soon said "Do," although the salesman promised me they were real. Go wild. All prescriptions that were created were checked in the U.S. and passed 100%. Bargain like mad.

Tian Li Toy City (Toy Market)
Hong Qiao (no nearby Metro).

This building is almost alongside the Pearl Market. It's through an alley and offers floors and floors of fake toys made in the style of the big brands, such as wannabe Legos and so on. When you finish laughing, you will have a ball. © 10/6711-7499.

Ya Xiu Market
58 Gong Ti Beilu, Sanlitan (no nearby Metro).

See "Department Stores," earlier in this chapter.

SILK & TEXTILES
Silk & Cotton Company
Wangfujing (Metro: Wangfujing).

This store is modern and not at all funky—it's right on Wangfujing and easy to shop for yard goods or finished scarves and a few clothing items. I bought silk polo shirts (for men) with knit collars for $25 each in soft gray-blue shades that my son went wild for—very Euro chic (and hand washable). On my last trip, I found an embroidered denim Mao-style jacket for $40. The silks are about $10 to $12 per meter.

Yuan Long

15 Yongdingmenwai (no nearby Metro).

Touristy—and how. But that doesn't mean it doesn't have some things of interest. The parking lot is filled with taxis and tour buses, and guides are licking their fingers, waiting for their kickbacks. It's way off on the edge of downtown in the southern part of the city, not that far from the southern gate of the Temple of Heaven, but too far to be worth considering unless you come here in a tour bus, which is a possibility.

The store sells a little of everything (while you're trapped) and has an excellent Chinese costume department—all reproductions and very, very expensive ($500). Other than that, it is not a good store and the system is disgusting. If you are taken here, expect to be taken.

Zhang Textile

China World Shopping Centre (Metro: Jianguomen).

If you adore Chinese textiles and garments, you will go nuts in this store, which is one of the largest galleries in the world specializing in Chinese antique garments. There's some touristy stuff, but the collection of textile hats and helmets alone is enough to make you weep with joy. Because of China's ethnic diversity, there is a wide range of styles. Also here are framed fragments as well as full garments, mandarin rank badges, and that old standby, slippers for bound feet. Aside from antiques, there are gift items and a selection of crafts.

WEB TIPS No website, although information about Zhang is available on numerous Beijing sites for tourists.

SKI GEAR

This is a winter shopping occupation, but because of the easy availability of down and the nearby ski resorts, ski clothing—and some equipment—is sold everywhere. There were mobs of *gwailos* (foreigners) buying out a shop in Ya Xiu Market that sells **North Face.**

SPAS & TREATMENTS

All of the fancy hotels have spa services, and usually you do not have to be a hotel guest to try them. A few hotels also have traditional Chinese medicine treatments.

The "in" spa of the moment is the E-Spa at the **Peninsula Beijing.** You may also book treatments in your room, but at least take a walk-through of the spa itself (and breathe deeply to get the scent) as it is gorgeous and soothing and a unique place to float past. **Anantara,** a famous Thai resort and spa firm, has a spa at the Commune by the Great Wall resort. Massages begin around $50, making this an amazing day out. www.anantaraspa.com.

TIANJIN

If you arrive by cruise ship or are meeting a cruise ship after a turn around in Beijing, you will actually leave from, or arrive in, the former pearl-fishing town of Tianjin, just 2 hours from Beijing if you drive. There is a new fast train that brings travel time down to an amazing 30 minutes.

Shopper's notes:

- **Mingzhu Fishing Village** is where the pearls are.
- **Yanghou**—in the Tang Gu part of town—serves as the foreign-goods marketplace, souvenir-hunter's market, and tchotchke place.
- **Ancient Culture Street,** in the Nanki District, is the leading tourist destination for shoppers and gawkers. It's one big TT (tourist trap), but a lot of fun. It's the best place for arts and crafts shopping and has some serious shops for antiques and indigenous crafts. Be sure to explore the side streets that jut off the main road.

Chapter 11

Mandarin Chinese: Useful Terms & Phrases

Chinese is not as difficult a language to learn as it may first appear to be—at least not once you've decided what kind of Chinese to learn. There are six major languages called Chinese. Speakers of each are unintelligible to speakers of the others, and there are, in addition, a host of dialects. The Chinese you are likely to hear spoken in your local Chinatown, in your local Chinese restaurant, or used by your friends of Chinese descent when they speak to their parents, is more than likely to be Cantonese, which is the version of Chinese used in Hong Kong and in much of southern China. But the official national language of China is **Mandarin** (**Pǔtōnghuà**— "common speech"), sometimes called Modern Standard Chinese, and viewed in mainland China as the language of administration, of the classics, and of the educated. While throughout much of mainland China people speak their own local flavor of Chinese for everyday communication, they've all been educated in Mandarin, which in general terms is the language of Beijing and the north. Mandarin is less well known in Hong Kong and Macau, but is also spoken in Taiwan and Singapore, and among growing communities of recent immigrants to North America and Europe.

Chinese grammar is considerably more straightforward than that of English or other European languages, even Spanish or Italian. There are no genders, so there is no need to remember long lists of endings for adjectives and to make them agree, with variations according to case. There are no equivalents for the definite and indefinite articles ("the," "a," "an"), so there is no need to make those agree either. Singular and plural nouns are the same. Best of all, verbs cannot be declined. The verb "to be" is shì. The same sound also covers "am," "are," "is," "was," "will be," and so on, since there are also no tenses. Instead of past, present, and future, Chinese is more concerned with whether an action is continuing or has been completed, and with the order in which events take place. To make matters of time clear, Chinese depends on simple expressions such as "yesterday," "before," "originally," "next year," and the like. "Tomorrow I go New York," is clear enough, as is "Yesterday I go New York." It's a little more complicated than these brief notes can suggest, but not much.

–Peter Neville-Hadley

A Guide to Pīnyīn Pronunciation

Letters in pīnyīn mostly have the values any English speaker would expect, with the following exceptions:

c ts as in bits

q ch as in chin, but much harder and more forward, made with tongue and teeth

r has no true equivalent in English, but the r of reed is close, although the tip of the tongue should be near the top of the mouth, and the teeth together

x also has no true equivalent, but is nearest to the sh of sheep, although the tongue should be parallel to the roof of the mouth and the teeth together

zh is a soft j, like the dge in judge

The vowels are pronounced roughly as follows:

a as father

e as in err (leng is pronounced as English "lung")

i is pronounced ee after most consonants, but after c, ch, r, s, sh, z, and zh is a buzz at the front of the mouth behind the closed teeth

o as in song

u as in too

ü is the purer, lips-pursed u of French tu and German ü. Confusingly, u after j, x, q, and y is always ü, but in these cases the accent over "ü" does not appear.

ai sounds like eye

ao as in ouch

ei as in hay

ia as in yak

ian sounds like yen

iang sounds like yang

iu sounds like you

ou as in toe

ua as in guava

ui sounds like way

uo sounds like or, but is more abrupt

Note that when two or more third-tone "ˇ" sounds follow one another, they should all, except the last, be pronounced as second-tone "ˊ."

Mandarin Bare Essentials

GREETINGS & INTRODUCTIONS

English	Pīnyīn	Chinese
Hello	**Nǐ hǎo**	你好
How are you?	**Nǐ hǎo ma?**	你好吗？
Fine. And you?	**Wǒ hěn hǎo. Nǐ ne?**	我很好你呢？
I'm not too well/ things aren't going well	**Bù hǎo**	不好

What is your name? (very polite)	**Nín guì xìng?**	您贵姓
My (family) name is . . .	**Wǒ xìng . . .**	我姓。。。
I'm known as (family, then given name)	**Wǒ jiào . . .**	我叫。。。
I'm [American]	**Wǒ shì [Měiguó] rén**	我是美国人
[Australian]	**[Àodàlìyà]**	澳大利亚
[British]	**[Yīngguó]**	英国
[Canadian]	**[Jiānádà]**	加拿大
[Irish]	**[Àiěrlán]**	爱尔兰
[New Zealander]	**[Xīnxīlán]**	新西兰
I'm from [America]	**Wǒ shì cóng [Měiguó] lái de**	我是从美国来的
Excuse me/I'm sorry	**Duìbùqǐ**	对不起
I don't understand	**Wǒ tīng bù dǒng**	我听不懂
Thank you	**Xièxie nǐ**	谢谢你
Correct (yes)	**Duì**	对
Not correct	**Bú duì**	不对
No, I don't want	**Wǒ bú yào**	我不要
Not acceptable	**Bù xíng**	不行

BASIC QUESTIONS & PROBLEMS

English	Pīnyīn	Chinese
Excuse me/I'd like to ask	**Qǐng wènyíxià**	请问一下
Where is . . . ?	**. . . zài nǎr?**	。。。在哪儿?

English	Pīnyīn	Chinese
How much is . . . ?	. . . duōshǎo qián?	。。。多少钱？
. . . this one?	Zhèi/Zhè ge . . .	这个。。。
. . . that one?	Nèi/Nà ge . . .	那个。。。
Do you have . . . ?	Nǐ yǒu méi yǒu	你有没有。。。？
What time does/is . . . ?	. . . jǐ diǎn?	。。。几点？
What time is it now?	Xiànzài jǐ diǎn?	现在几点？
When is . . . ?	. . . shénme shíhou?	。。。什么时候？
Why?	Wèishénme?	为什么？
Who?	Shéi?	谁？
Is that okay?	Xíng bù xíng?	行不行？
I'm feeling ill	Wǒ shēng bìng le	我生病了

TRAVEL

English	Pīnyīn	Chinese
luxury (bus, hotel rooms)	háohuá	豪华
high-speed (buses, expressways)	gāosù	高速
air-conditioned	kōngtiáo	空调

NUMBERS

Note that more complicated forms of numbers are often used on official documents and receipts to prevent fraud—see how easily 1 can be changed to 2, 3, or even 10. Familiar Arabic numerals appear on bank notes, most signs, taxi meters, and other places. Be particularly careful with 4 and 10, which sound very alike in many regions—hold up fingers to make sure. Note, too, that yī, meaning "one," tends to change its tone all the time depending on what it precedes. Don't worry about this—once you've started talking about money, almost any kind of squeak for "one" will do. Finally note that "two" alters when being used with expressions of quantity.

English	Pīnyīn	Chinese
0	líng	零
1	yī	一
2	èr	二
2 (of them)	liǎng ge	两个
3	sān	三
4	sì	四
5	wǔ	五
6	liù	六
7	qī	七
8	bā	八
9	jiǔ	九
10	shí	十
11	shí yī	十一
12	shí èr	十二
21	èr shí yī	二十一
22	èr shí èr	二十二
51	wǔ shí yī	五十一
100	yì bǎi	一百
101	yì bǎi líng yī	一百零一
110	yì bǎi yī (shí)	一百一（十）

English	Pīnyīn	Chinese
111	yì bǎi yī shí yī	一百一十一
1,000	yì qiān	一千
1,500	yì qiān wǔ (bǎi)	一千五百
5,678	wǔ qiān liù bǎi qī shí bāi	五千六百七十八
10,000	yí wàn	一万

MONEY

The word yuan (¥) is rarely spoken, nor is jiao, the written form for ¹/10th of a yuan, equivalent to 10 fen (there are 100 fen in a yuan). Instead, the Chinese speak of "pieces of money," kuai qian, usually abbreviated just to kuai, and they speak of mao for ¹/10th of a kuai. Fen have been overtaken by inflation and are almost useless. Often all zeros after the last whole number are simply omitted, along with kuai qian, which is taken as read, especially in direct reply to the question duoshao qian—"How much?"

English	Pīnyīn	Chinese
¥1	yí kuài qián	一块钱
¥2	liǎng kuài qián	两块钱
¥.30	sān máo qián	三毛钱
¥5.05	wǔ kuài líng wǔ fēn	五块零五分
¥5.50	wǔ kuài wǔ	五块五
¥550	wǔ bǎi wǔ shí kuài	五百五十块
¥5,500	wǔ qiān wǔ bǎi kuài	五千五百块
Small change	língqián	零钱

TIME

English	Pīnyīn	Chinese
morning	**shàngwǔ**	上午
afternoon	**xiàwǔ**	下午
evening	**wǎnshang**	晚上
8:20am	**shàngwǔ bā diǎn èr shí fēn**	上午八点二十分
9:30am	**shàngwǔ jiǔ diǎn bàn**	上午九点半
noon	**zhōngwǔ**	中午
4:15pm	**xiàwǔ sì diǎn yí kè**	下午四点一刻
midnight	**wǔ yè**	午夜
1 hour	**yí ge xiǎoshí**	一个小时
8 hours	**bā ge xiǎoshí**	八个小时
today	**jīntiān**	今天
yesterday	**zuótiān**	昨天
tomorrow	**míngtiān**	明天
Monday	**Xīngqī yī**	星期一
Tuesday	**Xīngqī èr**	星期二
Wednesday	**Xīngqī sān**	星期三
Thursday	**Xīngqī sì**	星期四
Friday	**Xīngqī wǔ**	星期五
Saturday	**Xīngqī liù**	星期六
Sunday	**Xīngqī tiān**	星期天

TRANSPORT

English	Pīnyīn	Chinese
I want to go to . . .	**Wǒ xiǎng qù . . .**	我想去。。。
plane	**fēijī**	飞机
train	**huǒchē**	火车
bus	**gōnggòng qìchē**	公共汽车
long-distance bus	**chángtú qìchē**	长途汽车
taxi	**chūzū chē**	出租车
airport	**fēijīchǎng**	飞机场
stop or station (bus or train)	**zhàn**	站
(plane/train/bus) ticket	**piào**	票

NAVIGATION

English	Pīnyīn	Chinese
north	**Běi**	北
south	**Nán**	南
east	**Dōng**	东
west	**Xī**	西
Turn left	**zuǒ guǎi**	左拐
Turn right	**yòu guǎi**	右拐
Go straight on	**yìzhí zǒu**	一直走
crossroads	**shízì lùkǒu**	十字路口
10km	**shí gōnglǐ**	十公里
I'm lost	**Wǒ diū le**	我丢了

HOTEL

English	Pīnyīn	Chinese
How many days?	**Zhù jǐ tiān?**	住几天？
standard room (twin or double with private bath-room)	**biāozhǔn jiān**	标准间
passport	**hùzhào**	护照
deposit	**yājīn**	押金
I want to check out	**Wǒ tuì fáng**	我退房

RESTAURANT

English	Pīnyīn	Chinese
How many people?	**Jǐ wèi?**	几位
waiter/waitress	**fúwùyuán**	服务员
menu	**càidān**	菜单
I'm vegetarian	**Wǒ shì chī sù de**	我是吃素的
Do you have . . . ?	**Yǒu méi yǒu . . . ?**	有没有。。。？
Please bring a por-tion of . . .	**Qǐng lái yí fènr . . .**	请来一份儿。。。
beer	**píjiǔ**	啤酒
mineral water	**kuàngquán shuǐ**	矿泉水
Bill, please	**jiézhàng**	结帐

SIGNS

English	Pīnyīn	Chinese
hotel	**bīnguǎn**	宾馆
	dàjiǔdiàn	大酒店
	jiǔdiàn	酒店
	fàndiàn	饭店
restaurant	**fànguǎn**	饭馆
	jiǔdiàn	酒店
	jiǔjiā	酒家
vinegar	**cù**	醋
soy sauce	**Jiàngyóu**	酱油
bar	**jiǔbā**	酒吧
Internet bar	**wǎngbā**	网吧
cafe	**kāfēiguǎn**	咖啡馆
teahouse	**cháguǎn**	茶馆
department store	**bǎihuò shāngdiàn**	百货商店
	gòuwù zhōngxīn	购物中心
market	**shìchǎng**	市场
bookstore	**shūdiàn**	书店
police (Public Security Bureau)	**gōng'ānjú**	公安局
Bank of China	**Zhōngguó Yínháng**	中国银行
public telephone	**gōngyòng diànhuà**	公用电话
public restroom	**gōngyòng cèsuǒ**	公用厕所
male	**nán**	男
female	**nǚ**	女

English	Pīnyīn	Chinese
entrance	rùkǒu	入口
exit	chūkǒu	出口
bus stop/station	qìchē zhàn	汽车站
long-distance bus station	chángtú qìchē zhàn	长途汽车站
luxury	háohuá	豪华
railway station	huǒchēzhàn	火车站
hard seat	yìng zuò	硬座
soft seat	ruǎn zuò	软座
hard sleeper	yìng wò	硬卧
soft sleeper	ruǎn wò	软卧
metro/subway station	dìtiězhàn	地铁站
airport	feījīchǎng	飞机场
dock/wharf	mǎtóu	码头
passenger terminal (bus, boat, and so on)	kèyùn zhàn	客运站
up/get on	shàng	上
down/get off	xià	下
ticket hall	shòupiào tīng	售票厅
ticket office	shòupiào chù	售票处
left-luggage office	xíngli jìcún chù	行李寄存处
temple	sì	寺
	miào	庙
museum	bówùguǎn	博物馆
memorial hall	jìniànguǎn	纪念馆
park	gōngyuán	公园
hospital	yīyuàn	医院

English	Pīnyīn	Chinese
clinic	**zhěnsuǒ**	诊所
pharmacy	**yàofáng/ yàodiàn**	药房/药店
travel agency	**lǚxíngshè**	旅行社

GENERAL SHOPPING TERMS

English	Pīnyīn	Chinese
Where can I find a ____	**nǎ lǐ yǒu ____?**	哪里有____ ?
shoe store?	**xié diàn**	鞋店
men's / women's /children's clothing store?	**Nán shì / nǚ shì / ér tóng fú zhuāng diàn**	男式 / 女式 / 儿童服装店
designer fashion shop?	**shí zhuāng shè jì diàn**	时装设计店
vintage clothing store?	**gǔ dǒng fú zhuāng diàn**	古董服装店
jewelry store?	**zhū bǎo diàn**	珠宝店
bookstore?	**shū diàn**	书店
toy store?	**wán jù diàn**	玩具店
stationery store?	**wén jù diàn**	文具店
antique shop?	**gǔ dǒng diàn**	古董店
cigar shop?	**yān cǎo shāng diàn**	烟草商店
souvenir shop?	**jì niàn pǐn diàn**	纪念品店
flea market?	**tiào zǎo shì chǎng?**	跳蚤市场?

CLOTHES SHOPPING

English	Pīnyīn	Chinese
I'd like to buy ____	wǒ xiǎng mǎi ____	我想买____
men's shirts.	nán shì chèn shān	男式衬衫
women's shoes.	nǚ shì xié	女式鞋
children's clothes.	ér tóng fú zhuāng	儿童服装
toys.	wán jù	玩具
I'm looking for a size ____.	wǒ yào ____ hào.	我要____ 号.
small.	xiǎo	小
medium.	zhōng	中
large.	dà	大
extra-large.	chāo dà	超大
I'm looking for ____.	wǒ yào ____	我要____
a silk blouse.	sī zhì kuān sōng shàng yī.	丝质宽松上衣.
cotton pants.	mián zhì kù zǐ.	棉质裤子.
a hat.	mào zǐ.	帽子.
sunglasses.	tài yáng jìng.	太阳镜.
underwear.	nèi yī.	内衣.
cashmere.	yáng róng shān.	羊绒衫.
socks.	duǎn wà.	短袜.
sweaters.	máo yī.	毛衣.

English	Pīnyīn	Chinese
a coat.	wài tào.	外套.
a swimsuit.	yǒng yī.	泳衣.
May I try it on?	wǒ kě yǐ shì chuān ma?	我可以试穿吗？
Do you have fitting rooms?	yǒu shì yǐ jiān ma?	有试衣间吗？
This is ____.	zhè jiàn ____.	这件____.
too tight.	tài jǐn.	太紧.
too loose.	tài sōng.	太松.
too long.	tài cháng.	太长.
too short.	tài duǎn.	太短.
This fits great!	zhè jiàn hěn hé shēn!	这件很合身！
Thanks, I'll take it.	xiè xiè, jiù mǎi zhè jiàn le.	谢谢，就买这件了.
Do you have that in ____	Nà jiàn yī fu yǒu ____	那件衣服有____
a smaller / larger size?	gèng xiǎo / gèng dà de hào ma?	更小 / 更大的号吗？
a different color?	bié de yán sè ma?	别的颜色吗？
How much is it?	zhè gè duō shǎo qián?	这个多少钱？

Index

See also Accommodations and Restaurant indexes, below.

General Index

Black 10 miles
↑
does not have to be
Zahitian